If It Was Easy,
They'd Call the Whole Damn Thing
a Honeymoon

"If Chelsea Handler and Dr. Phil had a love child, it would be Jenna McCarthy, whose fabulous *If It Was Easy, They'd Call the Whole Damn Thing a Honeymoon* is at once profane, irreverent, warm, and wise. This is the best kind of relationship advice book, one written by someone who is smart enough to follow and smart-ass enough to make you savor the journey. Brilliant!"

—Celia Rivenbark, bestselling author of
You Can't Drink All Day If You Don't Start in the Morning

"Hilarious, smart, and utterly addicting. Watch out, Nora Ephron."
—Valerie Frankel, author of *Thin Is the New Happy*

"Every relationship is like being fit, healthy, and happy—you have to work at it. Jenna reminds us of this with wit, insight, and self-deprecating humor. At the end of the day, you'll recognize yourself in these pages and applaud her honesty." —Lucy Danziger,
editor-in-chief of *Self* magazine and coauthor of
The Nine Rooms of Happiness

"An uproariously funny, deliciously satisfying, and completely accurate take on wedded bliss." —Tracy Beckerman,
syndicated humor columnist and author of *Rebel without a Minivan*

"When Jenna McCarthy turns her wicked wit to the, ahem, challenges of modern-day marriage, hilarity ensues. Anyone still in love with the oaf they married will find a lot to love here."

—Julie Tilsner,
author of *29 and Counting: A Chick's Guide to Turning 30*

continued . . .

"This should be required reading for all brides. No, make that required reading for any woman who has been snookered into believing that finding and marrying the right person will somehow catapult her into a fairy tale—complete with a snorting horse, castle, and prince. . . . An enlightening tour of the true realities of marriage, [McCarthy] amazingly pulls off the impossible: She helps us to fall in love with our farting, nose-picking, burping, sex-obsessed doofus husbands all over again."

—Alisa Bowman, author of *Project: Happily Ever After*

The Parent Trip

"Clever and irreverent."

—Janet Evanovich, #1 *New York Times* bestselling author

"Wildly funny, intimate, and ever-so-honest. Trust me, you won't want this trip to end." —Cheryl Richardson, *New York Times* bestselling author of *The Art of Extreme Self-Care*

"Funny, smart, and utterly original. Jenna McCarthy is the new Erma Bombeck." —Alexis Martin Neely, bestselling author of *Wear Clean Underwear!*

"You can't make this stuff up! . . . [B]rilliantly captures the hilarious insanity of motherhood and family. Whether you have little ones running around or just got pregnant, this book is for you."

—Gabby Reece, supermodel, volleyball phenom, and mom

If It Was Easy, They'd Call the Whole Damn Thing a Honeymoon

· · · · ·

Living with and Loving the TV-Addicted,
Sex-Obsessed, Not-So-Handy Man You Married

Jenna McCarthy

B

BERKLEY BOOKS, NEW YORK

THE BERKLEY PUBLISHING GROUP
Published by the Penguin Group
Penguin Group (USA) Inc.
375 Hudson Street, New York, New York 10014, USA
Penguin Group (Canada), 90 Eglinton Avenue East, Suite 700, Toronto, Ontario M4P 2Y3, Canada
(a division of Pearson Penguin Canada Inc.)
Penguin Books Ltd., 80 Strand, London WC2R 0RL, England
Penguin Group Ireland, 25 St. Stephen's Green, Dublin 2, Ireland (a division of Penguin Books Ltd.)
Penguin Group (Australia), 250 Camberwell Road, Camberwell, Victoria 3124, Australia
(a division of Pearson Australia Group Pty. Ltd.)
Penguin Books India Pvt. Ltd., 11 Community Centre, Panchsheel Park, New Delhi—110 017, India
Penguin Group (NZ), 67 Apollo Drive, Rosedale, Auckland 0632, New Zealand
(a division of Pearson New Zealand Ltd.)
Penguin Books (South Africa) (Pty.) Ltd., 24 Sturdee Avenue, Rosebank, Johannesburg 2196,
South Africa

Penguin Books Ltd., Registered Offices: 80 Strand, London WC2R 0RL, England

This book is an original publication of The Berkley Publishing Group.

The publisher does not have any control over and does not assume responsibility for author or third-party websites or their content.

PRINTING HISTORY
Berkley trade paperback edition / October 2011

Library of Congress Cataloging-in-Publication Data

McCarthy, Jenna.
    If it was easy, they'd call the whole damn thing a honeymoon : living with and loving the tv-addicted,
sex-obsessed, not-so-handy man you married / Jenna McCarthy. —Berkley trade paperback ed.
        p. cm.
    ISBN 978-0-425-24302-2 (alk. paper)
    1. Marriage—Humor.   I. Title.
    PN6231.M3M4 2011
    818'.607—dc22   2011011581

PRINTED IN THE UNITED STATES OF AMERICA

10   9   8   7   6   5   4   3   2   1

To Joe,

for loving me anyway

Contents

• • • • •

Contents

'Til Death Do Us Part Is a Really Long Time

All marriages are happy.
It's the living together afterward that causes all the trouble.

• RAYMOND HULL •

This book was born of something from which few good things (besides hot, furious makeup sex) ever come: a nasty, name-calling, knock-down, drag-out brawl with my husband. After we exchanged some particularly ugly insults and I lobbed a large cup of ice at his head, we did what the pros tell you never, ever to do (besides lob large cups of ice at your partner's head): We went to bed angry at each other. Pissed off, if we're being totally honest here. When we woke up in the morning, I looked at the man I've spent thirteen years assuming I will purchase adjacent cemetery plots with and I thought:

I hate you.

No, that's a lie. That's not what I really thought. What I really thought was:

I fucking hate you.

• • • • •

Now, as husbands go, I have to admit I did all right. Joe is unquestionably handsome, doesn't leave ragged toenail clippings scattered about the house, and has never once, in nearly five thousand days of togetherness, left the toilet seat up. He also knows his way around a grill, occasionally makes the bed (if you can call straightening the duvet and tossing some pillows in the general vicinity of the headboard "making the bed"), and is not addicted to porn, painkillers, or crystal meth. He's seen me naked on numerous occasions and still wants to have sex with me. All in all, he's a catch by pretty much anyone's standards.

And yet he still can make me madder than a bag of rabid badgers. From the ill-timed get-to-the-point-already hand gesture in the middle of a riveting play-by-play of my chat with the UPS guy to his incessant references to, fantasies about, and demands for sex, the guy seems hell-bent on personally driving me to the nuthouse. Sometimes, these things merely bug me; other times they are nearly enough to make me want to pack up and leave him. But I haven't and I won't, and there are three particularly compelling reasons for this:

1. He's a guy, and all guys are basically the same, and since I really don't want to die alone, if I got rid of him I'd just be trading in his sometimes-infuriating tics for someone else's, and I'm too old and tired to even consider that.

2. He puts up with all of *my* shit. (This really should not be underestimated.)

3. I love him.

· · · · ·

Like I said, my husband is a decent guy. No, he's a great guy. But living with the *same person* day in and day out, for years on end, is no confetti-dusted cakewalk. I once saw a comedienne slay an entire audience with this line: "When I said 'til death do us part, I had no idea it was going to take this long." Clearly she was joking. Mostly.

This book originally was going to be a blog post, maybe a magazine article. After the ice-to-the-temple incident blew over and I returned to my formerly happily married state, I posted a few queries—in newsletters, on my Facebook wall, around Twitter, on my blog—with a simple question: "What does your husband—whom you still love—do that drives you nuts?" The idea was to tease out precisely the sort of irritating behaviors that women who consider themselves "happily married" are *indeed willing to live with*. The replies were astonishing not only in their content and volume, but most of all for the utterly venomous tone these smart, funny, remarkably sane women used to describe their significant others' reasonably benign traits. "He eats ice cream every single night with the tiniest spoon in the house," lamented one. "Over and over *and over and over*—a kazillion fucking times a night—I have to listen to that spoon hitting the side of the bowl. He says he's been eating ice cream that way for forty-five years and isn't going to change. And yes, I love him."

These gals weren't talking about their lying, cheating exes or the buffoons that beat them; they were talking about the men they live with and continue to love. Their gripes ranged from merely amusing ("He only ever half-finishes a bar of soap!") to downright asinine (nipple flicking? *Really?*), and every last one made me feel infinitely better about my own enchanting Neanderthal. Nothing like peering over the neighbors' fences and catching a glimpse of their withered, pathetic excuse for a lawn to remind us all that the grass isn't always greener.

Here's the funny part, though: The women who contacted me weren't exactly tripping over themselves to confess their own annoying habits or less-than-desirable qualities. (Granted, I didn't ask. And to the helpful husbands who e-mailed offering to do it for them? Thanks for sharing! Now go write your own goddamned book.) Because we're perfect, right? Okay, not *perfect* exactly, but pretty damned close. I mean, relative to the men we married at least, and certainly according to our friends and a majority of the literature available on the subject. Wise and witty author Charles Orlando wrote a wonderful book with one of the best titles in all of literary history: *The Problem with Women . . . Is Men.* (What's not to love, right? Blame the guys! Obviously it's all their fault!) It really is a moving manifesto, filled with fun facts and packed with appalling confessions from the boorish oafs we can't help but love, as well as some not-very-gentle reminders—and these are coming from a guy, mind you—that it would behoove the male population on the whole to try to be a tiny bit less boorish from time to time. With all due respect to Charles, who may very well be on to something, the author of *this* book would like to add that the other problem with women . . . is women.

Honestly, we're never happy, are we? We tell our husbands we want them to surprise us with hidden love notes, flowers for no special reason, romantic dinner reservations, big honking diamonds. We want them to pick up after themselves without having to nag them to do it. We want them to turn off the goddamned TV and pay attention to us as we regale them with details of our day. ("And then the cashier said, 'I'm sorry, but we're out of the low-fat maple-nut scones,' so I wound up having to get a lemon poppy, even though those have like eight billion calories, and on top of feeling guilty about that I've been worried all day that I've got a poppy seed stuck in my teeth. Hey, do I? What do you mean, '*Do I what?*' Have a poppy seed stuck in my teeth!!!") We want them to not roll their eyes when we are on the phone and to promise us in writing that they would cook veggies for the kids every single day if we died tomorrow. We want them to lay off the gas pedal, roll up the windows, turn down the air-conditioning, fix the leaky faucet, notice our new highlights but not ask how much they cost, spend more, save more, spot the bag of moldy, festering lettuce in the crisper drawer and then throw it away, and once—just one bloody time—*ask for fucking directions*.

These things would indeed make us happy, wouldn't they? Not even all of them, maybe two or three. Or one. If he did just one, we'd be content. Right? Well actually, probably not. Because fundamentally—and bear with me as I'm going to tiptoe right out on a limb here—the marital minutiae we fight about has nothing whatsoever to do with money or messed-up hair or all of the rotting produce on the planet. We're not really *that bothered* by the stinky socks on top of the hamper lid or the sound of back-to-back episodes of *Throwdown Fishing* constantly droning in the background of our lives. If these insults were perpetrated by, say, the best friend we hadn't seen in a year or a beloved, dying relative, we'd either not notice them in the first place or at least find a way to overlook them. The problem isn't him, and it's not you. The problem is attempting to live in excruciating proximity with another full-size person who can't read your mind and also isn't a carbon copy of you.

Think about it: When you were dating—and going home at night to your respective living spaces—there wasn't all that much to argue about. When you did have the rare disagreement, you'd go all Hollywood and sigh happily and think *"He completes me,"* and clearly it was all that damned Renée Zellweger's fault. But when couples try to share one electric bill, they turn into a pair of Japanese fighting fish, those colorful, carnival-prize favorites that come one to a bowl for a simple reason: If you put two in there, they will immediately try to rip each other's gills off.

If you ever had a roommate, you're familiar with the basic cohabitation timeline. It starts out all hopeful promise, the two of you deciding amicably who will park where and who will pay what and shopping for a new shower curtain together at Target. She insists you take the bigger bedroom since you found the place; you accept since you were gracious enough to grant her boyfriend's pit bull regular visitation rights. You're neater and more courteous than you have ever been in your life, because you know how hard it is to find a good roommate. You wait patiently as her laundry festers in the washing machine for three days because, really, it's not worth arguing about or anything. She drinks your last beer, but you ate her last bagel so it all seems fair enough. You spend weeks trying to come up with a way to broach the subject of her luxurious twice-daily hour-long showers, which obviously aren't fair seeing as you have to pay half of the water bill. After a while you notice—or is it a new thing?—that she has this irritating habit of not closing the bathroom door when she brushes her teeth. The sound rather reminds you of a room full of wailing babies who are also scraping their tiny fingernails across a giant blackboard while they vomit, so you gently close the door for her, hoping she'll take the hint. She doesn't. One day she discovers P90X, and from that point forward she insists on doing her workouts every bloody night when you'd very much like to be watching *Glee*. You smile as you seethe and start socking away dough to buy your own goddamned TV, which you will keep in your bedroom, the bedroom you may never leave again. Then one day she comes home drunk and accidentally pees in your hamper, or uses the rent money you gave her to buy a pair of designer boots, or invites a bunch of her obnoxious friends over on the very night you told her you were planning to wax your mustache, and it occurs to you that you don't *have* to live like this. From this point, you wage many a minor battle before the final war, the one that will determine which one of you is going to borrow the van and hock your futon.

But marriage isn't that easy. You didn't just sign a month-to-month lease here; now you've gone and entered into an inexhaustible, legally binding contract to live with this one person (forsaking all others, for crying out loud! What were you *thinking*?) for all of eternity or at least until one of you is finally able to rest in peace. (Yes, my husband snores, and yes, there really is always at least a kernel of truth in jest.) When you said "I do," you weren't promising to honor and cherish him for the next five minutes or five years, but *forever*. That's a hard concept to really grasp when your hormones have taken you hostage and you're consumed with thoughts of honeymoon souvenirs and the jaw-dropping offspring you could produce together.

Let me give you an analogy. Imagine that the next time you go shopping for a handbag you discover there is a new law in effect: The very next purse you buy is going to be the last purse you are ever going to be allowed to own. (There could even be a tiny loophole where you *might* be able to return it, but it will be complicated and expensive and besides, by then you will probably be comfortably used to the stupid purse, even if it has definitely seen better days and no longer goes with anything else you own.) Obviously you are going to put great thought and effort into finding the best bag on the market. You claw your way through dozens of different models until you find the Goldilocks of purses: not too big, not too small, handsome, versatile, and priced just right. As you lift your eyes to heaven celebrating your good fortune in landing this dream bag, ask yourself how you think you might feel about it forty or fifty years from now. Then envision the bald, bitter, broke bastard who—if you're among the fortunate, slight majority—will still be sharing your bed.

So basically, you're stuck. The man you married is yours to have and to hold for the rest of ever, even if he starts chewing tobacco or decides to pierce his hairy nipple and buy a Corvette, because you very plainly said—or at least implied—you were in it for better *or for worse*. Sure, you could always get a divorce, but that's generally messy and costly and in many ways, redundant. (How, you ask? Consider that roughly 75 percent of women who divorce will eventually remarry and that, sadly, that second union is even more likely to fail than the first one—at an exponentially increased rate to boot. See? Redundant.)

I don't care how handsome or fabulous or funny the groom is, or how sweet and accommodating the bride, or vice versa. *Marriage is hard.* Mating for life? Totally unnatural. In fact, only about 4 percent of all of the five thousand species of mammals on the planet even attempt it. The rest of them shack up for anywhere from a single sexual encounter up until the kids leave the nest or the den, and then it's back to the free-wheeling polyamorous life. In the very small eternally committed camp you've got your beavers, some (but not all) bats, and Kevin Kline. Oh, and geese. Talk about faithful. If half of a goose couple dies, the surviving partner *never mates again*. That kind of loyalty just isn't in our genetic makeup.

And yet, no matter how difficult or deviant it is, we go for it anyway—out of loneliness or fear or sometimes even honest-to-God, soul-stirring *love*—and then we proceed to spend the rest of our lives driving another human being crazy.

In my worst marital moments, everything is my husband's fault. You know, for being a slovenly, sex-obsessed, single-tasking, remote-control-monopolizing, wannabe race car driver who half-finishes projects, can't remember a date, and doesn't listen to a word I say. He, in turn, accuses me of never shutting up, being impossible to please, focusing on the negative, and insisting on detailing—daily—the many ways in which he makes me miserable, as if a running gripe list were something I swore under oath to maintain when I said "I do." (I didn't?) When I manage to acknowledge something considerate or helpful he's done, he points out that I usually can't resist employing the ever-popular "Thanks, but" construction. ("Thanks for doing the dishes, but next time could you use Super Sparkle Clean to wipe the table and not Regular Sparkle Clean?") Fine, he's right, I'm a total bitch. But—and here's where the playing field gets leveled—he married me for better *or for worse*. So there.

Now, I'm not saying I think we're all doomed to coexist in eternal misery because we were never meant to mate in the first place. I'm also not suggesting that women should learn to settle, or work hard to cultivate their inner bitches just to annoy their annoying husbands back, or stop asking their partners for the things that would make them happy. And I wouldn't dream of telling a friend who's in a helplessly miserable marriage: "You made your bed, sister." I'm simply acknowledging that marriage isn't always easy and advising that we might want to start seeing it for what it really is: a wholly unnatural state that's difficult at times but frequently has several bright spots and is occasionally better than the alternative.

I've been with my husband for thirteen years, married for ten. Am I happy? Mostly. Back in my optimistic twenties, before I had experienced the joy of nuzzling up to another person's unbrushed teeth *every single morning* for fifty-two consecutive seasons, I would have thought that was just about the most depressing thing I'd ever heard, the emotional equivalent of being told your new $200 jeans make your ass look "fine." (And not the sort of "fine" followed by a long, low whistle and a request to see them in a puddle on the floor; I'm talking about the painfully curt, totally dismissive, good-enough sort of "fine" that leads you to purchase a gently used elliptical machine on eBay.) But after a while, reality sets in and you decide that mostly happy is good. In fact, relatively speaking, it's great. No, it's a Blessed-Virgin-in-your-grilled-cheese-sandwich sort of miracle.

Here's a two-part exercise you can use to confirm your own Mostly Happy Wife (MHW) status: Let's suppose, just for argument's sake, that your husband has this super-insane, god-awful-stupid, totally annoying thing that he does. (Okay fine, he's got eleventy billion. But we're talking about that one that he does repeatedly, the one that makes you want to chop off his head and stick a rusty dagger down the neck hole.) Mentally write his name and his infuriating habit/quality on a scrap of imaginary paper. In a minute, you are going to toss it into an invisible bowl roughly the size of Texas. But before you toss in your scrap, peer inside the bowl. Here's a glimpse of what you might see in there:

"Todd: Picks his nose and wipes it on his jeans."

"Carlos: Calls me by my mother's name when he is pissed off at me."

"Ruben: Eats peanut butter from the jar every single day *with his finger.*"

"Freddy: Carries toothpicks everywhere and thinks it is acceptable to gnaw on them in public."

Now you have two choices: You can throw your scrap of paper in the bowl and pick another one at random, or you can keep your own. (No, you can't throw your scrap in and bolt for the state line; that's cheating, not to mention weak.)

I'm going to guess that you've decided—perhaps grudgingly, but still—to keep your own lovable little scrap. Congratulations! You are indeed an MHW! (If you considered, even for a nanosecond, opting for the trade-in, you need counseling or an attorney, pronto.)

Part II of the Texas Bowl exercise is especially fun because you get to picture your fantasy guy. (Wait! Not yet; we're still talking about your husband.) Now, despite the flaw(s) you are still fixating on from Part I, chances are the man you chose to marry has some other quality that is lovely and sweet and endearing. Maybe he fixes your coffee exactly the way you like it, even though the entire barista community secretly mocks you and your maddening fourteen-point order. Perhaps he takes out the trash without having to be ~~nagged~~ asked, or makes a mean pot of chili. Maybe he simply doesn't routinely spray you with spit when he chews. Whatever. *Find* something. Got it? Good. Now picture your dream mate, the one from your recurring fantasies of domestic bliss and happily-ever-after. Could be Brad Pitt, Denzel Washington, the dude at the car wash, your sister's hunky husband, Marilyn-freakshow-

Manson if he floats your boat. Who am I to judge? Now, ask yourself: Exactly what do you think are the odds that Bradzelyn *doesn't* do the annoying thing and actually *does* do the charming thing? My hunch is that they're slim to none. Remember: No matter how sexy he is or how perfect he seems, there's at least one gal out there who loathes him deeply and wouldn't dream of putting up with his shit if you paid her. Your husband is no different (and conversely, there are women out there who will find him relentlessly alluring, as impossible as this may be to fathom at times), and you married him "for better or for worse." Unless he hurts you, has sex with someone other than you without your blessing, or smells really, really bad, chances are it's not worth trading him in.

This book was written to remind you of that, over and over, in glorious, honest, sidesplitting detail. I've sought input from women around the virtual world to detail the many maddening ways of the men we'd miss terribly should they be abducted by aliens.

You know how good it feels when you tell your best friend about a ghastly spat with your husband and she not only says just the right soothing, comforting thing but fires back with her own battle tale that's thirteen times more fabulous than yours in its horror? This book is her—but you can curl up with it night after night and laugh until you cry and your husband won't give you grief about yet another two-hour phone marathon with your best friend.

Joe always wonders why I frequently come home from my too-infrequent Girls' Nights Out feeling particularly frisky.

He probably assumes it's the booze, but here's the real reason: It takes only a few hours with some married friends, listening to them bitch about *their* dreadful husbands, to make me realize I dodged some nasty bullets when I landed mine.

So when my otherwise lovely life partner is relentlessly gnawing on my last frazzled nerve, I am going to conjure the best stories I've heard and try to be grateful anyway. To love him even if I'd much rather be folding laundry or enjoying a nice Pap smear. *To cherish him like I effing promised I would.* And when he leaves the empty lemonade pitcher in the refrigerator after he polishes off the last refreshing drop, or thoughtfully deposits his stinky basketball shorts directly *next to* the hamper, I am going to beg myself to remember that it could be much, much worse. To wit: Peppered throughout this book—plus in a final glorious roundup chapter at the end—are true tales from the marital trenches, here to remind us all just how good we have it. (Relatively, at least.) Just look for the handy "At Least You're Not Married to Him" icon. You'll laugh, you'll cry, you'll count your connubial blessings like you haven't since your honeymoon. You'll come to appreciate tiny gestures—your husband's putting on deodorant or actually replacing the toilet tissue roll after he's used the last square—that you may never have even noticed before.

On that note, a little heads-up to the dude who *never, ever brushes his teeth* and his wife loves him anyway: You might want to step it up in every other marital area possible. That gal's a keeper.

CHAPTER ONE

Can We Talk?
Obviously Not

If love means never having to say you're sorry,
marriage means always having to say everything twice.

· ESTELLE GETTY ·

Just last week, a newsletter I read regularly arrived in my inbox with a headline heralding this terrifying bit of news: COMMUNICATION KEY TO GOOD MARRIAGE. Heart racing, I clicked through to the story, vastly relieved to discover that it was referring to a recent study conducted by the National Association of Advertisers looking at the "marriage" between client and agency. I mean, can you *imagine* if they'd been talking about men and women and the actual holy sacrament of matrimony? (The study also pointed out the benefits of having an objective third party in the room, which would certainly come in handy in the domestic arena. "Why don't you ask *her* if that's what I said, asshole.")

Maybe it's just me. Maybe my relationship is truly unique in its never-ending struggle over the basic exchange of ideas

· · · · ·

and information. Remember that old *Far Side* cartoon, the one with the guy talking to his dog? Under the first picture is the caption *WHAT YOU SAY TO YOUR DOG*, and the speech bubble coming out of the guy's mouth reads something like this: "Okay, Ginger! I've had it! You stay out of the garbage! Understand, Ginger? Stay out of the garbage or else!" Under the next picture, which is identical to the first, there's the caption *WHAT YOUR DOG HEARS*; *that* bubble has this inside it: "Blah, blah, Ginger, blah, blah, blah, blah, blah, blah, blah, blah, Ginger, blah, blah, blah, blah, blah . . ."

Now I'm not calling my husband a dog exactly, but seriously, we do seem to have a hell of a time relaying ideas to one another. For many, many years, I operated on the assumption that Joe simply has a smaller capacity for both using and processing words than I do. If you want indisputable proof that my theory was wrong, ask him for details about the collapse of the S&L industry or the history of the Raiders or the plight of the beautiful but endangered red-shouldered hawk or anything else he's passionate and knowledgeable about, and he'll chew your ear until it's bloody. But if you want to know how he feels when we get denied the bank loan we desperately want, or what sort of legacy he hopes to leave behind when he's gone, or how he thinks his parents' divorce ultimately affected his ability to foster and maintain lasting, meaningful relationships, good luck getting a single intelligible nugget out of him. If someone came out with Conversational CliffsNotes for Relationships, I'm sure my husband would happily buy the entire series.

• • • • •

In addition to his aversion to verbalizing matters of the heart, Joe tends to be extremely stingy (he'd probably say "economical," but the divide over semantics is another episode of *Dr. Phil*) with his syllables when it comes to basic, everyday chitchat. Whereas I am not merely fond of but one might say driven to lengthy discourse, my husband holds on to his words as if they were hundred-dollar bills and he's hovering on the brink of bankruptcy. This verbal imbalance frequently results in exchanges in our home that sound a lot like this:

JOE: "Did you order the Office Max stuff?"

ME: "Well, I looked around and found the printer cartridge cheaper at Staples, but you had to spend fifty bucks to get the free shipping, so I did the math and realized if I bought some more stuff it would actually be cheap—"

JOE: "Yes or no?"

ME: "I have all of the stuff in my cart—"

JOE: "So, yes?"

ME: "Well, I still need to find the model number for the fax mach—"

JOE: "So, no?"

ME: "Oh my God, you are impossible to—"

JOE: "So, no."

In my multitasking mind, this is not a yes/no question. Sure, maybe the bottom line is that *I haven't ordered the goddamned supplies as of this particular moment in time*, but there are mitigating circumstances! Explanatory details! Titillating shades of expository gray! The shortest answer I could possibly give is that I haven't (and I'd be happy to explain why) but I will (and allow me to tell you when). Alas, my listening-impaired husband doesn't want a story; he wants an answer. A simple, clear-cut, one-word, yes-or-no answer. And while I understand this on a fundamental level, that tiny detail kicks my ass every single time.

" At Least You're Not Married to Him "

My husband starts all of his sentences with the word *no*. Even when he is agreeing with me, he will say "No . . ." It's like a transition word for him between thoughts or sentences. It's totally annoying.

CATHY

It's taken me many frustrating years to accept the fact that my husband believes "Yes" is an acceptable answer to questions such as "Should we stay at your dad's or in a hotel next month?" or "Do you want pork loin or chicken cacciatore tonight?" For the longest time I accused him of being passive-aggressive, but the reality is there's nothing aggressive about his typical sort of reply at all. It's 100 percent passive—and for the most part absent of malice—because he *truly doesn't give a shit* where we stay or what we eat. And the thing is, for reasons unknown to me and probably most women who aren't scientists studying the social-anthropological motivations behind universal female drives, I *want* him to give a shit. *If he loved me, he'd understand I'm tired of making every mundane domestic decision and at least pretend to care*, I silently seethe. The thought bubble over *his* head, of course, would probably read, *What's love got to do with it?*

If he didn't love me, would he have built me that kick-ass walk-in closet without even demanding a single square foot of real estate inside it where he might stash a handful of socks? Would he patrol our darkened street every other night making enthusiastic kissing noises in an effort to lure home the cat he doesn't really care for because he knows I can't sleep if she's not in the house? Would he agree to spend Christmas Eve sleeping on scratchy, ill-fitting sheets draped over a saggy air mattress just so that I can spend the holiday with one or another of my wacky relatives? Of course not. He loves me, but the truth is he couldn't care less where we stay or what we eat. *C'est la vie.* Or at least, *c'est ma vie.*

" At Least You're Not Married to Him "

My husband is a major pessimist! No matter how positive things are going, he can find the negative in it. Instead of saying that something is going to go well, he talks about everything that could possibly go wrong.

DEB

• • • • •

Sadly, the mere fact of Joe's devotion does not make conversations like this any less maddening:

> ME: "How was basketball tonight?"
>
> JOE: "Good."
>
> ME: "How many guys showed up?"
>
> JOE: "Eleven."
>
> ME: "Did they finish redoing the floors in the gym yet?"
>
> JOE: "Yup."
>
> ME: "How were they?"
>
> JOE: "Nice."
>
> ME: "Did you play well?"
>
> JOE: "I was okay."
>
> ME: "How did your ankle feel?"
>
> JOE: "Fine."
>
> ME: "Was Danny there?"
>
> JOE: "Yeah."
>
> ME: "Anything new with him?"
>
> JOE: "Not really."
>
> ME: [*to self*] *Well this is a whole effing heap of fun!* [*to Joe*] "Who else was there?"
>
> JOE: "The usual."
>
> ME: [*silently*] *The defense rests, Your Honor. No further questions.*

Because I write about relationships a lot, I get a ton of press releases on the subject. The headline on a recent one, sent out to announce the results of a series of studies, boldly proclaimed,

"Women write emotional e-mails while men prefer short, straightforward ones." This is news? Did the "researchers" spend actual money to come to this shocking conclusion? Or did one of them merely extrapolate when she noticed that her own inbox was filled with spousal responses that contained nothing but the letter K (Think, "Want to go out for dinner tonight?" "K"), as if the sender might be suggesting he is far too busy and important to go to the laborious lengths of typing out the entire word *Okay*?

Communication experts point out that conversationally, in addition to their desire to share excruciatingly minute details, women tend to key in on similarities ("My kid/mom/dog/housekeeper/ass fat does that, too!"), while men pretty much take everything they hear as a challenge ("Your kid/mom/dog/housekeeper/ass fat does that? Big deal—listen to what *mine* does!"). These same professionals insist that the way to motivate and persuade people of either sex is to talk about things they care about in ways that matter to them. Far as I can tell, that would mean the preceding conversation would have worked out swimmingly for Joe had I just put it this way:

"Want to tell me all about basketball while I give you a blowjob?"

Here's the irony of this ubiquitous situation: Advice on bridging the titanic communication gap between men and women has become its own billion-dollar industry. The category pioneer, *Men Are from Mars, Women Are from Venus*, is no longer just a book, it's an empire, complete with online magazine, dating service, wellness retreats, seminars, CDs,

DVDs, personal coaching, franchise opportunities, even a supplement line—because perhaps the sexes would finally get along if men would just get a little more choline bitartrate in their diets while women simultaneously upped their intake of ginger root and boron.

Call me cynical, but I'm thinking that if his-and-hers vitamins were the answer, we'd have read about it in *Shape* or seen an investigative Consumer Alert segment on *Dateline*. The gals at *The View* would be all over that, don't you think? Your favorite bloggers would be blabbing about it, your hairdresser would already be hawking it right at her station, and Oprah would resurrect her beloved show for one glorious encore where she would interview happily supplementing couples and then bequeath cases of the stuff to her audiences, packaged generously in the trunks of their new Mercedes-Benz sport coupes, not that I'm bitter. Picture the news teasers: "Groundbreaking new supplement fosters satisfying communication between men and women!" Who among you wouldn't tune in at six?

Alas, we don't need fancy vitamins, because I think I have the answer. I have actually figured out how women—the doers in most relationships—can turn the conversational tide without their partner's consent *or* cooperation. I know, we all want the guys to step up and "own" their part in our collective relational dysfunction. But life is short, and really, isn't the final result more important than how you get there? Because I believe it is, I present to you my radically simple, three-step process for successful marital communication:

1. Shut the fuck up for five lousy minutes. Face the fact that your partner really, truly, deeply doesn't care to hear a real-time report of your every thought or a detailed recap of your latest dream or phone call. "Had a funny dream" or "talked to your sister" will do just fine. If he wants to know any more, he'll ask. (Don't hold your breath.)

2. Go out and get some girlfriends, or start spending more time with the ones you've got. Once you commit to Step 1, this will be both easy and imperative, as you will have seven billion thoughts, hopes, and random musings floating about in your head demanding to be shared. The beauty of Step 2 is that your girlfriends actually *do* want to analyze your mother's motives for sending you that curt e-mail, and they *will* be equally and vocally disgusted when you tell them about the dirty look the cashier gave you when you tried to use a handful of expired coupons at Bed Bath & Beyond.

3. *Stop expecting your husband to be a chick.* The mere fact that he does not have a vagina—probably one of the more compelling reasons you married him in the first place— means that he does not, will not, and cannot keep your conversational pace. And even if he does, will, and can, he probably doesn't want to and will resent the hell out of you if you keep trying to maximize his verbal potential. Accept this about him, and he will worship you forever. (Silently, of course.)

Albert Einstein, the original genius, is reported to have defined insanity as doing the same thing over and over and expecting different results. Which explains why trying to have a simple chat with your spouse can make you feel like a lunatic. (You: "Want to go to Doug and Karan's for dinner on Friday?" Him: "Sure." You: "Great, I'll let Karan know." Him: "Let Karan know what?") In countless laboratory experiments, scientists have proven that rats that are rewarded for pressing a lever with a pellet of food *will continue to press the lever*. Why? Because their actions produce a positive response. It's a simple reward system. But if pressing the lever ceases to result in the desired pellet drop, even a lowly, filthy, sewer-dwelling rat will eventually abort what has obviously become a futile mission.

Women, not so much. "Honey, what's wrong? Do you want to talk about it? Come on, just tell me. *Please.* You know you can talk to me, don't you? Is it something at work? Did I do something? You know it's not healthy to bottle up all of your feelings. There obviously is something wrong, so just tell me what it is. You really will feel better. Come on, I tell you *everything.* Honestly, you are the most emotionally constipated person I have ever met. I might as well be talking to a wall. I *will* stop bugging you as soon as you *tell me what's wrong!*"

Rats.

We see our husbands slouched down on the couch, staring off into space, fingertips comfortably poised inside the waistband of their boxer-briefs, and we are powerless to resist.

"Whatcha thinking about?" we ask, hoping the question sounds more indifferent than intrusive—and praying the answer is "Oh, just how wonderful you are" or some variation thereof.

"Nothing," he mumbles back, and we instantly become irate. What a liar! He has to be thinking about *something*! How can you think about nothing? It's not humanly possible. If he's truly pondering *nothing*, it has to be in some sort of context, right? Like, "There's nothing good on TV anymore," or "Nothing is better than a quickie after lunch," or "There's nothing in the refrigerator except some sour milk and a few squishy grapes." I mean, who can think about nothing? Go ahead. Try to think about nothing, just to see if it can be done. I'm betting that in less than two seconds you'll remember that you forgot to check to see if you turned off the light inside the car after you brought in the groceries, and it's your stepmom's birthday next week and you didn't get her a card yet, and where the hell could that damned checkbook be, because now the phone bill is exactly six days overdue, and what if there really *isn't* a God?

We just can't stop at *nothing*.

As inexplicable as it seems to anyone with ovaries, guys the world over insist they really can achieve an instant alpha-wave brain state whereby all their erstwhile thoughts become suspended like fake flies in a cube of plastic novelty ice. They can do this day or night, alone or in a crowd, practically on command. Like the ability to pee standing up or go topless without getting arrested, it's simply a skill they have that most women don't. (Look on the bright side: We get multiple orgasms and the privilege of sipping fruity umbrella drinks without being mocked. A pretty fair trade-off, if you ask me.)

· · · · ·

"" **At Least You're Not Married to Him** ""

When we go to a zoo or any public event where animals are involved,
he puts his zoology degree to use (no, this isn't sarcasm; he really does
have a zoology degree), and he loudly "talks" to the animals. We wan-
der away, hoping no one will know he's with us.

TRICIA

There's a saying: Women marry men hoping that they will
change; men marry women hoping that they won't. When my
husband and I were in the thick of those delicious, giddy, lust-
driven early months of our courtship, do you think I was
constantly pleading with him to share his every innermost
thought or badgering him to "talk about the relationship"?
Hell, no. We were too busy having sex! Plus, I didn't want to
pressure him or seem needy or insecure. In fact, the first (dozen
or so) fights I can recall having with him were those first
(dozen or so) times I tried to convince him that we needed
to . . . all together now . . . *talk about the relationship.*

When one half of a couple has a burning itch that the other
doesn't have and therefore doesn't have the vaguest idea how
or where to scratch, eventually the itchy one will find someone
else who can do their soothing. My sister Laurie is like human
hydrocortisone cream to my chronically chafed soul. Despite
the three thousand miles and three time zones separating us,
somehow we manage to talk nearly every day. Of course we
both go to great lengths to downplay the frequency and duration of our chats to our husbands, whom we have jointly

dubbed the Phone Police. We'll be enjoying our daily heart-to-heart when one of the "officers" will enter the room. "Phone Police," we whisper before trying to slip the receiver soundlessly into the cradle. "Who were you talking to?" Joe always wants to know. "My sister," I half mumble. "Didn't you just talk to her yesterday?" he demands. "Yeah, so?" I ask belligerently. A man who successfully maintains most of his long-distance relationships through an annual phone call couldn't possibly understand.

I know that it is pointless to rely on my husband to satisfy my urge to analyze and dissect the mad and mystifying world, but every once in a while—like when my sister is asleep or off at a conference or her cell phone battery dies—I nevertheless give it a shot. And it never fails. Once I start to delve into the meat of a deliciously juicy story—one I've waited hours to share, so that the kids would be in bed and I'd have my husband's undivided attention—I am swiftly and systematically cut off before I even get to the good part.

ME: "Did you hear that Bob cheated on Shelly and he got
    the other gal pregnant?"

JOE: "Bob's an asshole."

ME: "I know! Isn't he the *worst*? He's despicable. He's slime.
    I don't even know what I'll do the next time I see him.
    God, I hope I'm not nice to him. I'll have to remember
    to try to be really nasty. If you see me starting to be
    nice, remind me, okay? Anyway, Shelly got this amazing lawyer—the guy's supposed to be an absolute

shark—and, wait a minute, don't you want to know who Bob knocked up?"

JOE: "Not really. Bob's an asshole. Shelly needs to get an attorney."

ME: "Shelly *has* an attorney, I just told you that, and we don't know the other woman anyway, but her kid plays soccer with Shelly's son and she's supposed to be this totally trampy bimbo with big fake boobs who hits on all the dads at—"

JOE: "Who's the attorney?"

ME: "How should I know? I'm just trying to tell you—"

JOE: "Do you know whose name the house is in?"

ME: "No, but—"

JOE: "What about any other assets?"

ME: "I'm going to go call Laurie."

Interestingly, and despite all of this, it has never been proven that women talk more than men. In fact, the frequently cited "women speak twenty thousand words a day while men utter only seven thousand" statistic turned out to have been completely unfounded—practically pulled out of thin air—although it's possible that is simply because no one's bothered to undertake the tedious task of actually counting how many words are spoken by a randomly selected mixed-gender sample of the population. And even if they did, someone else would get all pissed off and throw up her near-mute aunt Martha or annoyingly loquacious brother Larry as proof to the contrary, because of course there is an exception to every rule. I actually tried to find some legitimate statistics, but most of the research is liberally sprinkled with phrases like "collated meta-analysis" and "gender similarity hypothesis" that make my eyes glaze over and my brain turn to oatmeal. And that's fine, because I don't need a double-blind, placebo-controlled study to tell me what I already know: My husband and I are very, very different. Whether it's nature, nurture, programming, or perception matters not. It's not that he "doesn't talk" or "can't communicate," it's just that he *doesn't want to talk about the same things that I do*. He isn't interested in dissecting, emotionally and in agonizing depth, the many and varied reasons our friends Sam and Cindy have decided not to have children. He couldn't care less what the vet said about the cat's chronic eye-goop problem. (Allergies. Who knew cats got allergies?) He just wants to know (a) what we—and by *we* he means *me*—are supposed to do about it, and (b) how much it's going to cost. He will never, ever want to discuss a single title in the towering stack of books constantly threatening to topple my nightstand or debate the ethical implications of fictionalizing a memoir. (The only novel he's ever read is *Moby-Dick*, and trust me, we long ago tapped out the reading-group discussion potential there.) Ask him what he thinks happens when you die, and his go-to answer is, "Who cares? You're dead." And get this: The guy honestly doesn't give a rat's ass which celebrities have overdosed, or recently checked into rehab, or are rumored to be covered in cellulite. I know! And he doesn't even lord his moral superiority over me. It's enough to drive a wife insane.

Even though it's proven over and over to be a futile move,

* * * * *

because Joe and I both work from home I frequently toss out brief status updates such as, "I'm going to the grocery store after I get the girls." To me, this is a simple information-providing statement, one intended to prevent him from worrying when I haven't returned from school pickup in an hour. Nevertheless, as I am trying to wrangle the unwieldy, NASCAR-replica shopping cart our daughters insist we use while thwarting their persistent efforts to fill it with high-fructose, trans fat–filled goodies and not knock over any canned-goods displays or stooped-over little old ladies, almost without fail my cell phone rings, forcing me to dig frantically through the ridiculous quagmire of junk that has somehow found its way into my purse.

"Where are you guys?" Joe wants to know, sounding mildly alarmed.

"At the grocery store! I told you we were going after pickup," I say with all the patience I can muster.

"Okay, have fun," he chirps absentmindedly.

Fun? Oh yeah, buddy, this is a flipping spa vacation right here. One I'm sure you'll want to hear all about when I get home . . . right after you ask me where we've been.

" At Least You're Not Married to Him "

Imagine me at my desk and my husband, Brian, at home when the following argument ensues—verbatim—via instant messenger:

BRIAN: Wait a minute. It's next weekend? Why have you been saying weekend after next this whole week, then?

DEILIA: Because I'm talking about the weekend after next. Not next weekend. You have "this" weekend, "next" weekend, and "the weekend after next."

BRIAN: The next weekend after this past Monday was THIS weekend, not next weekend.

DEILIA: Yes.

BRIAN: Soooooooo . . .

DEILIA: This weekend is 3/13. NEXT weekend is 3/20 and the weekend after next (which is what I've been saying) is 3/27.

BRIAN: When you said "weekend after next" on Monday it meant next weekend.

DEILIA: Nope. On Monday it was this weekend. I would've said NEXT weekend.

BRIAN: Unless there was a weekend in between Monday and Friday, the next weekend would be this weekend. Just speak in dates for that stuff, okay?

DEILIA: You just said it yourself! Next weekend is THIS weekend. Why are you so upset???

BRIAN: EXACTLY. On Monday you said weekend after next.

DEILIA: Yes I did. Which meant not this weekend, not NEXT weekend but the weekend AFTER NEXT.

BRIAN: The NEXT weekend from this past Monday was THIS weekend.

DEILIA: Nope. That was this weekend. On Monday you would say "this weekend I'm going to go to the movies," right?

BRIAN: This weekend is the next weekend unless you are already in the weekend.

DEILIA: No. When you are talking about the weekend coming up, you say "this weekend." If you were talking about the previous weekend, you say "this past weekend."

· · · · ·

If It Was Easy . . .

BRIAN: "Next" means "closest future thing," especially on Monday.

DEILIA: No.

BRIAN: You have like a whole week in between.

DEILIA: You are a moron. This weekend is this week's weekend.

BRIAN: At the beginning of the week, what is the very next weekend?

DEILIA: This weekend.

BRIAN: !!

DEILIA: I want to kill myself right now.

BRIAN: I want to kill you right now. If this weekend is next weekend, then next weekend is weekend after next. That's how language works.

DEILIA: NO! On Monday I refer to this weekend. So if I was talking about two weeks out I would say weekend after next!

BRIAN: You just said that the very next weekend after Monday was this weekend. It's documented.

DEILIA: YES!

BRIAN: Scroll up.

DEILIA: So weekend after NEXT is not that weekend, not NEXT weekend but the one AFTER!

BRIAN: If THIS weekend is the NEXT weekend from the beginning of the week, then AT the beginning of the week when you say WEEKEND AFTER NEXT it means what it means.

DEILIA: I don't say NEXT weekend on MONDAY, I say THIS WEEKEND.

BRIAN: Then why did you say that the next weekend from Monday was this weekend?

DEILIA: Because it is the NEXT weekend in LINE which is referred to as THIS weekend.

BRIAN: So that makes it NEXT WEEKEND.

DEILIA: NO!!! If you were asking me out on a date on Tuesday what would you say?

BRIAN: I am sooo glad we aren't doing this verbally.

. . . . .

DEILIA: Me too.

BRIAN: We were not talking about Tuesday, we were talking about Monday.

DEILIA: So on Monday . . . you wouldn't say "Want to go out this weekend?"

BRIAN: I would never ask anyone out on a date that early in the week. That seems desperate as hell.

DEILIA: Because you know I'M RIGHT!!! I win.

BRIAN: It IS my fault. For not understanding that you don't think logically.

DEILIA

CHAPTER TWO

Sleep in Heavenly Peace, My Ass

Do you know what it means when you have a man
lying in bed next to you moaning and gasping?

It means you didn't hold the pillow down long enough.

• JOKE SO OLD MY DINOSAUR TOLD IT TO ME THE FIRST TIME •

If I were an Eskimo and the Huffington Post were selling ice, I'd still buy it by the igloofull. I can't help it; I'm a sucker for headlines like Gwyneth Paltrow Enlists Personal Trainer to Fix Her Sagging Ass and Tiger's Penis Issues Rebuttal. I mean, honestly. If you can resist getting sucked in by stories like those, you're a stronger woman than I am. So anyway, I was lurking around over there a few weeks back trolling for my daily fix, and because I am writing a book about marriage, you can imagine how excited I was to see this: The Secret to a Happy Marriage: Separate Beds? I Doubt It. The skepticism at the end was the part that hooked me, because frankly I've given the separate-beds idea a lot of thought and

• • • • •

I'm pretty sure it could be the answer to domestic bliss, at least between the hours of ten P.M. and six A.M.

The author of this particular piece, Dr. Michael J. Breus—also known as the Sleep Doctor, according to his byline—began by enumerating the countless terrifying ways that sharing a bed with a particularly disruptive partner actually can be hazardous to your health. Then he went on to list the many and compelling reasons to ignore the *potentially deadly risks* and go for it anyway. In addition to the obvious benefits of co-sleeping (sex and spooning, essentially), he holds up the results of a study out of Australia that found—and I am not making this up—that "men sleep better when they are sleeping next to someone else." Which simultaneously infuriates (what about *me*, dude?) and mystifies me. Because I find it hard to believe that my husband is getting a restful night's sleep when I am punching him every ten minutes and hissing at him to *roll the fuck over*. And if we're being honest here, I'd be sort of annoyed if he were.

The thing is, Joe snores. Not occasionally or delicately, either, I'm afraid. He's so damned contrite about it that I've even stopped believing that he's doing it intentionally just to piss me off. He's tried every single remedy I've angrily hurtled at him: nose strips, throat sprays, homeopathic remedies, palate guards, ergonomic pillows. The man willingly paid close to a monthly mortgage payment to spend a miserable night in a sleep clinic, where the doctors—upon vigilant observation—were able to rule out several life-threatening conditions including UARS (Upper Airway Resistance Syndrome) and OSA

(Obstructive Sleep Apnea). After much humiliating poking and prodding his heart was deemed robust, his septum arrow-straight. Eventually he was sent home with a diagnosis of MWCSBMSS (My Wife Can't Sleep Because of My Snoring Syndrome), otherwise known as NRMP (Not Really My Problem). Two weeks later I had a nice $150 pair of custom earplugs to help me deal with "my condition."

" At Least You're Not Married to Him "

My husband has to shake his leg or foot to fall asleep, every night. It makes it impossible to read in bed without feeling nauseous.

KRISTA

If only Joe's snoring was the singular thing preventing me from getting a solid stretch of rest. No, even on the rare silent night, trying to come to any sort of compromise regarding our bedroom's atmospheric conditions is harder than drowning a tractor-size helium balloon in a two-inch puddle. You'd think I was one of those anorexic, hairless cats and Joe was a fifteen-hundred-pound polar bear by the irreconcilable differences in our core body temperatures.

"Your internal thermostat is totally fucked up," Joe will insist. Why? Because I can't feel my extremities and it's a balmy fifty-five degrees in here? If you set up a hidden video camera in our bedroom, here's a glimpse of what you might see on any given evening:

. . . . .

Me, quickly slipping into my sexy camo sweatpants, thermal long-sleeve tee, and triple-ply chenille knee socks. I begin the elaborate process of removing and stacking the bed's dozen-or-so decorative throw pillows neatly on the window seat, hopping and performing mini jumping jacks in an effort to prevent my blood from freezing right there in my veins.

Joe, entering the room fully dressed. Ignoring my warm-up routine entirely, he proceeds to open all of the windows and *turn on the ceiling fan*. When he is finished, he artfully raises a single eyebrow at me (translation: "That's right, bitch. I want it nice and frigid in here when I come back in two hours.") before leaving the room to go watch TV.

I roll my eyes and shut the door, sticking my tongue out at him from behind the hinged slab of wood that separates us. Then I quickly and quietly close the windows and turn off the ceiling fan before bounding into the bed, where I frantically tug one sheet, two blankets, and the duvet-wrapped Permabaffle eiderdown comforter up to my quivering chin.

Joe returns minutes later under the guise of "getting his slippers," but of course he is there for one reason: to make sure *the windows are still open and the fan is still on*. They are neither.

"Really?" he demands, flipping the fan switch by the door.

"Really," I reply, daring to dart an arm out of the velvety warmth of my blanket mountain to flip the switch by the bed.

"Put on some clothes!" he barks. *Flip.*

"I'm wearing half of my pajama drawer and you're *not even in here*!" I bellow back, my teeth chattering audibly. *Flip.*

Joe, giving me the stink-eye: *Flip.*

Me, flashing a look of mock shock and flipping him a mental bird: *Flip.*

Joe, both brows raised, torso puffed up like a pissed-off gorilla: *Flip.*

Me, all Central Park crazy lady (the one with hot-pink lipstick smeared around the vicinity of her mouth who mutters to herself constantly): *Flip, flip, eff you, flip, fuckity, flip, flip, FLIP.*

"You have a serious problem," Joe grumbles, stalking back out of the room.

"Yeah, *you*," I mutter in perfect crazy-lady fashion. When he's gone I sigh in exasperated relief, tuck my head under the covers, and say a quick prayer to the slumber gods that I will be deep in my first REM cycle before he returns and flips the dreaded switch again.

I'll admit that being married to a human furnace occasionally has its advantages. When I underdress for an occasion—which you probably won't be surprised to hear happens frequently—Joe never, *ever* complains about relinquishing his jacket. In movie theaters (where *what in the name of the Holy Mother* is up with the arctic freeze? It's not like they're selling winter coats or even hot panini sandwiches at the ridiculously overpriced concession stand, even though I'd be inclined to buy both), he's been known to cavalierly wrap an index finger around the tip of my frozen nose. On ski lifts, he'll graciously offer the toasty pocket of his nearest armpit for me to thaw out at least a few fingers. And in the rare instances when we crawl into bed at the same time, he invites me to press my icy ass cheeks into his sweltering thighs and wriggle my wintry feet between his toasty calves—a sensory thrill that lasts approximately thirty seconds before I feel like I'm suffocating in a Nigerian sauna. I know; the *irony*. Naturally he's hurt and angry when I pull away from him.

"I thought you were *freezing*," he says incredulously, with mock-whiny emphasis on the last offensive word.

"I was before, but now I'm not," I huff, shuffling around the bed looking for a sliver of coolness on the mattress, any tiny patch where his body heat hasn't penetrated the eighteen-inch foam and spread like, well, wildfire. I usually fall asleep on the tippy-edge of my side of the bed, where accidental bodily contact isn't likely. Sometimes Joe will absentmindedly search for my form across the vast expanse of mattress between us in the middle of the night, tossing a huge, heavy, feverish hand (I call it the "hot paw") protectively across my midsection when he locates me. It's so sweet when he does this that I try to sound really tender and loving when I squirm away pleading with him to *get his fucking hot paw off me*.

My salvation is our bedmate, Sheldon. No, we're not that kind of kinky. Sheldon isn't a Siamese or a Shih-Tzu, either; Sheldon is a deliciously lofty six-foot bag of feathers. You know, a body pillow. Sheldon is the perfect sleeping partner as he is climatically stable, totally malleable, and blissfully silent. He also has never once "accidentally" poked me in the backside with his boner, a courtesy I appreciate more than mere words can express. Joe, as you might imagine, is not a big fan of Sheldon. In fact, he gets downright jealous when he tries to snuggle up to me and finds me swaddling Sheldon like a slab of prosciutto wrapped around a tiger shrimp. Which is why I named him Sheldon.

HARRY: With whom did you have this great sex?

SALLY: I'm not going to tell you that.

HARRY: Fine, don't tell me.

SALLY: Shel Gordon.

HARRY: Shel? Sheldon? No, no, you did not have great sex with Sheldon.

SALLY: I did too.

HARRY: No, you didn't. A Sheldon can do your income taxes; if you need a root canal, Sheldon's your man . . . but humpin' and pumpin' is not Sheldon's strong suit. It's the name. 'Do it to me, Sheldon; you're an animal, Sheldon; ride me, big Sheldon.' Doesn't work.

Turns out Shakespeare pretty much nailed it, because a body pillow by any other name—even Sheldon—still breeds massive marital resentment. But it *does* help block the occasional hot paw, so at least there's that.

" At Least You're Not Married to Him "

My husband wears socks to bed, but in the middle of the night, he slips them off. They usually stay in the bed until they either travel to my side of the bed, at which time I kick them back to his side, or they

fall on the floor. I refuse to pick them up. When he's out of socks, he's
out of socks.

ROBERTA

Apparently Joe and I are not the only couple out there with
"pillow issues." I am not particularly proud of this, but my
husband and I each still sleep with the (head) pillow we had
when we got married. Since they were never living things,
carbon dating isn't an option, but I will tell you that when we
met, *Married . . . with Children* was still in prime time. In
other words, they are well loved and extremely distinctive, so
getting them mixed up is not a problem. My sister Laurie,
however, regales me with tales of how even though she recently
bought brand-spanking-new, *identical* pillows for herself and
her husband, a certain one of these twin slabs of foam is dis-
tinctively hers. How does she know? Evidently *her pillow* has
two or three tiny little bumps that she (a) would recognize
anywhere, (b) has grown intimately fond of, and (c) cannot
sleep without. Laurie will call me absolutely irate to report that
Carl fell asleep with *her pillow* again and she had to "rip it right
out from under his listless head." (I told Carl he should write
a book about it. He's not the cursing type or I'd have sworn I
heard him call me a smart-ass.)

Just as pillow thievery is not conducive to remaining happily
married, neither, it would appear, is having separate and distinct wake-up times and methods. Now, my difficulty not only
falling asleep but *remaining there* once I've surpassed that first
critical hurdle is legendary. Deadline looming two worrisome

• • • • •

months away? Can't fall asleep. Kid gets up to go to the bathroom? I'm up. Squirrel scampers along the branch of the tree that is next to but not even touching the back fence? There go the last eleven winks. Ambulance or police siren screams by on the highway four miles away? *Dear God, where are the children?* Now I must race across the house, up the stairs and into their rooms so that I can be sure that they haven't sneaked out and robbed a convenience store or gotten flattened by a train. While I'm there, I might as well gently lay a hand on each of their tiny chests to confirm that they are rising and falling with robust regularity. A half an hour apiece generally is enough to convince me that I am not just imagining that they are tucked safely into their little beds and that they will probably make it through the night.

Because I am intimately familiar with the elusive nature of the beast we call sleep, I am the most considerate roommate a semiunconscious person could ever have. When Joe is in bed before me, I brush my teeth and wash my face in the guest bathroom. I take a painstaking thirty seconds to twist the bedroom doorknob the ninety necessary degrees to unlatch it, so that it doesn't emit a single audible creak. I tiptoe to the bed and peel back the covers gently, one layer at a time, so as not to shock his docile body with a massive, unexpected blast of arctic air. Then I crawl in like a burglar through a window, careful not to deploy more than a single bedspring with any given movement.

I think another reason I am so freakishly courteous is because of my ex-boyfriend Jake. (Jake is not his real name, but I am still friends with Jake and would like to remain so, so indulge me here.) During the three years I lived in sin with Jake we just couldn't seem to get the hang of sharing a communal bedroom. I'd turn in at my usual rock-star bedtime of eight thirty to read, passing out at some point shortly thereafter. Jake would come in to join me anywhere between midnight and sunrise the next morning.

"You asleep?" he'd ask, *not using his library voice or even his regular inside voice*, swinging the door as wide as it would go. As he would stand there letting his eyes adjust to the darkness, the hallway light worked like twin laser beams to carve matching holes into my retinas.

"Kitcha catcha shhhh shhhhhhhh arghhhhhhhhhhhh!" I'd stammer furiously, wrapping my pillow around my head and trying to resist consciousness.

"Oh, sorry, you *were* asleep!" he'd remark stupidly. I mean, what do you suppose would have made him think someone was asleep in there? The pitch-darkness? The dead silence? The large, lifeless heap slightly to one side of the bed?

I'd rock myself gently back and forth, hoping the rhythmic motion would bring sleep back, and softly repeat a soothing mantra to myself: *I hate you I hate you I hate you I hate you.*

"Okay, then! I'll just be super quiet so you can go back to sleep, okay? Think you can? Go back to sleep, I mean? Jen?" Jake was actually a nice guy. He just happened to have been born with a gene that would allow him not to wake if a plane crashed into the house and set it on fire. And even if he *did* galvanize when the firefighters showed up and carted him to safety, this same gene would allow him to fall immediately back to sleep on the cold, wet ground next to the wailing fire engine. Because he was built this way, Jake could not fathom when I repeatedly threatened to strangle him with the cord on his alarm clock.

A typical morning in our house looked like this:

5:47 (which was really 5:39 but he liked his alarm clock set exactly eight minutes fast, because this—he insisted—was how he "tricked" himself into getting up earlier. I'd have laughed at the absurdity of this but I was too busy crying.): *Blurp! Blurp! Blurp! Blurp! Blurp! Blurp! Blurp!*

Fiddle, rustle, *blurp!* Snap, crackle, *blurp!* Jesus effing *blurp!*

Finally he'd find the snooze button and the godforsaken blurping would stop. Literally within seconds, he would be sound asleep again. Naturally at this point I would be wide awake, so I would busy myself with the freakishly OCD task of making sure the colon between the clock's hour and minutes flashed exactly sixty times. (It did! Every time!) I would do this for nine hellish sixty-flash cycles in a row, my eyes burning from not blinking, before the inevitable repeat performance.

5:56 (technically, 5:48): *Blurp! Blurp! Blurp! Blurp! Blurp! Blurp! Blurp!*

Although I purposely bought him an alarm clock that offered the kinder, gentler wake-to-music option, he couldn't use it, you see, because he was apt to "incorporate the song into his dream" and sleep right through it. (I promised to punch him in the esophagus every nine minutes, but he couldn't get over this crippling dream-song fear.) And also, what if the radio station was experiencing technical difficulties at exactly 5:47, 5:56, 6:05, 6:14, 6:23, 6:32, 6:41, 6:50, 6:59, and 7:08 (which was actually 7:00, his intended wake-up time)? You really can't blame the guy for not wanting to risk it.

When I ended things with Jake, we agreed that he would stay in the house, so I packed my things and moved out. Even though we parted amicably, when I made my final sweep of the bedroom I couldn't resist resetting his alarm clock to the correct time. It was a tiny, vindictive little victory, and in hindsight, it's almost appalling how satisfying it was.

" At Least You're Not Married to Him "

He falls asleep on the sofa and when I try to rouse him to come to bed, he says okay and then won't get up to walk upstairs. I try to wake him and then he gets grouchy about me bothering him. After twenty years of being married and knowing his routine, I have stopped trying and now I just let him sleep on the couch. Usually, he wakes around one A.M. and comes to bed, where he wakes me up and says, get this, "Why didn't you wake me up to come to bed!?"

CINDY

The man I married thankfully (although not accidentally) is significantly more considerate than old Jake was. If Joe has to get up at some ridiculously unholy hour, he sleeps in the guest bedroom. If he merely needs to be sure he's awake by a particular but reasonable time, he'll program his phone to emit a single, subtle reminder tone. For this display of consideration alone, plus maybe the fact that he tells me constantly that he adores my body, I will never leave him.

If he's going to leave *me*, it might be because of the cats.

In my defense, it's not like I falsely advertised myself as a dog lover and waited to reveal my true cat-lady self until we got married. When Joe and I met, I had just moved from New York to Los Angeles. *With my three cats.* On Joe's very first visit to my apartment, my clowder of four-legged roommates took turns climbing into his lap, nuzzling his pant legs, and burrowing deep into his backpack.

"How many cats do you have?" he tried to ask nonchalantly.

"Just the three," I chirped.

"Oh," he replied. "I mean, that's great! I love cats. Really, you know, I just think they're great. [*pause*] So how old are they?"

"They're all about six," I told him.

Again: "Oh." And then: "How long do cats live, anyway?"

Eventually he must have decided that the cats weren't a deal breaker and asked me to marry him. I think he even grew to love them in his own way, and I am pretty sure I spotted a tear in his eye at each of their little kitty funerals. Two years ago, he didn't even gripe (much) when I suggested it was time to get our daughters a pair of kittens.

Although cats by nature are typically *crepuscular* (which sounds like it means "covered with festering, oozing sores" but really means "most active in the predawn, twilight hours"), Frick and Frack don't seem to have gotten the memo. They'll often decide to launch a rousing game of "Can't catch me, sucker!" right around midnight, and their preferred track runs, roughshod, directly over our bed. After four or five laps they tire of the chase and switch to swarming and circling in a repetitively concentric fashion about the bed, tamping down imaginary grass and looking for the perfect pair of resting spots. Joe finds this portion of the feline festivities utterly enchanting.

"Fucking *cat*," he'll growl, launching whichever one has dared to alight on one of his feet several yards into the air.

Thrilled that he's finally taken an interest in the game, Frick (followed in short order by Frack) will resume the sprint course with renewed vigor, tearing across our bodies and our heads indiscriminately and occasionally leaving a flesh wound in their mutual wake. Their process of settling down to snooze rarely takes them more than an hour or two, so I don't know why Joe gets so damned cranky about it. I mean, the love and affection those cats give him on a daily basis *more* than—oh, crap. Never mind.

I think it comes down to the fact that much like dogs and cats—or as we have recently established, people and cats—men and women just weren't meant to share a bed. It's not natural. But somehow it's gone mainstream.

In a way co-sleeping is actually a lot like the much maligned suntan. A long time ago, a "tan" was considered undesirable because having one was a sign that you made your living doing backbreaking labor in a field or some other blue-collar, al fresco venue. (Bear with me; this is relevant, I swear.) But with the advent of air travel, a new reality emerged. If you lived in Chicago and were showing off bronzed limbs in January, it could only mean one thing: You'd obviously just been on holiday in St. Bart's, you rich, lucky dog. Flash forward to the present, where the tan is once again out of vogue, because sporting one means you must be either too ignorant to read the thousands of consumer magazines telling you how sun exposure causes cancer, or too poor to fork over for one of the kabillions of broad-spectrum sunblocks on the market that those magazines informed you would be best suited to your skin type.

Sleeping with your spouse is sort of like that. Before the Industrial Revolution, when families tended to work the land they owned, it wasn't uncommon for a husband and wife to sleep in separate rooms. When you see this in movies depicting this era, you assume it's so that the husband could fool around with the nubile young chambermaid, but truly it often was simply a matter of having the space, a result of the hard-to-argue-with "Why not?" argument. The marital bed became a tradition only when couples moved from rural to urban areas and found themselves with limited real estate to work with. "Guess we'll have to bunk in here together," they probably said with a shrug when they eyed their new brownstone's "master" bedroom for the first time. (I'm guessing that this is when the anti-snore device industry took off as well.)

I don't want to freak you out or anything, but you may want to know that depression, heart disease, stroke, and respiratory failure are all associated with insufficient sleep. Not logging enough shut-eye also puts people at a greater risk for divorce and suicide (no data seems to be available for flying off in murderous rages, but I'm going to venture there's a link). The bottom line is, being tired sucks. It makes you grumpy, impairs your motor coordination, and leaves big, dark, unsightly rings around your eyes. Oh yeah, and it can *kill you*.

In the hilariously dead-serious HuffPo piece, the Sleep Doctor goes on to point out that according to surveys, 23 percent of married Americans sleep alone, and that double master bedrooms will soon, once again, be the norm in new-home construction. Although the author obviously intends to appall the reader with these details, I find them strangely comforting. In fact, the next time I can still hear Joe sawing imaginary logs with his fifteen-amp nasal chainsaw through my earplugs or the temperature in the room drops into the single digits, I will close my eyes and envision the brand-new, all-mine master suite of my dreams, which by the way will be painted Laura Ashley 110 Apple Blossom (the perfect pale pink), will be filled with two dozen flickering verbena-scented candles, and will be a continuous, climate-controlled seventy-six degrees day and night, all year round. In case you were curious, my dream master suite also has forty-eight throw pillows heaped atop a luxurious Tempur-Pedic mattress that comes with a self-heating feather bed and is wrapped in ten-thousand-thread-count Egyptian cotton sheets. The room itself boasts gigantic windows, a fireplace you can control remotely, and a walk-in closet that is the size of a 7-Eleven with a rotating shoe rack right smack in the middle of it.

Not that I've given this much thought.

. . . . .

• • •

CHAPTER THREE

"I Was Watching That!": Life with the Cable Guy

Today, watching television often means fighting,
violence, and foul language—
and that's just deciding who gets to hold the remote control.

• DONNA GEPHART •

He can do it alone or with his friends, drunk or sober, indoors or out. He'll indulge through his laptop, in the car, on a plane, and—in the most idyllic of instances—in a strange and far-away hotel room. He can (and frequently does) fall asleep doing it. Lying or sitting, with or without a snack and his hand tucked into the front of his pants, it's quite possibly the singular most versatile and enjoyable activity known to man.

And I do not mean *man* in the gender-neutral, all-encompassing, politically incorrect sense.

The inimitable Ann Landers once said, "Television has proved that people will look at anything rather than each other." In a way I guess that's a blessing in disguise, because it would totally freak me out if Joe spent even a quarter of the time he squanders watching TV just sitting there staring at me.

• • • • •

From what I know about addiction, I can confidently say that my husband does not have a TV-abuse problem. At least, not if my father is the yardstick by which he's being measured. When I was a kid, if my dad was home, the TV was on. "His" seat at the dinner table was the one that afforded the straightest, least neck-crooking view of the tube—which was *always* tuned to the news during dinner. The volume had but one setting: All the Way Up. The nonstop droning didn't bother us kids much, as not only did it preclude us from having to regale the table with daily tales of Catholic school soap eating and knuckle cracking, but it was also a great opportunity to point out birthday and Christmas wish-list items as they flashed across the screen. God love those clever marketers and their prime-time displays of beloved favorites like the Barbie Dream House and Baby Alive—because every girl should have a gamut of toys that represent what she probably will never have (a hot-pink convertible parked in front of her Swiss chalet), and also what she more than likely will (a small person in her care who makes indecipherable noises and is impossibly hard to keep clean).

❝ At Least You're Not Married to Him ❞

He simply cannot resist Tom Selleck. Long before TiVo and Hulu, my husband's sick days were filled with tomato soup and *Magnum, P.I.* on VHS. He taped over the one and only copy of my college graduation to get his own copy of "Tropical Madness" from season two; it must have been riveting because my sweet hubby learned nothing from that not-so-minor faux pas and later taped "Dead Man's Channel" over our wedding! Luckily, we had a duplicate wedding video, so the man I married is not the dead man in question. I think my feminist husband is drawn to Magnum's machismo—that overt swagger and unapologetic womanizing that is so far from his chosen reality. Despite being a poster child for evolution, those pre-PC episodes give my otherwise loving and respectful man a twisted lineage to his caveman roots.

SHELLY

Of course, my childhood was before the days of TiVo and remote controls, so many times I'd come home from being at a friend's house or more likely, the mall, to find my dad half comatose in front of some ridiculous show like *Maude* or *Barney Miller*. The watery remains of a Southern Comfort and ginger would be etching a permanent watermark ring on the table beside him.

"Hey, Jenna, while you're up could you do me a favor and change the channel?" he'd ask innocently. (Incidentally, Dad rarely meant "while you're up" literally; he'd use it even if I was asleep in my bedroom upstairs. While I was up, I also was welcome to refresh his cocktail, fix him a nice roast beef sandwich, or give the dog a bath, if the urge to do any of these things happened to strike.)

Since we had only four channels—the three networks plus a mostly fuzzy version of Fox you might be able to pick up if there was just the right amount of tinfoil wrapped around the rabbit ears—this wasn't an overwhelming task. I'd twist the dial six or seven times until he made his decision ("Is that your final answer, Dad?"), adjust the antenna to the sweet spot of maximum clarity, and be on my way.

What a difference a few decades makes. Now we've got *nine hundred channels* to choose from, and if we are so inclined we never have to watch another commercial as long as we live. No longer do we have to wait in eager anticipation for the occasional instant replay; we can watch any scene we'd like, frame by gloriously detailed frame, any old time we please. (If you haven't done this while watching *America's Funniest Home Videos*, you are absolutely missing out.) This combination of bottomless options and selective viewing has turned what was once an opportunity to relax or even cuddle on the couch into a highly charged competitive sport.

The key to winning the modern-day television Olympics, of course, is to acquire possession of the remote control and to retain it for the duration of the match. (And although the definition of a "match" is subjective, generally you're talking about any time period between a thirty-second commercial and a rainy four-day holiday weekend.) If your opponent manages to wrestle the remote away from you—through either bribery, physical threats, manipulation, the promise of sexual favors, or the withholding thereof—the odds of getting it back are infinitesimal. Once you no longer stand any chance of reclaiming the coveted clicker, you might as well go fix yourself a nice sandwich or give the dog a bath, because you lose. Game over.

I lose a lot, mostly because I don't care all that much. If I were single and childless, I would cheerfully count myself among the less than 0.01 percent of lucky Americans who do not own a TV. But because I am neither of those things, I have grudgingly joined the mind-boggling 99.9 percent of the people in

· · · · ·

this country who are the proud owners of nearly three sets each—machines we collectively watch with appalling frequency. According to the A. C. Nielsen Company, the most esteemed media research group in the world, the typical American logs more than five hours in front of the TV every single day. In case you're not a fan of math, I'll do the calculating for you: That's thirty-five hours a week, or seventy-seven days a year of uninterrupted idiot box watching. If Average Andy manages to keep up that prolific couch potato pace until he is eighty, he will have spent more than *thirteen years of his life* glued to the tube. Where, I ask you, is Michael Moore's blistering documentary about what *that's* doing to our society?

Call me a big, fat hypocrite, but I'm married and I'm a mom. So in addition to the SUV, the black lab, and the white picket fence, I own precisely the number of TVs I am supposed to own, even though I rarely watch any of them. I might be inclined to tune in more if I knew how to work the remote, or if there weren't such a disconcertingly large number of options to choose from, or if my husband didn't care if I also did something else—like balance my checkbook or write thank-you notes or check Twitter from my iPhone—while I was watching. But for some inexplicable reason, Joe not only is desperate for me to be his cable companion, but wants a full 100 percent of my uninterrupted focus to be on the television for the duration of the programming.

I do not understand this need at all. I mean, I get the bit about his wanting my company. You know, because we're married and we love to spend time together and if I'm watching the same show he is, ostensibly I'm not interrupting him every four minutes to ask him to do something around the house. It's the part where he minds when I multitask that confuses me.

"Want me to rewind that?" he'll ask.

"No, why?" I'll respond, intently focused on the laundry pile in front of me.

"Because you were the one who picked this movie and that part was really funny and you were folding that towel so I thought maybe you missed it," he says.

"It's okay," I insist. "I heard it. It *was* funny!" I say the last part out of courtesy and refrain from adding *I wanted to read, but you begged me to watch a movie so quit bitching about the movie I picked or what I'm doing while I'm watching it.*

"You didn't laugh," he pouts.

"I laughed on the *inside*, dear," I reply. "I'll try to be more vocal with my displays of hilarity from now on."

"Well, I have to rewind it now anyway, so I'll just go back to that part," he says.

"You ready?" he asks, when the sidesplitting moment in question is all cued up.

"Yup!" I tell him, continuing with the folding. Three or four minutes later I realize he hasn't hit the play button yet. If he is waiting for me to gaze meaningfully into the television set's lifeless electronic eyes, he's going to be there an awfully long time.

"You know what? I think I'm just going to go read," I say, because obviously boob-tubing is not something we were built to do as a team. He's got the TV tuned to *SportsCenter* before I am even on my feet. Joe knows I can't stand the sound of televised sports, so he courteously dons the headphones he gave me for Christmas one year (they were a mock gift because we both knew he'd be the one wearing them, and because he actually *does* wear them with loving regularity, they were the best gift he's ever given me). From this point forward, any attempts to communicate with him are strictly prohibited. It's hard enough for him to tear his attention away from the screen when he's *not* wearing sound-canceling headgear. Should I dare to require his input or consideration then, there's usually a great show of locating the remote and finding and pressing the pause button before he'll look at me with a dramatic sigh, because clearly I should know that a man cannot watch, listen, and talk at the same time. When the headphones are in place, I could run through the room naked with my hair on fire and unless I stopped to smolder directly in front of the screen, my bare-assed pyrotechnic show would go entirely unnoticed.

" At Least You're Not Married to Him "

He can't sleep without the television blaring, or more accurately he takes the *position* that he can't sleep without the television blaring. Which is complete and utter bullshit because what is the first thing he does upon boarding a plane, sitting in the passenger seat of a car, watching a movie in the theater, or reading a book to his kids? You guessed it: fall asleep. Seriously, he is a strong sleeper. He sleeps deep and long but insists that the white noise and white light of the

• • • • •

television remain on until he is into a solid REM cycle. So in order to keep the peace I do one of two things: One, attack him when I get into bed and insist he turn off the TV; or two, wait until he's asleep and then turn the damn thing off myself.

VICKY

As frustrating as it may be to try to watch TV with my husband, it's picnicking in Versailles compared to trying to watch it solo. I'm not saying that Joe is smarter than I am, or that he orchestrated this intentionally just so that I would never, *ever* watch TV of my own accord, but you need an advanced engineering degree to watch a simple sitcom in my house. I discovered this the hard way the first time Joe went out of town after having set up our high-tech new "home theater system." (The one I still argue should have come with a popcorn maker or *something* useful and deserving of the name.) He made me diagrams and cheat sheets, but I couldn't make heads or tails of them. It wouldn't matter, he assured me, because if I got stuck, all I had to do was press the handy "help" button on the $400 universal remote and it would walk me right through any possible scenario. Turns out the professed "help" button isn't so helpful if you're the sort who gets lost trying to find the bathroom in Best Buy and you wouldn't know a coaxial cable from a crossover conduit if your very life was riding on the correct answer.

"Is the TV on?" the remote asks right off the bat. Already I am stumped. I study the TV. The screen is black but there's a little light in the corner. Since "I'm not sure but I think so" isn't an option, I hit YES.

· · · · ·

"Is the PVR on?" it wants to know.

I'm sure it would help if I knew what a PVR was, but I don't. I look around the media cabinet for something that says PVR on it, but I can't find anything so I randomly select NO.

"Is the AV receiver on? Is the video monitor set to output 6? Is the DVD/VCR set to input mode? Is the remote sensor window blocked? Do you want to restore factory settings? What's the square root of 4,309,782, who was the eleventh president of the United States, and if I offered you a million dollars, could you define the word *the*?"

Go Zen, I tell myself as I randomly answer YES and NO to thousands of bewildering questions. "*Now* is the PVR on?" it asks at one point, and I think I hear it sigh. I start to feel the way I always do at the optometrist when he asks me to cover one eye and tell him whether A or B looks sharper, clearer, better. My personal theory is that since *they look exactly the same* it is unmistakably a trick question, a way of seeing if you're paying attention. "Yes," I tell the remote control this time. "Now the PVR *is* on!"

Suddenly—and I am not just saying that for dramatic emphasis, believe me; it really does happen out of nowhere—the impossible happens: The television set turns itself on. Surely this is merely a miraculous coincidence and not the result of something I've done. If it's the latter, I'm actually bummed—because it's not like I could reproduce the winning sequence if you held a gun to my head.

Slightly shaken by this unexpected turn of events, I begin scrolling through the online TV guide, which features incomprehensible portions of the titles of the roughly one thousand shows I have the luxury of choosing from. I've made it to 277 when the phone rings.

"You're still awake?" Joe asks. I look at the clock and it's more than an hour past the time I normally turn in.

"Oh, yeah, I was just reading," I lie. I refuse to admit how I spent the last several hours.

"I was just going to leave you a message asking you to record something for me while I'm gone," he says. "It's super easy. Want me to walk you through it?"

"Can we do it tomorrow?" I ask. "I'm exhausted." And if I have to look at that godforsaken remote again tonight, something is going to get broken.

" At Least You're Not Married to Him "

My husband has this awful habit of pulling out back hairs with his fingers while we're watching TV. He just reaches behind his neck to his back and yanks them out one by one. We'll be sitting there watching *True Blood* when all of a sudden the couch jerks with this crazy force of him pulling his back hairs out! He doesn't have a hairy back, just a few stray hairs, which he only feels the urge to remove when we're watching TV together. It is beyond gross.

DEILIA

This may come as a shock to you, but it is universally accepted (by most people with penises at least), so you might as well get used to it: Once a man has pressed the power button on the TV, he is officially "watching it," for all of eternity or until he manually turns it off himself, whichever comes last. (Power outages don't "count" as an active act of disengagement, either. Just so you know.) You might think because he is fast asleep, has gotten into the shower, or just boarded a plane for a two-week business trip on another continent that you might then be free to change the channel or—if you're feeling *really* ballsy—turn the thing off entirely, but you'd be wrong.

"Did you turn off the TV?" he'll ask in a terrifying Hannibal Lecter voice.

"Well, um, yeah, I did—" you'll stammer, confused.

"I was watching that!" he'll roar from the puddle of drool/steamy bathroom/faraway tarmac, frightening the bejesus out of you because you'd have bet your last dollar that you were well within your legal/marital television operating rights when you assumed control. Do not even try to rationalize with him by pointing out that he was unconscious or in a different time zone, because the conversation will turn preschool on your ass before you can say Hanna-Barbera.

"Honey, you were not watching that," you'll say with a small chuckle, as if you are both mature adults who can laugh and admit when they are being patently ridiculous.

"Was too!" he'll bellow, huffing and planting his hands on his hips dramatically. (You won't be able to see this over the phone, but trust me—he's doing it.)

"Were not," you'll say incredulously. Well, he wasn't!

"Was to-oooooo!" he'll shout, eyes closed and index fingers

stuck in his ears. To answer your unspoken questions: Yes, you married him, and no, it's not worth divorcing him over unless you want to stay single and celibate forever, because eventually you would have this exact conversation with every other man on the planet.

" At Least You're Not Married to Him "

When I'm in bed watching TV, he'll come in and try to persuade me to change the channel to something we "both" like. I'm not stupid. What he means is that he wants to change it to something *he* likes.

MIKEY

Now, I know lots of people—some of them even women—who like to watch TV in bed. As you could probably surmise, I am not one of them. I like to go to bed early and get up early, and I can't sleep unless I'm in silent pitch-blackness, so it just wouldn't work. Joe has begged many, many times over the years to get me to *just try it*, but I always stand firm on this one. He even attempted to woo me with the compelling argument that it would be "really fun for the girls to climb in here on Saturday mornings and watch cartoons." It's hard not to hate a man who can easily sleep through the SpongeBob theme song, but my husband really does have many redeeming qualities, so I try to fixate mostly on those. No matter what Joe's argument is, I know I will win as soon as I whip out the sex card, the one that conveniently details the scores of studies that have found that couples who have TVs in their bedrooms have less sex than couples who don't.

I am sure it is because he is so deprived of bedroom entertainment (and I'm mostly talking about the televised kind here) at home that Joe acts like an inmate who's just discovered his cell has a free cigarette machine whenever we walk into a hotel room.

Before I've even had a chance to scope out the honor bar or check to see if the last guests left anything good in the safe, he is sprawled spread-eagle on top of the comforter (he obviously doesn't read the studies where they report the sorts of things they find on there), looking a bit like a hairy, mannish Angel with his remote control "gun" pointed at the TV. It matters not if the room's set is smaller and older and has far fewer bells and whistles than any of the models we have at home. To Joe, the ability to indulge in this beloved pastime from the unparalleled comfort of a bed ranks up there with winning the Heisman Trophy, the Nobel Peace Prize, and the super lottery all in one day.

My husband, an astute guy who knows how to play any situation to his advantage, has picked up on the fact that "vacation rules" are quite different from "home rules." They must be, if the wife who is a veggie-pushing nutrition Nazi at home will give in to her family's pit stop pleas for Doritos and Yoo-Hoo and then actually be cool enough to call it dinner.

"Wow," he'll say, sucking the powdery processed cheese from his fingers. "I'm proud of you." *For relaxing your ridiculously rigid standards for the first time in possibly ever*, is the part he is wise enough not to say out loud.

"Whatever," I reply breezily. "We're on vacation!"

Totally abusing my laid-back holiday attitude, he will try to squeeze as much TV time into any given getaway as I'll allow. Every time we return to our hotel room, he molests the set like it's his long-lost, war-torn lover. He begs me to order room service, thinking I'll be impressed with his big-spender façade, when really the fantastical idea of watching TV and eating in bed—at the same time—is almost more than he can bear. If I protest, he flings my words back at me like poo in a monkey cage.

"Come on, honey," he pleads. "We're on vacation."

Lots of wives complain about husbands whose nonstop channel surfing makes them dizzy and nauseated. I once read an article—and it was pure speculation, mind you, not a scientific exposé—that suggested that a man's inability to settle on one channel could be merely an extension of his evolutionary need to expose himself to as many women as possible in the (subconscious) hope of maximizing reproductive success. In other words, more channels equal more chicks. Another theory suggests that channel surfing is just another of the many ways a man—the aggressive hunter to our more laid-back gatherer—is built to explore. Perhaps Joe is more evolved than most, because when it comes to television he's not much of a surfer. In fact, I'd say if anything he's a loiterer. Something on a random channel will catch his eye—a stock market ticker, a black-and-white movie with cowboy hats, anything to do with sports or nature, a big voluptuous pair of knockers—and he'll be spellbound for hours.

One day he appeared to be watching a screen saver of a forest. It piqued my interest only in the is-that-TV-broken-or-is-he-really-watching-a-screen-saver? sort of way.

"Whatcha watching?" I asked.

"It's a documentary about birds," he replied.

"Is it interesting?" I prodded.

"Not really," he admitted.

"Oh," I said. "So why are you watching it?"

"I want to find out what happens," he answered. "Besides, I've got an hour invested in it already."

What I wanted to say is, *Dude, we have at least 899 other channels! Cut your losses! That's already an entire hour of your life you'll never get back!* But that combination of hopefulness and loyalty is rare and sweet, when you think about it. So instead, I did what I always do: I said good night and crawled into bed with Sheldon, the cats, and my book and prayed for sleep to come quickly.

. . .

CHAPTER FOUR

What's Cooking? (I'm Gonna Go Out on a Limb and Say Me)

> Anybody who believes that the way to a man's heart
> is through his stomach flunked geography.
>
> • ROBERT BYRNE •

Heart disease may be the number one *actual* killer of women in this country, but the whole orchestrating-of-the-meals thing has to be the number one killer of their little spirits. I mean, honestly. Unless you're Rachael Freaking Ray and somebody is paying you to come up with a crowd-pleasing spread under a certain price point night after identical night, what is there to love about the gig? To be fair, I am sure there is at least one woman out there who wakes up each day eager to show her family how much she cares for them through a new and innovative display of culinary wizardry. I would genuinely love to meet her and shake her flour-dusted hand. Then I'd like to shove a flaming lamb chop into her annoyingly chipper pie hole.

• • • • •

My friend Jill owns a restaurant that makes the best chicken you have ever tasted in your life. Somehow the wonder chefs over there can take a boneless, skinless slab of poultry and turn it into a mind-blowing series of multiple orgasms for your taste buds. Lunch or dinner, on a sandwich or à la carte, served alongside an award-winning bottle of wine or a glass of tap water, this stuff is the best of the breast, bar none. When Jill's Place began selling its signature spice blend, I bought it and I even used it, but my chicken still tasted like, well, chicken.

"You're holding out on me," I accused Jill over yet another plate of perfect poultry one evening.

"What are you talking about?" my friend demanded, the picture of innocence.

"There obviously is some ingredient or technique you use to make your chicken taste like this," I charged, shoveling in another impossibly delicious bite.

"We just season it and grill it," Jill insisted.

"Liar," I replied.

I begged and pleaded; and Jill continued to deny employing any steroid abuse, so I dared her to come over to my house and prepare it right in front of me. I bought the organic, free-range chicken myself, so that she wouldn't be able to inject it with some sort of tenderizing flavor booster on the sly. When Jill arrived, she prepared the chicken just as she'd instructed me and cooked it precisely the same way I had. As usual, it was orgasmic.

"I don't get it!" I cried. "I did every single thing you did! I used your damned spice rub and I even got the kind of pan you have at the restaurant. Do I need to be wearing checkered pants and nurse shoes? Is it the hair net, because I'll get one. Just tell me, what am I doing wrong? What's the secret?"

"You have to cook it with love," Jill said, shaking her head sadly. Honest to God, that's what she said.

Well, fuck me, then.

I don't love cooking. I used to, back in another lifetime when I was doing it for other appreciative adults and had untold hours to scan cookbooks for ideas and peruse gourmet markets for inspiration and exotic ingredients. Once I had kids, putting a meal on the table became a chore that ranked up there with getting my annual mammogram or cleaning the oven on the intrinsic-joy scale. Like most working moms, I had managed to assemble a meager arsenal of five or six family-friendly meals—meaning the kids would eat them without threatening to puke or actually puking—that I cooked and served on a continual loop. It got to the point where the kids knew what day of the week it was by what was on the table.

"It's taco Tuesday *again*?" they'd moan. The only day that was a universal crowd pleaser was Saturday, also known as "breakfast-for-dinner day." On BDD they could have any breakfast item of their choice—cottage cheese, fruit, French toast, pancakes, waffles, hash browns, bacon, omelets, or green eggs and ham if it meant quiet acquiescence. I bought an appalling selection of cereals, hoping to entice my family to the uncooked side. Occasionally it worked, which did slightly mitigate the pain of having to fire up the oven the other six days.

" At Least You're Not Married to Him "

When I go grocery shopping I'll typically buy myself a couple of special treats, something I like to nibble on from time to time. At the same time, I'll buy my husband a few treats I know *he* likes, so that he'll keep his hands off mine. I've even been vocal about it. "Please don't eat my stuff. I bought you your own." Does it help? Absolutely not. He even knows I'll get mad about it, so now he tells me that he ate my stuff and he'll pick me up some more on his way home. If you think I tell him not to bother, you're wrong. Making him go into a grocery store is his punishment.

SUSAN

When we were first married, Joe didn't cook and I didn't expect him to. Once the kids came along, however, I began to plead for his help. Not with the actual adding-heat-to-ingredients part, or even the shopping, slicing, dicing, battering, breading, puréeing, pulverizing, or cleaning up. What I wanted more than anything else was for someone else to plan an occasional menu, to say, "Tonight we are having *this.*" What a dream that would be, to have an assignment I could carry out on autopilot. No more torturous self-doubting parade of "Will everyone like this?" or "Has it been a week since we had it last?" or "What should I serve with it?" *Not my problem,* I could say. *I just work here. But I'll be sure to pass your complaint along to management.*

Because I didn't exactly relish the hours I spent slaving over the proverbial hot stove, I tried to minimize them by cooking in bulk. I'd buy twenty-pound turkeys for our little family of four (only two of whom actually had full sets of teeth), stuff as many meatballs into the Crock-Pot as it would hold, bake a dozen potatoes at once. I wouldn't just make enchilada pie, I'd make *four* enchilada pies! My theory was that if we could live off leftovers for a few days at a stretch, I could whittle my time in the kitchen down to a reasonable two or three evenings a week.

What I failed to factor into my brilliant plan was the fact that Joe doesn't like leftovers. Actually, that's not technically true. He *likes* leftovers, he just prefers to eat them all on the first night you cook them.

"Take this away from me," he'll say, pushing the serving bowl toward me.

"Just stop eating," I reply.

"I can't," he says with a shrug, pulling the serving bowl back toward himself.

"Are you still hungry?" I ask him, this time reaching for the bowl myself.

"Actually, I'm stuffed." He groans, leaning back and rubbing his annoyingly flat abdomen for effect.

"Then *stop eating*," I growl.

"Wish I could," he replies sadly, dumping the entirety of tomorrow night's dinner on his plate.

" At Least You're Not Married to Him "

I have never heard someone chew a sandwich the way my husband does. I promise that you have heard it from your home and you were probably thinking to yourself, *Gosh, what is that sound?* It's my husband

eating a PB&J. Every time he does this, I instantly think of the look on
Nick Lachey's face in the first season of *Newlyweds* when Jessica Simpson asks if it's chicken or tuna. I firmly believe his sandwich sounds are
the reason I have lines on my forehead, because I make that face every
single time.

AMANDA

Worst of all would be when he would walk in the door at the
end of the day with a grocery bag, because invariably—and I
am talking roughly 127 percent of the time here—it would
contain nothing but beer.

"Would it *ever* occur to you to call me and tell me you were
stopping at the store and ask if we needed anything?" I'd rage.
At any given time I have no fewer than four different shopping
lists going, one each for the farmer's market, the "regular"
grocery store, Costco, and the super expensive mostly organic
specialty market. And even when I go to each of these places,
I forget stuff all the time, even stuff that was on my stupid list!
I don't care if you saw me unloading $600 worth of consum-
ables just this very morning; the odds are that we still need
something. And even if we don't, I'm going to make you pick
up something heavy—like the thirty-two-pound tub of kitty
litter or a case of water bottles—just to make it worth your
while.

It was a long and exceptionally random string of events that
finally led to my kitchen salvation. Unbeknownst to me at the
time, it began when I was pregnant with my first daughter and
we bought a new house that happened to have a pool. It was
a balmy ninety-nine degrees the day of the open house, and

that pool glistened like a cartoon hero's oversized front tooth. I am fairly certain that if you look up "How to Hook a Sweaty, Hormonal Home Buyer in the Summertime" in any real estate manual, you'll find a photo of that piece-of-shit, owner-built, godforsaken pool.

The ballooning hose running nonstop into the corner of the thing should have been a tipoff, but it wasn't until we got our first $500 water bill that we realized if pools were ships, we had the fucking *Titanic* docked right in our backyard. Well, we'd just have to get it fixed, that's all there was to it. *Immediately.* In a big, fat, pregnant-lady panic I called every pool repair company in a hundred-mile radius and started scheduling estimates. To my horror, after a cursory inspection every single one of them systematically refused to touch the thing.

"We don't know when it was built or what it's made out of or if it even has a proper foundation," was the general consensus. (To their shared credit, for the price of a fleet of Range Rovers, several were willing to have the existing pool removed and replaced with a brand-new model.) In other words, *Good luck with that colossal money-sucking hole in your yard, chubs.*

The bulldozers showed up the next week. I stood in the kitchen, sweat pooling in and around my newly massive cleavage, weeping openly for the floating *SkyMall* table tennis set I would never have, the legendary water polo parties I'd never host.

"What about an outdoor kitchen?" Joe asked one night as we stood on the freshly tamped mound of dirt where my overpriced Pottery Barn double-wide lounge chair was supposed to go. You know how they say the way to a man's heart is through his stomach? I'm thinking a knife to the chest would be a lot faster.

"Ooh, just what I always wanted," I said with an extra dose of sarcasm. "*Two* kitchens!"

"Jenna, you know I love to barbecue," he replied. "I'd totally cook all the time if we had a kitchen outside."

I didn't believe him for a second, but he had some compelling arguments. First of all, our inside kitchen sort of sucked, so this would make life better for both of us. Second, if we built a kitchen instead of putting in another pool, I wouldn't have to play neighborhood lifeguard, which—now that it was a little cooler outside—sounded like a relief. In the end I negotiated an al fresco fireplace in exchange for a beer tap, and the whole thing sounded way better than the current dirt pit I was tired of looking at, frankly. *It's all about resale value*, I justified to myself. If I wound up getting an occasional cheeseburger or veggie kabob out of the deal, it would be one of those unexpected little delights of life, like finding that something you were already going to buy is on sale, or discovering one last Tic Tac stuck to the inside lid of the box when you thought it was empty and you were desperately craving one and a half calories of minty freshness.

" At Least You're Not Married to Him "

I call him the food economist. This has nothing to do with nutrition or finances or cooking. No, it is all about the way he eats his food. No matter what he eats, he plans it out in his mind so that each item on his plate is eaten in one of two ways, and which way depends on how much he is enjoying his meal. For instance, if he loves everything on the plate (say a nice rib eye, potatoes au gratin, and grilled asparagus), he will eat everything in unison, rotating bites of each but maintaining the exact proportionate quantities of each so that his last bite may include all elements of his dinner, or at least, so he can then decide which to eat last. It's maddening. Sometimes I have to reach over and grab that last mushroom just to fuck with his organization.

ELIZABETH

Within a year's time we had a new baby and a new kitchen.

"What do you want me to cook tonight?" Joe would ask eagerly several nights a week, the picture of the helpful, enlightened superdad.

"Something, anything, I don't care," I'd mutter resentfully. I know, he was offering to cook and I should have been grateful, but I wasn't. I was a ravenous nursing cow, and here we were with *two kitchens* and I was still having to make the dreaded call on what we were going to eat for dinner. Only now I had to do it balancing a squirming newborn on my padded, postbaby hip while yellowish milk dripped from my nipples. (Forget the condom talk. *This* is the image they should show in high school sex ed classes.)

For a while this was how it worked: I'd shop for all of the food and assemble the day's menu. An hour or so before dinnertime, I would hand Joe a platter containing a hunk of the marinated animal flesh du jour, then proceed to sauté the veggies, toss the salad, boil the requisite starch, assemble the necessary condiments, fold the napkins, set the table, and dole out an assortment of beverages. Proudly manning a shiny variety of high-tech appliances with a frosty draft beer in hand, Joe would gingerly lay the meat onto the hot grill (five to thirty seconds, ranging from a single small pork loin to multiple chicken breasts or some nice carne asada). For the next ten to forty minutes, he would be free to talk on the phone, check his e-mail, watch a few snippets of the news, catch some ESPN highlights, or play with the kids until it was time to "check the meat" (fifteen seconds). He might have to repeat this burdensome inspection phase two or three more times (thirty to forty-five seconds) before it was officially time to remove the cooked flesh from the flame (ten seconds) and carry it to the table (twenty-five seconds).

Make no mistake: If I sound like a bitter, miserable hag as I reminisce about this time period in our marriage, it's *because I was a bitter, miserable hag during this time period in our marriage.* I may have tried to hide it—I genuinely can't recall if I had any will at all at the time—but even on a good day, I am sure my miserable hagness was never far from the surface. Like many modern-day moms, I was working, shouldering approximately 98 percent of the new-baby burden, keeping up the house, sleeping an average of two hours a night, and still trying to fulfill what I felt were my wifely duties (provide sex and dinner, mainly). So while he was "helping" with dinner, Joe's total time contribution to any meal averaged about two minutes and five seconds, and that's being patently generous. If you factored in the time I spent doing related meal-preparation minutiae like circling the grocery store looking for a parking spot, comparing prices, reading ingredient lists, waiting for the ninety-eight-year-old lady in front of me to painstakingly *write out her goddamned check and record it in the accompanying check register* (Dear God, why? I mean, I know she has nowhere to go and nothing to do, but does she have to bring me down, too?), cruising the neighborhood for an hour because the kid had fallen asleep on the way home and she needed her nap so there was no other choice, loading and unloading the groceries, and searching online for recipe substitutions when I opened the lid on the sour cream container to find a mass of furry blue goop where creamy white deliciousness should have been, let's just say it's pretty clear who was doing the lion's share of the work. (Ahem. Roar.) Compounding my agony was the fact that my friends, my mother, my stepmom, and one very envious sister constantly, woefully bemoaned how "lucky I was" all the flipping time because my husband "cooked." I began to think they should congratulate me on how much "money I'd made" each time I traipsed down to the bank to deposit my beloved's latest paycheck.

"Most guys don't cook at all," Joe would argue if I dared to suggest he step up his efforts a notch or two.

As much as I hated to admit it, he sort of had me there. Still, I wasn't about to let him off the hook.

"Big deal," I'd huff. "Most women don't work *and* take care of the kids *and* keep the house as immaculate as I do!" *So there!*

"Yeah, but you're the only one who cares about the house being immaculate," he'd point out with an annoying combination of accuracy and matter-of-factness.

It was usually right around this point that I would come to my senses and realize that things were never going to change, so I'd better learn to just suck it up and be grateful for whatever measly contribution I could get. The vocalization of this highly evolved sort of epiphany usually sounded something like this: *"Oh my God I fucking hate you and I am totally not ever doing your stupid laundry or shopping for goddamned groceries again EVER so good luck with that, jackass!"*

Of course that was a total pack of lies, and I kept doing the stupid laundry and the goddamned grocery shopping and the hateful, mind-numbing meal planning because apparently I was the only one who cared about a clean house and also not getting scurvy. (True story: When I met Joe, the only food in his house was a twenty-pound bag of pierogies. If you're like I was and have no idea what a pierogi is, picture a potato-filled ravioli dumpling, your basic nutrient-free, white flour gut-bomb. Purchased in bulk, the lowly pierogi may be the one convenience food that is even cheaper than and inferior to ramen noodles.)

This is where my story of culinary deliverance takes on an ironic edge Alanis Morissette would appreciate. If you recall, we now had *two kitchens* merely because what I originally felt was my home's most compelling feature turned out to be a mirage. To my great disdain I continued to serve as the primary kitchen wench—until the fortuitous day that Joe discovered the convergence of food and television in the form of the Food Network. I wasn't there when it happened, but imagine how you'd feel if you discovered that two of your favorite things in the world—like petit fours and pedicures, or *Dancing with the*

Stars and dirty martinis—had somehow been rolled into a delicious model of one-stop shopping. Talk about televangelism!

I didn't even notice it at first, because as I may have mentioned, I don't watch much TV. But one day I was scrolling through the TiVo lineup looking for something to occupy the girls and I noticed a bunch of strange titles: *Boy Meets Grill. Throwdown with Bobby Flay. 30-Minute Meals. Diners, Drive-ins and Dives.*

"I saw a bunch of cooking shows scheduled on the TiVo thingy," I mentioned casually later that day. "Do you watch any of those?"

"Sometimes, a little, I don't know, yeah," Joe stammered. He sounded guilty, like I was his mom and I was grilling him—so to speak—about the baggie full of funny-smelling parsley I found in his jacket pocket.

Relieved that the only breasts he was ogling after I went to bed belonged to dead chickens, I let it go. Then my birthday rolled around.

Joe likes to wrap presents in newspaper. To be extra ironic, he likes to wrap *my* presents in the sports pages. Anyhow, as I tore through a piece about our local high school football team, I very nearly went into early cardiac arrest when it became clear that I was now the proud owner of the latest Williams-Sonoma cookbook, simply titled *Grilling*. If the steak on the cover had been a man, it would have been Hugh Jackman, his bronzed body dewy with sweat and wearing nothing but a smile. My mouth immediately started to water. But really? A fucking *cookbook*?

"I know what you're probably thinking," Joe said, rushing to preempt my disappointment. "But I am going to make everything in that book for you. Every week I want you to pick something new and I'll make it. *And* shop for all of the ingredients. *And* clean it all up."

For once, I was speechless. I didn't even screw it up by pointing out the still unfair six-to-one weekly division of labor. I gushed and fawned appropriately, and proceeded to dog-ear the pages of the most delectable-looking recipes. *Something is always better than nothing,* I reminded myself. *And those scallop and mushroom brochettes better rock my little world.*

" At Least You're Not Married to Him "

My husband makes these gross things I call "scrumples" where he crumples a napkin at the end of a meal and sometimes blows his nose in it and sometimes even kind of wipes his tongue with it if he has snotty mucus. I hate it. He leaves the crumpled napkin on his dirty plate. If he hadn't cooked the meal (he's a chef)—and he does cook every meal—it would be grounds for divorce or a Lorena Bobbitt move at the very least. I hate the scrumples but I love him.

DIANA

Before long I noticed that Joe was cooking—or at least, contributing to the cooking—more than once a week. A lot more than once, in fact. I started to get cocky, even grocery shopping without a list. As long as I bought some sort of meat, he could figure out what to do with it and make it taste good. The positive impact of this skill on our marriage truly cannot be overstated. The kids became so accustomed to our tag-team efforts in the kitchen that rarely did we enjoy a meal without having some version of this conversation:

Kids: "Who made the steak?"

Us: "Daddy did."

Kids: "Who made the asparagus?"

Us: "Mommy did."

Kids: "Who made the rice?"

Us: "We made it together."

And that's pretty much how it worked. Until one night, something funny happened: I made a casserole. There was nothing inherently amusing about the casserole, but the conversation that followed was one for the books.

Kids: "Who made the chicken?"

Us: "Mommy did."

Kids: "And who made the noodles?"

Us: "Mommy did."

Kids: "But . . . then who made the broccoli?"

Us: "Actually, Mommy made that, too."

They looked at each other, then back at us, not for one moment buying this preposterous story.

"Mom, you can't make a whole dinner *all by yourself*," my six-year-old finally blurted.

"Yeah!" her four-year-old sister agreed, as if that settled it and we were just a pair of liars in cahoots.

Was this really happening? Did those years and years *and*

years and years of doing all of the miserable grunt work by myself mean nothing to the little ingrates I had birthed? Did they *really* think that I was incapable of pulling off a simple supper without their father's help?

"Actually, it's not that I *can't* make an entire dinner by myself," I finally replied. "I just don't usually want to." As understatements go, that may have been the mack daddy. But at least I'd gotten across the message that I was relinquishing some of the cooking by choice and not out of incompetence.

Joe's gotten to be a creative and almost intuitive cook. No longer does he have to measure out the requisite teaspoon of salt or tablespoon of olive oil. Gift-giving occasions have become a delightful excuse to purchase exotic kitchen tools (who knew you needed different spatulas for fish, burgers, and veggies?) and splurge on frivolous but fun items like a panini press or a bamboo pizza peel. Sure, now that he's a "pro," there is some suffering to endure. "Did you put more salt in this than usual?" he'll ask after dipping a spoon into a pot of some-thing-or-other that I'm simmering, clearly implying a leaden hand. "Want me to flip these?" he'll offer, inspecting the pan-cakes I'm making and all but suggesting that I don't recognize when a bubbling circle of batter is ready to be turned. He'll stir my sauces, adjust the stove burners, add and remove lids, even suggest additions and substitutions. As annoying as it is to be micromanaged by him, I take great comfort knowing that if anything tragic should happen to me, at least my chil-dren won't be eating Lucky Charms for dinner every night.

· · · · ·

. . .

CHAPTER FIVE

Domestic Bliss and Other Big Fat Lies

Marriage is not just spiritual communion;
it is also remembering to take out the trash.

· DR. JOYCE BROTHERS ·

My husband has superhuman eyesight. It's true. We'll be zip-ping down the highway at eighty-five miles per hour and he'll casually remark, without even pulling his eyes from the road in front of him as he drives, "Wow, did you see that baby hawk on the roof of that barn?" Hell, half of the time I didn't even see the *barn*. Or we'll be hiking and he'll suddenly freeze and put a finger to his lips, his other hand pointing to what turns out to be a tiny lizard sunning itself on a rock a dozen yards up the trail. He can read road signs in their entirety before I can even make out the letters, can spot a familiar face in a crowd of thousands, and as far as I know, has never walked through a spiderweb, even when it's pitch-dark.

So you can imagine why it is relentlessly frustrating to see him standing before the refrigerator, door swung wide, scratching his head and staring blankly into the Warhol-esque interior.

"Guess we don't have any milk," he'll say with a shrug.

"I don't know, maybe it's hiding behind that *massive gallon of white liquid on the top shelf right in the front*," I like to respond warmly. "Did you check there?"

The most frustrating aspect of living with a victim of Male Pattern Blindness is the disease's unpredictable nature. For instance, although my poor husband apparently isn't able to see the brown, festering lettuce in the main crisper drawer or realize that the lemonade pitcher no longer contains a single molecule of liquid when he puts it back on the shelf, he has no problem finding the last slice of leftover pizza that I wrapped in tinfoil, scrunched into a ball in an effort to camouflage the telltale triangular shape, and hid in the far corner of the bottom shelf on the door, behind the maraschino cherries that may have actually come with the refrigerator.

Sometimes I actually feel bad for him, like when he asks where we keep the vinegar or the vacuum bags, as if he lives inside some funhouse Costco where every night the sadistic manager rearranges every single item so that he can never find what he's looking for. The other night, it was ear drops. Our daughter woke up complaining that her ear hurt, and for the first time in possibly *ever* she serendipitously made this announcement while standing slightly closer to Joe's side of the bed. The unwritten but also unconditional rule in our house is that if one of the children chooses *you* to do her midnight bidding, you get up and deal without complaint. To Joe's credit, he did precisely that, murmuring sweetly to her that it would all be okay, Daddy would just get her some of the nice ear medicine, and it would feel better in no time.

Rumble, crash, fumble.

"Medicine drawer," I mumbled, trying not to fully emerge into consciousness.

Clang, clatter, bang.

"White box with blue lettering, right side, toward the front," I called, a bit louder this time.

Thump, thud, boom.

"Size of a deck of cards only fatter, next to the Children's Motrin!" I shouted, totally awake and furious at myself for not having ESP so I could have left the damned ear drops out on the counter before I went to bed. I endured another several minutes of this maddening ruckus before throwing back the covers angrily and marching into the bathroom where Joe stood peering into the open medicine drawer. After hugging my daughter gently and apologizing for the fact that she was in pain, I tenderly shoved my husband out of the way to have a look myself and—lo and behold—the white, card-deck-size box with the blue lettering sat like a snake coiled and ready to strike, right there in the front, right-hand side of the medicine drawer. *Next to the Children's Motrin.*

When I ask him to unpack the kids' backpacks, he'll stack the respective contents on the nearest counter, because he has absolutely no idea where anything "goes." (Hint: 90 percent of it "goes" into the trash.) Sometimes I'll be lying in bed and suddenly I'll think to myself, "My God, I am the *only person in this house who knows where the spare sheets are*! What would they do if something happened to me?" I've even asked Joe this question, and his response is usually something like "I'd throw away three-quarters of the shit you hoard in this house so I could actually find something when I needed it." Because obviously, it's my fault for recklessly putting the medicine in the *medicine drawer*.

Although my husband may complain about all the "stuff" I "hoard," when it comes to food, the man I married throws nothing away. Expiration dates are meaningless, mold is but a slightly bothersome topping to be scraped away, and that salad dressing nobody liked? Oh, that will make an *excellent* marinade.

"Pasta doesn't go bad," he'll insist, and, "It's just the crusty stuff around the mouth of the container that smells funny; the milk inside is fine."

Of course, I'm the exact opposite. I take that whole "best by" business seriously. I put those dates on my mental calendar and promptly toss the contents on the appointed day. I have learned to do this when Joe isn't home, because frankly the sight of my husband digging through the trash to salvage some hardened heels of bread could be the nail in my libido's coffin.

"Where's the rest of the turkey we had the other night?" he'll ask. He's referring, of course, to that "other night" six months ago, also known as Thanksgiving.

"Dunno, honey," I say absentmindedly. "Maybe I ate it or something."

" At Least You're Not Married to Him "

My husband won't throw *anything* away, ever. I live with old ripped
sneakers ("I'll use them for gardening"; we have a lawn guy), socks
with holes ("I can sew them"; he doesn't know how to sew), ancient
photography equipment ("Digital is a fad"), magazines dating back to
1979, sleeveless frat T-shirts, and a few cables the puppy chewed
through. The worst part is that he works from home and if he sees me
carting anything to the trash, he follows me out and brings it right back
into the house.

LEAH

I am not blaming my husband for his inability to find anything
in our house, really. I am sure that a social anthropologist
would be able to explain why, evolutionarily, it made no sense
whatsoever for a man to be able to locate anything specific
within the cave. "Back in the woolly mammoth days," the wise
scholar would tell me in the gravest of tones, "if the hunter
went into the den to retrieve his bow and arrow, he would be
endangering his family by alerting the enemy as to their where-
abouts. Therefore, he learned to stay several protective paces
from the entrance to the cave, where he would throw his voice
onto a faraway boulder as he bellowed, *'Hey honey! Where'd
you put my goddamned bow and arrow?'* "

If gatherer-girl got pissed when this happened—and I'm
going to bet that she did—her hulking hunter-husband
would launch into his lecture about the dangers of his job
and how *lucky she had it* being able to stroll through the

• • • • •

fields, chatting with her bitches and picking berries while he was out risking life and limb and slaying big, burly bison all day. And sadly, without the benefit of Wi-Fi or Wikipedia, she couldn't even shut him up by informing him that *80 percent of all of their food was gathered, not hunted, thank you very fucking much.*

> ## " At Least You're Not Married to Him "
>
> Although I've been happily married for seventeen tears, it drives me nuts that my wonderful, giving husband continually leaves his skivvies on the bathroom floor. It is especially gross after he's come back from a fifty-mile bike ride during the brutally hot summer. Does he think his undies will magically walk to the laundry basket themselves? The funny part is we've talked about it and he truly believes most of the time he puts them in the hamper.
>
> **SUE**

I should interrupt myself here by saying that although Joe may not have an intimate working knowledge of our home's interior or a majority of its contents, compared to most men he does do a lot around the place. Especially considering—as he is quick to point out—he really couldn't care less if the beds ever got made or the laundry got put away. *If you died tomorrow, I'd never make the bed or put a single article of clothing away ever again,* he tells me. (Well, not with actual words or anything, but believe me—he tells me.) He could live happily ever after pulling clean clothes from a mound on top of the dryer, so the fact that he will go so far as to transfer a stack of folded items into their respective drawers is, in his mind, an act of loving selflessness. Or more specifically, foreplay.

This is not a quantum leap. Just last year, a fascinating study found that the more household chores people do, the more sex they have. (Go ahead, put the book down and go tell your husband that. I'll wait.) Now, had the study focused exclusively on how housework pays off for otherwise reluctant guys, *of course* the findings would have made perfect sense. I am pretty sure I'd be willing to give it up on the spot if I saw Joe wielding a Swiffer or emptying the dishwasher of his own accord. But here's the part that stumped me: The study found that for *both* men and women, more housework equals more sex.

As a compulsive Type A neat freak who has been known to make the bed around her snoring husband in the morning, I find this hard to believe. According to this theory, considering the staggering number of hours I already log sorting socks and chasing crumbs and plumping pillows each week, I should be having more sex than a billionaire in a brothel. Am I to believe that I'd be getting significantly more action if I just added some *more* scrubbing, scouring, sweeping, sponging, and straightening to my endless daily to-do list? Would a gleaming toilet bowl or streak-free windows—made that way through my own tireless efforts and an excess of elbow grease— make me feel ever more frisky? Even more discouraging to consider, is my housekeeper swinging from her ceiling fan at night in a pair of crotchless chaps while I am passed out wearing earplugs and flannel Hello Kitty pajamas?

The researchers (a man and a woman; no word on whether they were having sex with one another) admit that they were surprised by their own findings, ultimately chalking them up to something called the "multiple spheres" hypothesis, which suggests that people who "work hard" also "play hard." Interestingly, the same study also found a positive correlation between time spent at the office and frequency of sex—and reportedly they mean sex with the regular old ball-and-chain at home and not a few quickies in the supply closet with a cute administrative assistant. The way the researchers explain it is that compared to "normal folks," both workaholics and vacuum addicts are better at prioritizing their time to make room for the things they enjoy.

I am pretty sure my cleaning habits do not lead to more sex. In fact, I wouldn't be surprised if Joe considers my meticulous nature (what he calls my anal relentlessness) a serious cock block. Regardless of his take on my tidiness, I do know that I'm not easy to live with. I like everything done a certain way (mine), and I like everything to *look* a certain way (spotless). I hang clothes according to color, constantly twist cans in the pantry so that the labels are facing outward, and alphabetize things—like appliance manuals and the kids' books—that have no business being alphabetized. When the *Hold Everything* catalog comes, I attack it with the lustful eagerness of a teenage boy diving into his dad's latest forbidden issue of

Playboy. I realize that it shouldn't make me want to claw my husband's eyeballs out when he loads the dishwasher haphazardly (when everyone knows you always load back to front and never place two glasses side by side) or doesn't close his sock drawer the last half-inch *every single godforsaken time he opens it*, but it does. It really, truly does.

"It must suck to be you," Joe will say, not even meanly. And sometimes I do wish I were one of those easygoing, roll-with-it types, but I'm just not. Occasionally I'll try to force my square self into a round hole by making a public declaration such as, "Tonight I am going to leave the dishes in the sink until morning!" Most of the time, my resolve lasts less than eight minutes. Remember in the movie *The Crying Game* when Forest Whitaker recounts the poignant parable of the frog and the scorpion? (It's the second most memorable scene in the movie, right after the part where the dude finds out his girlfriend has a penis.) In the story, the scorpion asks the frog to carry him across the river because he can't swim. The frog is afraid that the scorpion will sting him, but the scorpion reminds him that if he did, the frog would sink and they would both die. Finally the frog agrees to serve as the scorpion's water taxi. Halfway across the river, wouldn't you know? The goddamned scorpion stings him! Before the frog sinks to his death, he demands to know why the scorpion would do such a foolish thing. "I'm a scorpion," the predator replies. "It's in my nature." It's an admittedly depressing and obscure analogy, but I totally get what the scorpion is saying. It's just hard not to be what you are.

- - - - -

" At Least You're Not Married to Him "

The thing that drives me the most nuts about my husband is that when he opens up a drawer or cabinet door to either retrieve something or put something away, he NEVER closes it. I'll come into the kitchen after he's put away dishes and it will look like that scene from *The Sixth Sense*.

WELMOED

Joe and I used to have this one recurring fight that was so stupid I almost can't bring myself to put it in writing, but I will because there's a good lesson in it somewhere, I think. Joe has a favorite sandwich that he likes to make, and he makes quite a mess doing it. Because he is not actually a Neanderthal, and because I've trained him well, he even wipes down the counters and puts all of the ingredients away when he's finished making it. Then, after he polishes off the sandwich, he brushes the crumbs into the sink and puts his plate in the dishwasher. Hard to complain about that—right?

Wrong. For approximately ten years, I would watch this ritual, waiting until the precisely perfect moment to say casually, "Don't forget to rinse out the sink, please!"

"Does it really matter?" he'd ask.

"Yes, it *does*," I'd reply. "If you do it right away, it takes three seconds. If you don't do it right away, the crumbs harden and stick like little globs of glue and then I have to use a Brillo pad to get them off." Those stuck-on crumbs had become symbolic, an emblem of all of my unheard pleas and unmet needs.

· · · · ·

"Big deal," he'd mutter.

"Exactly!" I'd shout, because when you have the exact same fight 6,392 times, you tend to pick up right where you left off the last time. "It shouldn't be a big deal and it *wouldn't* be a big deal if you'd just rinse the fucking sink when you were done! We've got the little sprayer and everything! How hard would that be, honestly?"

But time after infuriating time he'd forget, and I'd march into the kitchen in a huff and resentfully scour away the evidence of his passive-aggressive hatred for me.

"You do it on purpose, don't you, just to piss me off?" I accused him one day.

"Do what?" he asked, a shoo-in for Best Actor in a Clueless Role.

"Leave your crumbs in the sink!" I bellowed.

"You really believe that, don't you?" he asked, shaking his head and sounding genuinely hurt. "You actually think that I go through my day trying to think of hundreds of tiny little ways to irritate you. You give me way too much credit, Jenna. I'm not that conniving. Having a spotless sink just isn't important to me, so I forget. I know it *should* be important to me because it's important to you, but you have a lot of little 'things,' you know? It's hard to keep track of them all."

Can you imagine? Playing the wise-and-rational card on me? The nerve! But I had to admit, I did sort of sound like a paranoid, insecure, and impossibly demanding nut-job when he put it that way. And I felt bad that I'd accused him of malice where there was none, but the important thing was that after that perfectly compelling little speech of his, *he stopped leaving crumbs in the sink.* I am not even making this up just to make him look good. Even though he was right that I did have "a lot of little things" that bugged me, and even though he had convinced me that he wasn't borrowing extra crumbs from the neighbors so he could sprinkle them in the sink as part of an ongoing, evil plot to annoy me to death, and *even though I essentially admitted that I was being difficult and the crumbs weren't that big a deal in the grand, overall scheme of the eternity that was our life together,* in the end I got what I wanted: a stupid clean sink. I'll be damned if I can figure out exactly how, but I'm just going to keep my mouth shut and my head down and appreciate it while it lasts.

" At Least You're Not Married to Him "

For ten years my husband has not picked up a wet towel, washed ketchup off of a dish, changed a lightbulb, or remembered trash day without a friendly "How many times do I have to tell you?"

JENNY

I have a male friend who told me—in confidence and under threat of a lawsuit if I identified him by name or distinguishing characteristics, so for these purposes I'll call him Sally— that men have figured out a foolproof way to get out of doing any dreaded housework:

"We suck on purpose," Sal told me, speaking without

permission for his entire gender. "We know that if we do a really bad job at something, you won't ask us to do it again. Once I actually pretended that I couldn't fold a simple hand towel in quarters. I just sort of scrunched it up in a wad and set it on the towel pile with a flourish and a triumphant 'There!' My wife hasn't asked me to fold the laundry once since then."

Joe is no Sally (and that's not a sentence I ever thought I'd need to write). He is an adept towel folder and knows the secret to streak-free windows (newspaper, not paper towels). He doesn't "suck on purpose" just to get out of doing the job. He doesn't have to, because he tells me to my face that since there's no way he could ever do any task to my unreasonable standards, he's just not going to do it at all. And since he's more or less right, it's really hard to argue the point.

When I was in college, I preferred male roommates to female ones for several reasons: They had sex with strangers more often, which meant they were more likely to stay out all night and therefore not be at home eating my food. (And when they *were* home, they'd never touch my fat-free cottage cheese or home-made negative-calorie cabbage soup anyhow.) They didn't care about décor, so I could hang whatever I wanted on the walls. They rarely borrowed, ruined, or lost my favorite skinny skirt. I am not sure if I was just a lot more blasé back then or it's simply because I was drunk for the majority of that four-year stretch, but I don't recall constantly being bothered by my guy room-mates' little domestic insults. You know, the never-made beds, the pile of dishes in the sink, the stinky socks on top of the wash-ing machine (because lifting the lid or locating and then actually using a hamper would require herculean effort), the offhand admissions of oh-yeah-actually-I-*did*-drink-your-last-can-of-Diet-Coke-sorry. Now that I think about it, it must have been the booze, because that shit makes me mental on a daily basis.

Apparently I have a thing that drives Joe crazy, too: I like to use the lights in the house. I know, it's selfish and indulgent, but it's a little luxury I sometimes like to afford myself. Because of this, my husband has nicknamed me the "light leaver-onner" and has made it his personal mission in life to circle the house whenever he is home, turning off every light in his path. The criteria he uses to determine whether a certain light should be switched off is simple: If it's on, it should be off. Regardless of the time of day, whether the light in question is serving any sort of purpose, or who might be using it at the time.

"I'm in here!" I shout from my perch on the throne, fumbling for the toilet paper I can almost make out in the shadows.

"I'm in here!" I yell, head in the dryer, my voice echoing in my ears like I'm trapped in a cartoon cave with a yodeler.

"I'm in here!" I roar from the bathtub, searching for somewhere to place my razor before I sever a critical artery in the now pitch-darkness.

I should probably thank him for reducing our electric bill and being concerned about the environment and helping to preserve our natural resources so that our daughters will have lights someday. He's probably thinking that without those lights, *their* husbands will have nothing to go around turning off. It's sweet the way he wants to preserve the tradition, don't you think?

• • • • •

• • •

CHAPTER SIX

Gee, Honey. Are You Sick? I Never Would Have Guessed.

I love being married.
It's so great to find that one special person
you want to annoy for the rest of your life.

• RITA RUDNER •

I was lucky enough to betroth myself to a man who is as healthy as a horse and has the immune system of a garlic-loving superhero to prove it. *Thank God.* Because when a runny nose is attached to a body that doesn't also have a uterus, I think it's safe to say the world is going to hear about it.

I'm not stereotyping here, am I? I have to believe I'm not, as pretty much every guy I've ever known—including the one who sired me, several I've lived with, and the one I eventually married—seems to follow the exact same script when he's

• • • • •

under the weather. He never has a "little cold" or a "touch of the flu." He is never just sick; he is urgently, unreservedly, violently, pitifully, painfully sick. He could be dying, in fact. Nobody has ever felt as bad as he is feeling right this minute. Ever. He pretty much invented sick, or at the very least has single-handedly elevated it to a new extreme. At the first sign of excess nasal moisture or the faintest rattle in his chest, you might as well prepare yourself for the full-on shuffle-moan-woe-is-me routine, because if this were a wedding, the organist would have just hit the first unmistakable notes of "Here Comes the Bride." (I realize that there is a chance that your spouse is among the handful of men who make up the exception to this rule. If that is the case, put down this book immediately and go scour YouTube for the BBC3's "Man Cold" episode of the hilariously snarky and wonderfully inappropriate *Man Stroke Woman* show, featuring what I only wish were an exaggerated account of a man suffering from an acute viral upper respiratory tract infection. You know: a cold. It's a side-splitting little skit that has more than four million views as of this writing because at least that many women can relate to it. Watch the episode, then shut the hell up and count your blessings.)

" At Least You're Not Married to Him "

When he has a cold he stuffs the ends of tissues into his nostrils so that they hang down like white flags of surrender. He thinks it's func-

• • • • •

tional and remembers doing that when he was twelve. Was I dreaming? How can this be the sexy hunk I lusted over last week?

DEBORRAH

When a man (maybe not *your* one-in-a-kazillion mate) falls ill, all of the symptoms typically strike at once and with thunderous force. Male Instant-Onset Illness (MIOI) typically features a mild and generic litany of contradictory complaints, including but not limited to agonizing sniffles and congestion, excruciating fatigue and insomnia, piercing constipation and diarrhea, and unbearable sweats and chills. The cumulative effect of these symptoms is a sort of zombielike trance, which he will perfect by pacing around the house in his female partner's immediate shadow.

"Unnhhhhh," he moans, shuffling his slippers across the tile dramatically. Even if he is normally the poster boy for perfectly coiffed metrosexuals, his absurdly disheveled hair is standing on end in striking Cosmo Kramer fashion. His wife looks at him, wondering if he actually went to the trouble to locate and employ some sort of styling product to achieve this look. Then she turns away and proceeds to ignore him, because the groaning is annoying as hell and furthermore she is pretty sure five minutes ago he was a normal, symptom-free human being.

"Unnnnnnnnnnnnnnhhhhhhhhhhhhhhhhhhhhh," he repeats, louder and longer this time, perhaps pressing the palm of his hand to his forehead, because guys never seem to understand that (a) you test for fever with your wrist, not your palm, and

(b) it is a well-known scientific fact that you cannot be the judge of your own temperature.

If I refuse to acknowledge it, it'll go away, she says to herself foolishly as she picks up her pace in an attempt to put some distance between herself and the godforsaken moaning.

"Unnnnnnnnnnnnnnnnnnnnnnnnnnnnnnnnnnnnnnnnnnnhhhh-hhhhhhhhhhhhhhhhhhhhhhhhhhhhhhhhhhhhhhhhhhhhhhhhhhhh-hhhhhh, sniff, snortle, [*hacking, phlegmy, here-comes-a-lung cough*]."

"You sick?" she asks, stopping, defeated. Shadow Boy bumps right into her back.

"I dink so," he replies, plugging his nose from the inside by pressing his tongue into the back of his throat, in an effort to give his voice an air of crippling, incurable congestion.

"Sorry to hear it," she says with a kindness she does not feel, stepping slightly away, just in case. "Want me to make you some tea?"

"Ogay," he sniffles. "Ed baby sub soup?"

"Sure, yeah, tea and soup, coming right up," she mumbles through gritted teeth.

Shadow Boy somehow manages to separate himself from her. He shuffles into the living room, moaning periodically so that nobody in the house accidentally forgets that *he is very, very sick*, and plops down onto the couch. The joyful sounds of *SportsCenter* fill the house.

She brings him his soup and his tea. He thanks her meekly before asking for a bigger spoon, the salt shaker, some crackers, more sugar, the phone, a few magazines, his woolly socks, and a blanket. She finds herself hoping—for a brief moment and while simultaneously wondering about their collective health insurance coverage—that he will require hospitalization sooner rather than later.

" At Least You're Not Married to Him* "

My hubby returned from an out-of-town business trip and you would have thought he had a stage-four end-of-life disease. I brought out throat lozenges plus the Vicks and told him to put a little dab inside each nostril to help clear his head. What does he do? He smears a huge glob of it under his nose. Five minutes later he appears in the doorway shouting "My EYES, I got it in MY EYES, the fumes, *oh my God*!" I told him it was a personal spastic issue and that I couldn't help him anymore. I liked him better when he had pneumonia. At least then he was so sick, he was quiet.

TERI

*or frankly, *her*

I posted a query on my blog asking women how they deal with a sickly spouse, and though an overwhelming majority offered some version of "I try to stay far, *far* away," one lady actually got a little pissy with me. "Who doesn't like a little pampering when we're not feeling well?" she demanded, sneering at me with her words. "I offer juice, tissues, cold medicine, a cozy bed, *and* DVDs," she added. (If you look closely, you can almost *see* the words *you heartless bitch* right there at the end.)

Another gal took a decidedly practical stance. "I don't bend over backward to take care of him, but I do bring him food and drinks. I can't have him flat-out die on me, can I?" And then there's my friend Jenny, who has honed her convalescent duties down to a single word: "Porn. In a man's world, it solves everything. At the very least, it'll occupy his tiny mind for a little while."

Whether you ignore him, wait on him hand and foot, head out of town for a few days, or distract him with back-to-back showings of *On Golden Blonde*, try to keep in mind that it's not his fault he's a big fat pansy-ass. He's *inherently* not good at managing discomfort because he hasn't been groomed for it virtually since birth the way you have. Between wrangling your pendulous breasts into a constricting wire-trimmed undergarment on a daily basis, regularly having thousands of tiny hairs ripped off your body with strips of molten wax, repeatedly wedging your mostly flat and plainly rectangular-shaped feet into triangular footwear perched on top of twin four-inch spikes, and let's not forget occasionally expelling a creature the size and shape of a large watermelon (sorry, a watermelon *with shoulders*) out of your vagina—or alternately, having the watermelon person or people pulled out through a man-made gash in your abdomen—you know what pain is. And it's not a little tickle in the back of your throat or a blocked freaking nostril.

I am sure I don't need to bring this up, but I will: When the woman of any given house comes down with a cold, somehow the world continues to turn. Beds get made, lunches get packed, permission slips get signed, laundry gets washed, pets get fed, work gets finished, bills get paid. No one is mopping your brow as you accomplish these tasks because—and you can't really put too fine a point on this—*nobody realizes that you are sick*. It's not that you don't feel lousy, because you do. Of course you do! But what good does it do you to belabor that? Or to announce it every five minutes? Or even to acknowledge it yourself? You're not being a martyr, and most of the time your clueless life partner isn't intentionally being an insensitive cad. It's just that because of your aforementioned experience with bras and waxing and high heels and childbirth, you can take it. You can't afford *not* to, because last time you checked they weren't giving away five extra hours of daylight with every box of Kleenex. So you pop some pill or another and you power through, and somehow, magically, you get it all done.

In marked contrast to your stoicism, when your husband develops a raging ninety-nine-degree fever, he will likely be rendered immediately immobile and expect you to morph into Florence fucking Nightingale. Even though we live in the third millennium (and we know that we do because we all have vague memories of all that unwarranted Y2K hoopla) and you've never *once* met him at the door with his slippers and a highball, one of the side effects of MIOI is a sort of hallucinatory state in which the patient believes he has time-traveled back to the 1950s and has himself a nice little housewife to attend to his every irritating need.

This is where you must tread very, very carefully. Because if you act like the bitch you want to be and accuse him of—

gasp—exaggerating his symptoms, it will cause the "illness" to linger for several weeks or longer. No one knows the precise pathology behind this phenomenon, but trust me, it's a time-tested fact. You see, guys have figured out that there are certain distinct benefits of being sick. Consider these quotes from some legendary men:

> I reckon being ill as one of the great pleasures of life, provided one is not too ill and is not obliged to work till one is better.
>
> —*Samuel Butler*

> I enjoy convalescence. It is the part that makes the illness worthwhile.
>
> —*George Bernard Shaw*

> 'Tis healthy to be sick sometimes.
>
> —*Henry David Thoreau*

Where are the nudge-nudge-wink-wink quotes from Erma Bombeck, Marie Curie, Eleanor Roosevelt, Gloria Steinem, or Jane Austen extolling the benefits of being unwell? Where are the inspirational posters emblazoned with quotes like this: "If you want to test a woman's capacity to really get shit done, get her sick. You'd be amazed at what a coughing, hacking, feeling-like-hell female can accomplish." What? They don't exist? Exactly my point.

I had always assumed the whole poor-poor-pitiful-me routine must have its roots in some sordid sexy-nurse fantasy. Even though most of us were raised with terrifying images of female caregivers like Louise Fletcher's callous Nurse Ratched in *One Flew Over the Cuckoo's Nest* and Kathy Bates's psycho Annie Wilkes from *Misery*, the stereotype persists. (I blame it on the Halloween costume people, who in recent years have managed to make even pirate and inmate outfits slutty.) But maybe that's not it at all. Maybe men walk around shouldering a burden I can't fathom. Maybe they all go through life feeling like they need to be big and brave and productive and protective every waking minute of every single day, so when their noses seem to have sprung a tiny leak, they see it as a sanctioned break from the rigors of their self-imposed power prisons. If that's the case, we women need to band together to show them that is it much, much worse on the outside and that their little "vacation from life" won't be the all-expenses-paid Caribbean cruise they're envisioning.

Consider the child who is allowed to stay home from school because she has a tummy ache. If *you* stay home from work to cuddle with her on the couch and eat ice cream and watch movies together all day, what do you suppose are the odds that she'll feel better tomorrow? Or the next day? I can't be the first to point out to you that *your husband is not very different from a child*—yours or anyone else's. So looking at it that way, the trick is to ever so subtly make being "sick" a living hell for him. You know, so that he will realize there's no benefit to remaining unwell and recover quickly so that you can all get on with your perfectly busy lives.

Here are a few things you can do to help him get back on his feet with head-turning speed:

Call his mother (or your mother; whichever one he likes less). If she lives nearby, explain that you're worried about leaving him alone—which you have been forced to do, since you're doing double duty and all—and were wondering if she could sit with him for a few hours a day. If she lives out of town, tell her she can help by checking in frequently via phone and e-mail.

Refuse to have sex with him until he has been symptom-free for a week. It's amazing how a man who is too weak to fetch his own aspirin can muster enough energy to grope/proposition/fling himself on top of his partner, but somehow they seem to manage it. "Sorry, pal, but look how miserable *you* are," you might chastise gently. "I'd be crazy to expose myself to whatever nasty bug you've got!" Once he realizes that coughing preempts coitus, he'll be tripping over himself to embark on the road to recovery. In the interim, unless he is robustly ill (or his "symptoms" are keeping you up all night), try to resist the urge to decamp to the guest bed or couch. Having the bed to himself could fall into the reward category and effectively negate the no-sex threat.

Send the kids in to entertain him. Nothing says "get well soon" like a couple of rugrats jumping on you, right? Pump them up on lots of sugar and send them in with very full mugs of steaming beverages. Make sure they tell him, "Mom says we need to be in here as much as possible to cheer you up!" After a few days of this, he should come to realize that being vertical and productive is the far less painful option.

Hide the remote control. I know, this one is cruel and really will require herculean effort on your part not to give in, because the whining and complaining will actually worsen in the short term. Also, it's best to initiate this plan when the kids aren't home, as he will spew obscenities like the lead thug in the dirtiest Quentin Tarantino flick you ever saw and make an upsetting mess tearing up the house looking for his beloved clicker. He'll accuse you of hiding it (the nerve!), and he may even bribe you with offers of spa vacations and shopping sprees if you'll just give it back—or at least help him find it. Be strong! Remember, you're doing this for his own good. Desperate times call for desperate measures. If televised delights are taken away from him, the only other perk to being sick is a license to eat all of the junk food he can possibly shovel into his mouth. Which brings us to:

Clear the house of all junk food and refuse to buy any more until he is 100 percent well. This is easy to pull off, as you will use the "you need to eat healthy, *healing* foods" line of reasoning that's impossible to argue with. Strip the pantry and refrigerator of his tasty favorites such as salami, Doritos, and those disgusting frosted circus animal cookies he insists on having in the house, and replace them with a hearty assortment of nutrient-dense goodies like liver, wheatgrass, radishes, boiled cabbage, low-sodium chicken broth, and canned, unsweetened goat's milk. Continue to drink wine, eat steak, and enjoy dessert as you normally would, insisting that you need to keep up your precious strength. This isn't being unkind; it's helping to motivate him toward wellness. Bottoms up!

Make sure whatever cold medicine you give him has the words *may cause drowsiness* on it. This won't do anything to shorten the duration or severity of his symptoms, but it could buy you a few minutes of silent relief. Administer this medication in the late afternoon so that you can have a few hours to yourself after the kids go to bed and before you turn in.

Threaten to call a doctor. Few things strike fear into the heart of a grown man like the thought of donning a paper gown and having a stranger (in all likelihood another man) palpate his flesh or, heaven forbid, puncture it with a needle. You can lead up to this one gradually, dropping casual comments like, "If you're not feeling better by Friday, I think you should go to the doctor." Obviously he's a big boy and the boss of himself, and you can't *make* him go, even when Friday rolls around. If he resists, having an arsenal of vague and ambiguous questions such as "Have you read that prolonged fever is associated with erectile dysfunction?" can be enormously helpful in encouraging him to be proactive in his own health care. (By the way, the doctor card works great with sick kids, too—and you can be totally sly about it. "Do you think maybe I should call Dr. Black?" you can ask, looking gravely concerned and slightly perplexed, as if the situation may indeed be out of your hands. Brace yourself for the inevitable, "You know what? I think I'm starting to feel better!" More often than not, it works like a charm.)

Get sick yourself. This move is the trickiest of all of to pull off, because you probably don't get sick easily, and on the rare occasion that you do, you aren't adept at broadcasting your misery. Whenever I manage something brutal like projectile vomiting or severe diarrhea, Joe occasionally notices and responds (even if he was praying to the same porcelain god just hours before me) with a steady stream of Gatorade and the luxury of having the whole entire bed to myself. It's not much, but it's better than listening to *him* moan and hurl.

CHAPTER SEVEN

The View from the Passenger Seat . . . Sucks

As we were driving, we saw a sign that said
"Watch for Rocks."
Marta said it should read "Watch for Pretty Rocks."
I told her she should write in her suggestion to
the highway department,
but she started saying it was a joke—
just to get out of writing a simple letter!
And I thought I was lazy!

• JACK HANDEY •

From the endless train of ridiculous research studies that cross my desk, one of my favorites of late was this one: WOMEN MORE ATTRACTED TO MEN IN EXPENSIVE CARS. That was the actual title of the news release, which I even skimmed—mostly because I thought there must be more to it than the obvious—before promptly filing it in my handy "no shit" folder. Apparently a team of university psychologists showed a group of women photos of a man sitting in a sleek silver Bentley and another guy in a battered Ford Fiesta. The women were then asked to rate each man on a standardized scale of attractiveness. Not surprisingly, the women found the Bentley boy significantly more handsome than the Ford fellow, never mind that they were the *very same person*. None of this was surprising in the least, including the brief mention of a corollary study in which this time the men were asked to rate women in various vehicles. Not at all shockingly, what kind of car the woman drove or what shape it was in or probably even whether it was on wheels or blocks mattered not in the least to the men; they judged each gal on face and figure only, her choice of automobile utterly irrelevant.

Call me shallow and materialistic, but I get this. To Joe, a car is a tool for carrying crap, and because he is both handy and adventurous, a truck is a must. He drove an old, gold, too-small-for-his-frame Ford Ranger when we met, and he never looked sexier to me than the day he upgraded to the brand-new, gleaming white F-150. It was no Rolls Royce, but it was rugged and manly and had that delicious new-car scent and a CD player. He was *hot*.

That was eight years ago. Today the outside is scratched up, the tailgate is bent, and the inside is coated in dueling layers of dust and dog hair.

"It's a *truck*," Joe says when I complain about the filth and the stink. "It's supposed to be dirty."

So most of the time we take my car, which isn't a minivan but close. It's more of a station wagon–SUV hybrid, but at least it's got leather seats and a moon roof. It runs great and has never given us a single headache, so I know that I'm stuck with the stupid thing for at least another hundred thousand miles. This used to infuriate me—I like change!—but I've come to a place in my marriage and in my life where I have realized that it really doesn't matter if I'm driving a Pinto or a Lexus; a car is just a vehicle of transport, sort of like a hot dog is to ketchup. It's an armor designed to protect my family from the dangers of other, bigger cars and keep us dry in a rainstorm. It's a climate-controlled wagon for hauling groceries and small bodies from one place to another. Oh, and it's also a great sparring spot.

Many years ago I wrote an article about relationship conflict for a national magazine, and one of the sources I interviewed—probably a Ph.D. or a famous clinical researcher or bestselling author—told me something I have never forgotten: "When you want to bring up a touchy subject with your spouse," the communication guru told me, "do it in the car." The reasoning he used to substantiate this advice sounded like something you'd hear from a wilderness guide before taking off on a solo stint through the grizzly-riddled back country: "Men perceive direct eye contact as a challenge," he went on to explain. "So the same information will be received as significantly less hostile if you're not looking directly at him when you deliver it." After years of careful observation, I've come up with another equally compelling motivation for always limiting your sex, money, child care, politics, and religion discussions to the car: Chances are, you're already fighting anyway. At least if you're me.

* * * * *

" At Least You're Not Married to Him "

He has a Starbucks obsession. He absolutely cannot pass one without filling up; it's just not an option. This is combined with the fact that he has to stop every hour on every single road trip we take. Just yesterday we were driving three hours and he had to stop twice for coffee. I didn't talk to him for an hour. I love him but I do not always like him.

MARYELLEN

Pretty much every single knock-down spat I've had with Joe has either started or seriously escalated in the car. Remember the ice-to-the-temple incident at the very beginning of this book? Well, here's what was happening in the moments just prior to that culminating moment of marital excellence: It was a beautiful summer day and the whole family had been invited to my friend Tami's birthday barbecue. Tami is an event planner and her husband Mark owns one of my favorite restaurants in town, so their parties are always over the top, with spectacular food and great music and every detail carefully considered. I'd been looking forward to it for weeks and had even rented wacky costumes for all of us so that we would totally rock the hippie-fiesta theme. So there we were in our sombreros and waist-length wigs and love beads, having a lovely time, when our youngest daughter proceeded to launch into what was predictably going to be one of the more impressive meltdowns of her little four-year life. Joe, who has a zero-tolerance policy for tiny tantrums, immediately whisked her from the room to frighten some compliance into her. When they rejoined the party, I took the child we have nicknamed LBS (for Low Blood Sugar) into my lap and basically force-fed her, knowing that once she got some food into her system she'd be a new, happy person. Of course I was right, and the rest of the festivities passed without incident. At the party's end, we packed up our new tie-dye T-shirts and the rest of our copious gear and loaded ourselves into the car.

"You coddle her," Joe spat at me as soon as all four doors were shut.

"I just know how she gets when she's hungry," I replied simply, reaching for the radio button. I knew where this was likely to go, too, and I was hoping some decent music could defuse the situation. "I knew her mood would change once she'd eaten," I added.

"It doesn't matter!" my husband shouted at me, pounding the radio's power button off for emphasis. "She needs to learn that she can't just throw a tantrum because she's hungry."

"I agree," I said, struggling to remain calm. "But I didn't think a birthday party was the best place to teach that particular lesson. I just wanted to calm her down and get her fed. And for the record, I don't think *anyone* would consider feeding a child the same thing as coddling her." I reached for the radio button, thinking that we'd each just had a chance to explain our take on the situation and could put the discussion to bed. But evidently, Joe wasn't finished.

"That's just putting a Band-Aid on bad behavior," he accused, smacking my hand away from the dial.

I sat there shocked.

"Did you just . . . *smack my hand*?" I asked incredulously, struggling to remain calm and reaching for the dial. Again, he blocked my move. Rage boiled inside me like a cauldron of bleach and ammonia and a dozen other incompatible toxic chemicals. I wanted to shout ugly four-letter words at him but the girls were in the backseat, so it was imperative that I remain as composed as could be.

"Are you kidding me?" I hissed, using the hand closest to his to hold it down and reaching for the dial with my free hand. The minute I had the music on, he snatched his hand from my grip and snapped the power back off. Because hurtling the sort of insults we were both thinking ("You are *such a fucking asshole/ bitch!*") was out of the question, instead we continued to take out our joint frustration on the radio dial like a pair of surly, sugared-up kindergarteners: On. Off. On. Off. On. Off. On. Off. *All the way home.*

Mature, I know.

I am not proud of our embarrassingly adolescent behavior, nor am I condoning it. I'm merely sharing this story to illustrate one of the principal drawbacks of the car fight: You can't walk away. (At least not until you arrive at your destination, where hopefully one of you won't lob a cup of ice at the other's head.)

" At Least You're Not Married to Him "

My husband loves his cars more than he loves me, even though he swears that's not true. He meticulously cleans, waxes, and shines them at least once a week, and heaven forbid if it rains I have to listen to him go on and on about how God hates him and it always manages to rain when he washes the cars. If I did anything to one of his cars I'd be hiding underneath my bed like a scared dog.

MARA

Over the years, Joe and I have driven thousands of miles in agonizing silence, and I've demanded he *pull this car over and let me out because I refuse to be stuck inside it with him for another second* more times than I can count—although to his enormous credit, he's actually given in to this insane demand only once. The funniest bit about *that* time is that neither of us can recall what we were fighting about. We were kidless and carefree and enjoying an idyllic vacation in Hawaii. Each day prior to World War Three had been better than the last, filled with a year's worth of sun and sex and delicious sleeping in. It was our last night and we were on our way to the island's most romantic dinner spot, and we are both pretty sure we weren't fighting when we left the hotel or why would we have gone to dinner at all? So somewhere between beautiful point A and even lovelier point B, The Fight broke out. There we were, zipping along this winding island road in our vacation-splurge convertible, verbally abusing each other at the top of our lungs.

"Just let me out of this car!" I remember screaming. "Do you hear me? I mean it! I cannot sit next to you for another minute. Pull over and *let me out!*"

To my part relief and part horror, he twisted the wheel and drew the car to a screeching, gravelly stop. I flung my door open and stumbled out, smoothing my skirt and my hair and wondering what the hell would happen next. Joe didn't even give me a second sideways glance as he peeled away. I leaped into the middle of the road, where I stood violently and repeatedly shooting him the full-body double-bird. I convinced myself I saw him watching me in his rearview mirror.

I knew I was closer to the restaurant than the hotel behind me, so I walked the rest of the way. I spotted the empty convertible in the parking lot and thought to myself, *That son of a bitch is inside eating! Well, I'm not sitting out here while he enjoys the best food on this island. I'll just go in there and sit down like I own the place and eat my food and ignore him. That'll show him.* He had the keys and I didn't have a dime on me. What other choice did I have?

Just as neither of us remembers what the fight was about, neither can recall how it ended. We both just know that by the end of the meal, somehow we were talking and laughing about the fact that he'd dumped me on the side of the road. I have a feeling we'll laugh about that one for a long time. As long as it doesn't happen again.

" At Least You're Not Married to Him "

I love my husband but he seems to thoroughly enjoy picking his nose—and I'm talking *digging* here—in the car, with me right beside him. It's so gross.

AMANDA

From our home base on the central California coast, Joe and I have driven to and around Montana, Mexico, and the Mojave Desert. We've circumnavigated the entire island of Ireland, each of us sitting on the "wrong" side of the car while driving on the "wrong" side of the road. (Which, it should be noted, makes quarreling significantly more dangerous.) We've had car-guments in countries whose language we don't speak, frequently over my appalling inability to decipher foreign road signs. We've bickered about music, the internal car temperature, which route is indeed fastest, his incessant need to be the leader in any string of vehicles, and occasionally where to stop for food. (My feeling: Burger King is best, McDonald's will do, and Wendy's is acceptable for an emergency potty stop only; *never* for eating.) Fortunately, my map-reading skills are stellar, because I hear a deficiency in that area can be fodder for some epic spats.

We don't need a three-day trip to fall into auto-argument mode. Even a typical ten-minute drive to Costco can go like this:

Me (tucking my arms into the body of my shirt for warmth): "Brrrrr! I didn't realize it was so cold out!"

Joe (rolling down all four windows): "Cold? It's got to be at least fifty-five degrees out! It's beautiful! Practically balmy!"

Me (shivering and realizing that he's locked the windows in the down position): "Could you unlock the windows or at least put mine up for me?"

Joe (grudgingly complying): "I need fresh air. Don't you need fresh air? How can you not need fresh air?"

Me (turning on the radio): "I'm going to just keep a blanket in the car."

Joe (switching the radio to CD): "You keep saying that, but you never *do* it."

Me (fast-forwarding the CD he's chosen to the track I prefer): "Whatever. I *will* do it. Hey, I'm starving. Can we grab a hot dog before we go into Costco?"

Joe (noticing that I've stealthily turned on the heat and snapping it off): "Why didn't you tell me you were going to want to eat? I didn't factor in eating time."

Me (picturing "Costco run" blocked off in his Outlook calendar): "I didn't plan it, I just realized I was hungry. Besides, I want a lousy hot dog, not a hand-rolled sushi platter and a chocolate soufflé. And if you'd been ready to go when you *said* you'd be ready to go, we'd have time to eat a dozen hot dogs!"

"Why don't we see if we have time for the hot dog *after* we shop?" he suggests, leaning heavily on the gas pedal, as if to prove that he is going to do everything in his power to make sure I get my death rocket. Now, Joe swears that he doesn't tailgate just to piss me off, and since he is the most honest man I have ever met, I'll have to concede that he truly must not realize his own unconscious need for vehicular vengeance.

"Honey, honey, *honey!*" I sputter as I see the rapidly approaching rear bumper of the truck in front of us. I am gripping the oh-my-God bar above my head furiously with one hand; the other is splayed firmly against the dashboard, bracing for the imminent collision.

"What?" Joe barks, easing up on the gas just a hair and

putting a few comforting inches between our bumper and the truck. "That jackass is going fifty in a sixty-five, and he just switched lanes to get in front of me and hit his brakes. I'm just encouraging him to move over."

"Why don't you just go around him?" I ask. The very man who lives for the thrill of passing semitrucks in the pitch-darkness on curvy, two-lane highways has suddenly lost the will to overtake another automobile? I find this hard to believe.

"Don't need to," he says, speeding up again. "He'll move."

I close my eyes and pray. *Dear God, I know I haven't been over to visit you there at church in a really long time—oh by the way, happy belated birthday to your son!—but if you could see fit to make sure I make it home alive, I'd really appreciate it. You know, for the kids' sake and also so that I can continue to do your will here on Earth, which I promise I am going to start doing if you let me live. Love, Jenna. I mean, Amen.*

I suppose you are wondering why I don't just get behind the wheel myself. The thing is, I am a perfectly good driver—until my husband is in the passenger seat. I don't know what it is about having his physical presence up there next to me, but whenever he is there I'm a nervous wreck. I plow through red lights, stop at barely yellow ones, and bounce along the center line of reflectors like a drunken kangaroo on casters. For this reason (and admittedly, the half dozen fender-benders and handful of speeding tickets on my record), Joe thinks I am unfit to operate anything motorized. And since his driving record is pristine—minus that one speeding ticket he got in Bumfuck, Montana, which he paid cash for on the spot so there's no actual record of it ever happening—it gets me nowhere to point out the well-documented fact that men break the law more, drive more aggressively, receive more traffic tickets, *and* get in more accidents than women (who aren't me) do. So I shut up and hang on and pray silently and occasionally let loose with a spontaneous, terrified obscenity.

For a while, I thought my iPhone was going to be the simple solution. I could almost completely tune out what was going on around me—even the bumper-kissing action on all four sides of the car—as long as I was surfing the web or checking the weather or texting or playing hangman or responding to e-mail. This, of course, quickly began to drive Joe insane.

"Who are you texting?" he'd demand angrily, obviously bitter that I was allowed to do it and he wasn't because he was behind the wheel.

"My boyfriend," I'd answer, poking him playfully in the ribs. "Come on, why do you care what I'm doing? I'm bored over here. I have nothing to do! I might as well answer a few e-mails. It's called being productive."

"No, it's called being *rude*," was the reply. "I'm right here. Talk to *me*."

"We're going to be in the car for hours," I remind him. "We'll run out of stuff to talk about, so I'm saving some of it for later. Besides, you don't mind if I'm reading a magazine or flipping through a catalog even though they make me totally carsick, so what's the difference?"

"It's just different. It's like talking on your cell phone in public. It's disrespectful."

So we frequently ride along in annoyed silence, him whistling some Creedence Clearwater Revival tune he's got in his head (is there anything more annoying than gratuitous whistling?), and me having to fight every urge in my body to *not look at my iPhone*.

"This is fun," I might say, unable to resist my innate need to be sarcastic.

After endless debate and compromise, it's come to this: I'm allowed to drive only if I am violently carsick, in which case Joe always quickly and wisely hands over the keys. I occasionally—and covertly—check my iPhone for new text and e-mail messages, but I reply only if something is urgent or work-related or relevant to where we are going at the given moment. Joe will never stop tailgating, and pointing it out only intensifies his need to do it. If I play the *freezing* card, I sometimes win the windows-up war. (If Joe suspected I was trying to preserve a blow-out while compromising his precious comfort, he'd install an eject button beneath my seat.) Regarding the climate issue, it turns out there is a solution—and it will only cost us about $65,000. Apparently they make cars with individual "climate zones" that each passenger can control. I can picture us zipping along the highway in our luxurious mobile greenhouse, frost covering Joe's side of the car while warm moisture drips down the windows on my side. It's an absurd image, but at least we are both smiling in it.

• • •

CHAPTER EIGHT

Why Don't We Get Drunk and Screw?

*Sex: the thing that takes up the least amount of time
and causes the most amount of trouble.*

• JOHN BARRYMORE •

When you stood at that altar or beneath the diaphanous branches of that romantic willow tree or beside those gently lapping waves or under that stunning chuppah your parents paid a fortune to festoon in seasonal foliage, you said some version of the words "I do." You promised, before God and family and possibly a curious squirrel or an oblivious sand crab, to love and cherish the man standing beside you. Forever. The part you didn't say out loud was this: "I solemnly swear not to grope or be groped by anyone but the guy in the monkey suit—the one who looks slightly sweatier and more faint than all of the others who look just like him—for the rest of my life or at least until he ceases to have

• • • • •

a pulse."* What other reason is there to get married? The tax break isn't enough to make it worth it; if you're desperate for companionship, you could always get a dachshund; and if your answer is "to start a family," we're back to the groping thing. All of that being the case, the odds are, by default if for no other reason, your husband would very much like to rub his naked body against yours from time to time. If you're lucky, you'll want to do the deed with the exact same frequency for the exact same duration in the exact same position using the exact same props, potions, and method of contraception as he does, every single time.

Yeah, right. Good luck with that.

But thanks to that one tiny clause unique to the marriage contract, you are each other's single option when it comes to getting lucky. No other relationship you have operates within such strict confines. I mean, you love your hamster, you cherish your friends, you obey your boss, but the only living creature on the planet for whom you *forsake all others* is your spouse. Right? You could go out and get thirty more hamsters or three hundred more friends or switch jobs tomorrow, and

---

* Of course, there are exceptions to every rule. Maybe you married your gay best friend because neither of you was getting any younger and you both wanted to have kids, or perhaps the common bond you share with your partner is that neither of you has a single carnal need or desire, so you're in one of the billions of supposedly happily sexless marriages CNN is always reporting on. If either of these is the case, feel free to skip right to the next chapter; there's very little for you here.

• • • • •

it's not like your other hamster/friends/bosses are going to take your kids from you and demand lifelong financial support. For the most part, the more the merrier!

Let's look at the intimate exclusivity business in terms to which most women can relate: If people were clothes and clothes equaled sexual partners, you would be the *only shirt* hanging in your husband's metaphorical closet. When the man wants to "get dressed," you're it. And if he's like most guys, he would like to get dressed every freaking day. (The nerve, right?)

Again, I don't mean to stereotype. I am sure there are plenty of women—I even know one myself—whose husbands can't keep up with their turbocharged libidos. For all I know there may even be guys out there moaning to their buddies that their nymphomaniac partners "never just want to cuddle." But from many years of my own unscientific research—usually involving copious amounts of wine and a handful of outspoken girlfriends—it seems like the most common marital scenario is the one in which the wife believes her husband wants sex 24/7, and the husband feels like his wife could go the rest of her life without ever doing it again.

"I'd have sex with him *all of the fucking time* if he would just be nice to me and help a little more around the house," she grumbles frequently.

"I'd be nice to her and help her around the house *all of the fucking time* if she'd just have more sex with me!" he fires back. (It's worth noting that another study out of the University of Oxford—and this one was wholly separate from the sex-and-sweeping-correlation one—found that the more willing a guy is to chip in with the household chores, the more attractive a woman will find him—which could potentially lead to more sex, so clearly he should make the first move here and pick up a goddamned broom. Am I right?)

Here's what I find amusing about all of this: At one point in time, it's entirely probable that this composite couple was having sex *all of the fucking time.* Isn't that how most relationships start out? I can recall weekends where Joe and I left the bed only to refill the chip bowl or use the john. Anthropologists explain that the novelty of new love causes both partners' brains to release the neurotransmitters dopamine and norepinepherine, which basically are nature's amphetamines. When these love drugs are coursing through our veins it causes our hearts to race, makes us alert and immune to fatigue, and basically turns us into lust-driven hussies. *Sleep, schmeep! I'll sleep when I'm dead. Now get over here and penetrate something!* It's the honeymoon phase and everyone knows it doesn't last—if it did they'd call the whole damned thing a honeymoon. Scientists have actually determined that this passion-fueled, impossibly idealistic stage lasts exactly, on average, two years, six months, and twenty-five days. (I know, that seems long to me, too.) After that point, guys in the defining study admitted they pretty much stopped trying to pretend to be tidy or feign even a semblance of interest in anything their ladies might be saying, and the gals confessed they no longer really gave a shit if their partner found them attractive. I might be paraphrasing the findings a bit here, but that was the gist.

Looking at this data and factoring in my own hindsight,

• • • • •

here's what I can't help but wonder: Was there a gradual wan-
ing of desire that nobody noticed? A moment of total neutral-
ity? And how do you go from a dozen prolonged, romantic
romps in a weekend to two quickies a month without noticing,
if nothing else, that you have several extra hours of free time
on your hands and that it's been ages since you had to call your
OB/GYN for an emergency urinary tract infection prescription?

" At Least You're Not Married to Him "

If I refuse to have sex more than twice in a week, my husband accuses
me of being "stingy." I've tried to tell him that most husbands are lucky
to get sex twice a *month*, but he doesn't believe me. Imagine that!

MARA

The experts won't come out and say how much sex we should
be having, but most agree that married couples who are reasonably healthy and have partners who engage in thorough, con-
sistent grooming practices should at least be having *some*. (And
folks who do it less than ten times a year or less are considered
to be in "sexless marriages," which basically means those ten
times don't even count.) There's a saying that goes something
like this: "Sex is only ten percent of a marriage. Unless you're
not having it; then it's ninety percent."

There are several subtle indicators Joe uses when he wants
to let me know it's been too long since we've been biblical. For
instance, when *every single thing* out of my mouth earns a

suggestive reply, it's time. (Me: "Honey, could you please pass the sausage?" Joe: "Oh, I've got your sausage right here, baby." Me: "Did you fix the dishwasher yet?" Joe: "Oh, I'll fix *your* dishwasher, hot stuff.") And though my husband is characteristically affectionate, when I can't bend over to scoop the cat litter without getting goosed or brush my teeth without being fondled, the guy really needs some action. Sometimes—although not as often as with the other methods—he resorts to a simple whispered "Can we *please* have sex tonight?" It's enough to break a girl's heart, I tell you.

Newsweek did a big exposé on who's actually getting the most action, and it turns out it's not who you might think. The rich, powerful CEO who folks assume can get as much ass as he wants in fact scores a dozen fewer times a year than his fresh-out-of-undergraduate-school son with the starting salary in the high twenties. Think your party-loving single pals are doing it around the clock? Turns out those of us who have forsaken all others fornicate with our singular option an average of seventy-one times a year. Spinster Sue and Bachelor Bob—with their limitless fields of potential partners—get off just forty-six times in that same time span, or less than once a week. Inexplicably, the profile of the most sexually active Americans includes a penchant for PBS, a disdain for organized religion, and two or more kids living at home. Really, the only *not* surprising part of the whole study was the finding that there is a positive correlation between exposure to pornography and frequency of sex. (What? Watching other people have sex makes you *want to have sex*?)

• • • • •

Whereas poor Joe gets turned down more often than a stolen credit card, neither of us is able to recall a single time that he's rejected my advances. He can be filthy, buried in work, furious at me, engrossed in a riveting playoff game, running a 104-degree fever, have one arm trapped under a boulder the size of a pickup truck, or all of the above, and it matters not; if there's even a whisper of a chance I might be up for a tangle, my husband will be stripped down to his boxer-briefs faster than you can say "Hokey Pokey." (As long as there's TiVo available in the playoff example.)

Not long ago, Joe and I had been enjoying one of our rare but lethal marathon battles. It was probably day four of the total and absolute mutual silent treatment—I'm talking not even a whispered "Rot in hell" behind the other's back—and though I'd sort of forgotten what we were fighting about, I was positive that I was still waiting for an apology. You know, for whatever heinous thing he'd done. So anyway, it happened to be a Saturday and the girls got invited to play at a friend's house. It wasn't five seconds after I'd shuffled them out the door before my husband turned to me—practically molesting me with his limpid, lecherous eyes—and propositioned me with this winning pickup line:

"Wanna get naked?" he asked.

Are you fucking kidding me?

"Are you fucking kidding me?" I replied. "I don't even want to *talk* to you until I get an apology."

"I have nothing to apologize for," he shrugged.

Here's the thing: I write a regular sex column, and I've

interviewed some of the foremost researchers on the subject in the world. I know on an intellectual level that giving in at this moment and enjoying a nice tryst with my life partner would be the best thing in the world for my marriage. Physically, we'd feel less stressed afterward and both get a better night's sleep. Emotionally, we'd be flooded with bonding hormones that would make the whole spat seem silly in the first place. Practically, we could quit walking around on razor-sharp eggshells and commence with the regular business of running a household. There was only one reason *not* to respond with a giddy "Take me now or lose me forever": Stupid, selfish pride.

"Hrumph," I replied, storming into my office and slamming the door and proving once and for all that Joe is unarguably right every time he calls me a stubborn pain in the ass. Sorry, but I can't be pissed off and turned on at the same time. It's just not possible.

" At Least You're Not Married to Him "

We never kiss at all anymore. I'd love to make out and cuddle again like we used to, but there's just no going to first or second base. With him it's all or nothing—so it's usually nothing.

CATH

Here's the thing about sex: Innumerable articles and books have been written about it, and there are untold ways to do it. Thanks to HBO, YouTube, and skanky, aspiring "actors" everywhere, you can watch *real people doing it* from the comfort of your office or your living room couch. If the parts God gave you aren't enough to send you screaming over the edge, there is a bottomless assortment of wedges, whips, cuffs, clamps, rings, swings, dildos, and DVDs you can buy to blow your randy little mind. If you're not quite in the mood, a strategic drop or two of a certain sort of lube will have you begging for it within minutes. (And if you're not familiar with Zestra— or Liquid Gold, as I like to call it—get thee to the Internet, pronto. That stuff is libido in a bottle, and no, I am not a paid spokesperson, but if you work for Zestra and would like to have me on your payroll, we should definitely talk.) You probably couldn't imagine—and wouldn't believe—what your neighbors are doing over there in that seemingly innocent backyard hammock. And that gal sitting next to you on the bus, the one with her nose in her laptop who appears to be diligently working? That's not a spreadsheet on the screen; it's porn. Sex is used to sell everything from beer to breakfast cereal (oh, come on, you haven't noticed the sultry way the cream is being drizzled over the firm, ripe peach on the box?), and urban legend even suggests that there are steamy subliminal messages in every single Disney movie ever made. (Think about it: *Bambi*? *Pocahontas*? *Lady and the Tramp*?)

And yet in a poll posted on the survey site TheSkinnyScoop .com, 81 percent of the women who responded admitted they'd rather get a back massage than get busy with their husbands. (The other 19 percent work for Zestra, I'm guessing.)

Since copulation is meant to be a delightful deed for all

involved parties, you'd think we'd be tripping over ourselves to get into bed. Instead, women in particular seem to spend the majority of their time and energy deflecting advances, avoiding innuendo, and coming up with excuses not to get naked.

"I'm too tired."

"I'm too fat."

"You didn't shave tonight."

"I haven't shaved in a week."

"The kids are awake."

"The kids could wake up."

"*Modern Family* is on."

"The dog is watching."

"It's too cold in here."

"It's too hot in here."

"I'm too drunk."

"I'm too sober."

"Aunt Flo is in town."

"You never listen to a word I say and you spend too much time at the office and I'm sick of picking up the constant trail of shit you leave in your wake because you don't have an ounce of respect for me and I did *not* want a toaster oven for my birthday!"

Comedian Billy Crystal is famous for saying that women need a reason to have sex; men just need a place. The only reason that this is funny is because it is true. A male friend of mine—a well-known author who is married to another well-known author—recently regaled me with the following private exchange he had with his wife:

· · · · ·

HIM: "Hey, honey, let's have sex!"

HER: "I'd love to but I'm really tired and I have to . . . Hey, did I tell you what happened when I went to—wait, I have to write something down before I forget—and by the way you never asked me how my day went today and did you get my thirty-five texts because I don't recall you sending *me* any, which I have to say really hurts my feelings—"

HIM: "Get in the bed."

HER: "Wait, we have all of these things to talk about!"

HIM: "Now!"

HIM [*to me, earnestly*]: "This really happened, I swear."

ME [*to him, solemnly*]: "I don't doubt it for one second, buddy."

" At Least You're Not Married to Him "

My husband is *always* "in the mood." He wants to know over six A.M. coffee if we are doing it that night. That is the last thing on my mind. I got home the other day around lunchtime and of course he wanted to go have sex. He even said I could close my eyes and think of someone else. Jeeeeeez! Are all guys this way?

LYNN

It's a widely accepted belief that human beings—men in particular—were not meant to be monogamous. Think about how the male body was designed: When he is stimulated, which barely takes more than a hearty wind gust in some cases, he quickly and effortlessly produces millions of sperm cells. If one of those lucky little sperms fertilizes a waiting egg, nothing really changes for him. His body doesn't stop producing more sperm, which means he can go on to fertilize another egg, and then another, and another and another and on and on indefinitely or until he catches something nasty and the resulting rash makes it too painful to even wear pants, let alone even *think* about finding and seducing another hapless egg. For the ladies, it's a whole different story, one you can't understand fully unless you have been pregnant or at least tuned in to the Learning Channel's *A Baby Story* a few times.

In scientific circles, it's repeatedly noted that males—of pretty much every species that has ever been studied—who have lost interest in their sexual partner consistently rebound with astonishing prowess *when given the opportunity to hump new and eager partners*. The phenomenon even has a name, the Coolidge Effect, in honor of the illustrious former president. According to legend, as Calvin and his wife were touring a poultry farm, the first lady asked the farmer how so few roosters could produce so many fertile eggs. The farmer replied that the roosters copulated all day long, day after day.

"Tell that to Mr. Coolidge," Mrs. Coolidge reportedly said.

Thusly informed, the president asked the farmer, "With the same hen each time?"

"No," said the farmer. "Each rooster has dozens of hens to choose from."

"Tell that to the First Lady," Coolidge is said to have replied.

Ba dum bum ching.

• • • • •

Even us ladies with our one lousy egg a month would benefit from having not just a single partner but a stable of baby-daddies on hand to help stoke the fire, mow the lawn, and cover the cost of our brood's combined braces, broken bones, and car insurance tabs. We could mate with a smart guy this year and an athletic guy next year and a breathtakingly handsome guy the year after that, and maybe—just maybe—one of the resulting offspring would become rich and famous and buy us a castle in Italy in which to luxuriate in our golden years.

And yet, even though it doesn't make sense for people of either gender to limit their sexual exposure to just one other person, here we all are, reading books and lighting candles and popping pills and shimmying into crotchless chaps and slutty nurse outfits (er, some of us) in an effort to make marital sex remotely resemble the stuff we see in the movies and therefore assume everyone else is having.

When the planets align perfectly and everyone is showered and shaved and the kids are asleep and all of the laundry has been put away and it's not too late and I'm not under the gun of an imminent deadline, I enjoy consistently excellent sex. And if we're being honest here, after a decade and a half of practice, Joe and I are pretty . . . efficient. What I'm saying is that sex is fun and doesn't consume hours of my precious time. It's physically beneficial for both of us—relieving stress, burning calories, boosting immunity, and even reducing the risk of having a fatal heart attack—and we're almost always nicer to each other afterward (at least for a few minutes). So why, for the love of lube, does it take such a herculean effort to get me to give in to it in the first place? And why on earth should my poor husband have to beg me to put down my boring book and do the one thing in the world that I can do to him that nobody else can?

Here's a metaphor for the best explanation I can come up with: Imagine I was walking down the street and a guy in a big overcoat walked up really close behind me and whispered into my ear, "Pssssst. Lady. You want some air? I got all sorts of air right here. This is good shit, too. You want some? I'll give you a good deal." Do you think I would be tempted by this in the least? Of course not! I can get air for free any old time I want. My house is filled with air. I can't imagine *paying* for air! At the end of the day, sex is pretty much like air. I take it for granted because it's always right there, at my disposal. It's not like if I decide I'm not really in the mood, I couldn't change my mind in five minutes. Anatomically, women are blessed. We don't get spontaneous erections that demand satisfying, and if we go a week or ninety without experiencing the physical release of orgasm, life chugs right along. Not like the poor ferret. Did you know that a female ferret will die if she goes into heat and can't find a mate? It's true. Can you imagine if that were the case with humans?

ME: "Joe, get in here right now and do me!"
JOE: "I'm watching the game. It's almost over."
ME: "But I'm going to *die*!"

JOE: "I need something to eat—I didn't have lunch at all today and— Aw, crap. Overtime! Gimme fifteen more minutes, okay?"

ME: "Dying . . . (*gasp*) . . . over . . . (*wheeze*) . . . here . . ."

JOE: "Hey, honey, do we have any more of that really good spicy Dijon mustard? The kind with the seeds in it? I was just going to make a sandwich and I used the last of the jar that was in the fridge yesterday."

ME: [*dead*]

JOE: "So no? We don't have any? Damn. I guess I could use mayo. Do we have any mayo?"

ME: [*still dead*]

Of course, that scenario would play out only if he happened to be watching a sporting match when I went into do-me-or-die heat. In every other instance, it would look like this:

ME: "Joe, get in here right now and do me!"

JOE: "On my way!"

I hate to admit this for fear of being judged by the company I keep, but several of our friends' marriages have been ripped apart by infidelity in recent years. Every single time this happens, my first thought is, *Really? You're throwing your family and your house and your lifestyle away . . . over sex?* I mean, I realize that good sex is great and great sex is spectacular, but we're talking about a relatively minute fraction of your time, even if you're doing it daily. (And guess what, cheaters? It may be extraordinarily exciting now, but call me again in eighteen months or so and we'll see how that's holding up.) If you really stop to think about the act itself—how downright ridiculous it is to repeatedly jab at a hole in another person's body with a body part of your own—it's almost shocking that the whole subject gets as much play as it does.

People often complain (most loudly after they've been busted having one of the aforementioned affairs) that their married sex has gotten old and routine. Well, frankly, so has brushing your teeth after lo these many years, but you keep doing it because it's good for you. Besides, that's why God invented vacation sex! You surely have noticed that the same old routine you rely on at home is approximately 380 percent more exciting when you're performing it anywhere else. This is, of course, because someone else has been cooking for you. Plus you may have finally been able to put your feet up for five minutes, possibly sleep in, and maybe even read a steamy book or trashy magazine. My sister swears that three days is the *minimum* for any getaway, as it takes two days to fully relax and catch up on your sleep before you even want to think about being intimate. If you commit to going somewhere glorious (or hell, even somewhere crappy—as long as there's no kitchen, it'll do) a few times a year, you'll have those superlative sessions to conjure up when you need a little mental push to do it back at the ranch. And even if you have one or two ho-hum getaway trysts, they're still a hell of a lot more fun than couples therapy.

• • • • •

• • •

CHAPTER NINE

It's Only Money, Honey

Money will buy you a fine dog,
but only love will make it wag its tail.

• KINKY FRIEDMAN •

I grew up very comfortable, financially. Even though Dad was a high school dropout, he was a brilliant man and a tireless worker. With his brother he started a hugely successful—and enormously profitable—custom home-building business. As I grew, so did the size of our own home, along with the number of fancy new cars in the driveway. My family had a weekend house and a very large boat (the snooty might call it a yacht) and several pretty cool toys including a dune buggy and a couple of Jet Skis. We went skiing in the winters and island hopping in the summers, and I am pretty sure I was the only sixteen-year-old junior in my high school driving her very own candy apple red Porsche 944. (Hey, Porsches were cool in the eighties.)

I know what you're thinking. Spoiled rotten brat.

• • • • •

But here's the thing: Other than the cars and the boat and the toys and the trips, you would never have known we had money. (I know that sounds absurd, but I'm talking about the day-to-day realities of living here.) My mom wasn't dripping in jewels or designer labels, Dad insisted on buying his own clothes at Pic-N-Save, and the invariable answer to "Can I have it?"—whether "it" was a magazine subscription or the hot-pink beach cruiser I wanted more than I had ever wanted anything in my life—was an emphatic *No.* We went to matinees and sneaked in our own candy, and traded hand-me-down clothes with our cousins. New clothes were an infrequent luxury—purchased only out of absolute necessity and always plucked from the clearance rack. Even then, we'd have to leave the bags in the trunk if Dad was home and sneak them into the house later. ("Are these new shoes? Goodness, no! They've been sitting in the car for a week!") Going to Red Lobster for the early bird special was considered a major splurge, and we never, ever ordered appetizers or dessert. Mom ran the house and Dad's business, and you got the distinct feeling she felt dramatically underpaid in both positions. There was much talk of saving for rainy days, but even during a deluge I couldn't get anyone to fork over for a Walkman. Our parents reminded us all of the time how much everything cost and, frequently, how entitled and ungrateful we were.

I am not complaining about any of this or looking for sympathy; in retrospect, I agree that I was a spoiled rotten brat and unquestionably I had far more than most. What's more, I was a sassy little back-talker and didn't deserve most of the stuff

I pined for anyhow. I am including this peek into my fiscally conflicted childhood for one reason only: It may help explain my lingering love-hate relationship with money.

When I began earning my own dough, I embraced my parents' financial lessons and rebelled against them at the same time. I lived below my means—in shitty, unsafe apartments decorated with thrift-store finds—so that I could sock away cash and also pick up the occasional obscene dinner tab. I brought brown-bag lunches to my hoity-toity magazine job and shopped at god-awful sample sales so that I could at least remotely resemble my well-heeled colleagues; then I'd take a cab home with my bags because I worked hard and I deserved it. By the time I met Joe, I was pulling in an impressive salary and had squirreled away a sizable lump in my savings account, too. Because we were in that lovey-dovey new-lust phase where the other person's quirks (that will be maddening someday) still seem delightfully charming, Joe was tickled by the fact that I would take the time to clip and use supermarket coupons and then spend $200 on a pair of jeans.

His amusement didn't last very long.

I was in an extreme shabby-chic phase when we bought our first house, and Joe—who'd grown up in the country—was appalled at my foolish, squandering ways.

"You didn't pay for that, did you?" he asked earnestly, inspecting the rusty, dented watering can I'd picked up at an antiques store. I was planning to use it as a planter, and I thought it was just darling.

"No, honey, they gave it to me for free," I replied sarcastically. Well, I mean, honestly.

"I hope so," he muttered. "Next time we go to my dad's, you should poke around in the shed. It's filled with a bunch of banged-up, corroded crap. You'll love it."

The epithet for the recurring economic debates in our house became "form versus function." (You can probably guess which one I favored.) Joe would come into the house, filthy from working in the yard, and look as if he were actually going to sit down on the creamy white linen sofa.

"Ah, ah, ah," I'd scold. "Get a towel if you're going to sit in here!"

"I can't even sit down on my own goddamned couches," he'd roar. "Who the hell buys white couches?"

"I do!" I'd yell back, and the game would be on.

" At Least You're Not Married to Him "

My husband is the biggest banking hypocrite ever. We are both spenders, no doubt about that. Neither of us pines over making purchases; most times we just do it. But I do not have exorbitant tastes, dress well, or eat out often. My indulgences come with the big red Target emblem or from a big-box store, and 85 percent of the time they are for my children. My husband, on the other hand, spends as he pleases, but only makes purchases for himself and takes enormous amounts of money out of the ATM. The worst part is that he constantly monitors my purchases, demands to know how I spent $598 at Costco (we have four kids who eat like six adults, dumbshit) and $18 at Walgreens (a prescription and Red Vines, thank you very much), and why I wrote a $100 check to the guy who has been coaching our kids' soccer for six years (annual fees). Meanwhile, he is completely unsupervised in his own spending. As you can imagine, I suspect that the bulk of his money goes to greens fees and hamburgers. I really don't want to know, or else I would.

VICTORIA

When we married, the very fact of our separate checking accounts drove Joe mad. We lived like a pair of very civil and laid-back roommates—he'd pay the mortgage and the car insurance, I'd pay property tax and all of the utilities. Because this allowed me some measure of control, I would have been perfectly happy to continue this way forever, but Joe felt a burning need to establish financial solidarity. Though we agreed that "our money" belonged to both of us, we couldn't seem to settle on a mutually satisfying accounting system.

"We should have one joint account," Joe would gripe. But my husband was unconditionally loyal to the little mom-and-pop bank where he had once worked, and I liked the convenience of my behemoth institution. (We had online banking *and* cooler checks.) And then there were the logistics: Who would keep the register? Who would be responsible for the monthly balancing? Would we pay bills my way (immediately upon their arrival) or Joe's way (file them away to be paid at the last possible minute)? It was all too much.

Eventually he wore me down and I agreed to try a joint account—if I could keep my own for the trial period. I wrote one check out of our joint account. It bounced.

"This is why two people can't share one account!" I wailed, indignant. "You didn't record the last check you wrote and I was stupid enough to believe the balance in the register was accurate! I have never bounced a check in my entire life!"

"Well, now you have," Joe said agreeably, clearly not as traumatized by this blemish on my otherwise pristine record as I was. After that I would write checks from the account at his request, but I refused to use it otherwise. Eventually he closed the joint account and we came up with the system we use now, which is that Joe pays all of the bills from his personal account and asks me for money when he needs it. I don't even have to look at all of those bothersome bills, a perk that has made giving up my precious control infinitely easier.

We had the banking thing dialed in, but that wasn't the last of our money issues. I became acutely aware of this the night Joe made the following gruesome announcement over an otherwise lovely dinner:

"We need to create a family budget."

My skin prickled, the hair on the back of my neck stood straight up, and I broke out into an uncomfortable and unattractive full-body sweat. I'm the person who, when she sees a Do Not Touch sign, has to *immediately* stroke the off-limits object. Rules and restrictions piss me off, so telling me not to spend money was just asking for disaster.

"A what?" I asked, feigning vacuity. On some subconscious level, I am sure I knew this was coming.

"We have nothing saved for our retirement," Joe was fond of reminding me. "We spend more money than we make."

"Your highlights cost *how much*?" Although I was appreciative that someone in the house was concerned about these things—and grateful that it didn't have to be me—I certainly didn't want anyone poring over my receipts, calculating how often I actually used my health club membership, or worst of all, putting the kibosh on my monthly pedicure.

Joe began establishing the dreaded budget by enlisting a financial planner I'll call Satan. After great effort and expense, Satan charged us the equivalent of several hundred cups of designer coffee to tell us that *we spend too much money*. Believe me, the irony of this shocking epiphany was not lost on either of us. In particular, the Angel of Darkness suggested we eliminate our child care budget (which included the cost of preschool) entirely. The fact that we'd have significantly less money without the income our jobs produced while the kids were being cared for by someone else didn't seem to be taken into consideration. Though we were going to be allowed to continue to eat (in moderation), Lucifer also recommended not just curtailing but eradicating the *entire* personal-grooming category. Now, I'd consider walking around with ragged toenails for just about any worthy cause, but revealing my sad salt-and-pepper roots was just not going to happen. The Antichrist would just have to peddle her sensible living plan somewhere else. Like Mars.

Thankfully, even Joe realized the absurdity of Beelzebub's recommendations, and I was allowed to continue to enjoy regular meals *and* maintain my lifelong charade of "naturally" sun-kissed tresses. We agreed to the pleasantly unrestrictive plan that we would "try to be more frugal." I still had to submit all of my receipts to my husband, but Joe agreed to a no-judgment policy. To show my team spirit, I started to stretch out the time between hair appointments—fortunately I have a pretty nice assortment of hats and look okay in most of them. I even let my beloved *New Yorker* subscription expire.

I also started paying for some stuff with cash. Nothing major or illicit, just things I'd rather not have to admit to buying. Before this I was the poster girl for credit cards, the gal who swiped her plastic to buy a single greeting card or a scoop of ice cream. I didn't charge exorbitant things I couldn't afford, and I paid the bills in full each month (well, technically Joe paid them—but I made sure I didn't spend outside of our means), but I liked my cards for the easy record keeping and of course the frequent-flier miles. But now that someone really *was* taking note of every lip gloss and latte I bought, I felt like Big Brother was breathing down my neck in every checkout aisle. Tiny cash purchases here and there were like a few stolen bites of someone else's dessert: They didn't really count.

"I'm not trying to get you to cut back on spending so much as I am trying to get an idea of where all of our money goes," Joe told me sensibly when he clued in to my petty-cash habit.

"Fine," I grumbled. "But if I get grilled about a single pack of Trident, I'm going back to the squandering-cash plan."

I found it interesting—but not all that surprising—when I read the results of a recent global study by the infamous media giant Nielsen. This time the researchers determined that women will fare far better in the current recession than men

• • • • •

because, quite simply, we put less emphasis on money. Rather than judging our worth and potency by our bank balance, women derive their happiness from *personal relationships and meaningful communication*. In other words, as much as we gals may pine for a rock the size of a golf ball on our fingers or a glistening new Viking range or those slutty clip-in Jessica Simpson hair extensions, we've also discovered—long before our blockheaded partners—that money can't actually buy happiness. It just lets you look better in your misery.

" At Least You're Not Married to Him "

My husband spends all of *my* hard-earned money on his boat. We are at about $10,000 at this point. He continually asks me for more money for his boat and lovingly calls me his "sponsor." It probably has strengthened our relationship because his extended time on the watercraft continues our "How can I miss you if you won't go away?" philosophy of marriage, but it is still annoying.

HANNAH

Even if your partner is the generous sort, here's what happens when you are working with a field of pooled resources: You can't just go out and buy whatever the hell you want. (I know!) For instance, Joe believes you should wait until your current car is officially pronounced dead, and then go out and pay full price for a brand-spanking-new one, which you will then be expected to drive into the ground. Using Joe's method, one might have the privilege of driving two or three different cars in a lifetime. Conversely, I was raised to believe one should *never* purchase this year's model ("It costs you 20 percent of the price just to drive it off the lot!"), but to buy a well-maintained two-year-old vehicle—preferably from an eighty-seven-year-old grandchildless woman who only used it to get to her weekly bingo game up the street. You would then drive it for exactly two years before trading it in for another gently loved toddler model, thereby dodging the bulk of that bothersome depreciation.

"Why would I want to buy someone else's headache?" is Joe's cynical argument whenever I buck for a trade-up.

Because of this, I am the proud owner of a nine-year-old SUV. The goddamned thing works perfectly and has never caused us a day's headache. It's only got 75,000 miles on it (because where the hell do I go?), and I am sure it has another ten years of life in it, possibly more. The mats are stained and ratty, there are Goldfish crackers and bits of string cheese ground deeply into the seats, and it doesn't have any of the fancy bells and whistles—like built-in DVD players in the headrests, an in-dash navigation system, or gloriously heated seats—that they've come out with in the past decade.

I drop hints about wanting a new car frequently. These "hints" include e-mailed links to Craigslist listings and one-day-only tent sales; laborious, gushing descriptions of other friends' new cars and all of their swanky features; and casual statements like "For the love of Lexus can I please just get a new car?" I know I am setting myself up for failure here, but

I have fantasies of being awoken on my birthday with some bogus request to come see the new birds' nest in the yard or to check out some silly thing the dog is doing in the driveway. When I shuffle outside in my slippers, I rub the crusty gunk out of my eyes to find a brand-new (well, two-year-old) Mercedes parked out front. Of *course* it's wrapped in a giant, obnoxious red bow. A flying pig winks at me from behind the wheel.

Now, I make my own money and could easily go out and buy myself a new car any old time I please. (Well, maybe not *easily*, as I am really bad at all of that tedious paperwork rigmarole and have a habit of signing things I haven't quite read, but you know what I mean.) But I haven't and I am almost positive that I won't, and not because I believe that blessed Benz is ever going to appear on its own. I know, in fact, that it isn't. But until Joe goes out and buys the motorcycle I don't want him to have, I just don't have enough ammo to do it.

" At Least You're Not Married to Him "

My husband was about thirty pounds overweight when—with his thirtieth birthday fast approaching—he decided to diet! Exercise! Get in shape! Most would chalk this up to being an early-midlife-I-should-get-healthy crisis. But no. It wasn't for his health. It was because the only thing homeboy wanted for his thirtieth (not sixtieth) birthday was an *oil motherfucking painting* of our family to hang over our nonexistent fireplace. He lost more than thirty pounds and said that once we got the oil painting done, he would stop dieting and eat whatever he wanted

● ● ● ● ●

again. His birthday was in June and there have been no plans for an oil painting and there never will be. He's still exercising and being healthy because I've seduced him with a trip to Hawaii in the fall. Because seriously, I'd rather dole out the cash it's going to take to see Maui than have to stare at our family in a painting on a wall where a fireplace will never exist.

MEGAN

My friends Jenny and Rob have an interesting way of handling their money. And by "interesting" I mean "Holy shit, this seems wacked to me, but hey, if it works for them, who am I to argue with it?" Jenny and Rob have been married for nearly two decades and they still keep all of their money separate. They both make around the same salary and each writes dozens of checks a month, for *exactly half* of all of the household and family expenses. When Jenny wanted to repave the driveway and Rob didn't really think it was all that urgent, Jenny saved up her own money to get the job done. Jenny drives a beater and wears fabulous clothes; Rob pilots a tricked-out Saab and hasn't been spotted in a new shirt since his teenage kids were toddlers.

"That really works for you?" I asked Jenny earnestly.

"Totally," she replied. "You know what the best part is? When we buy each other gifts, they're really meaningful. I mean, if you get Joe some sweater he doesn't like, he doesn't just have to wear it, he has to wear it knowing that he paid for half of it."

Jenny had a point—and it would sure make things simpler if they ever got divorced, knock on wood—but I still had concerns. What if one of them broke an arm or got cancer and couldn't work? What if the house needed a major repair and one of them couldn't afford their half? What if Rob had some massive midlife crisis and went out and bought a dozen fat gold chains or decided to get hair plugs?

Jenny just laughed. "We're still a team," she insisted. "Neither of us would do anything the other was really opposed to with our money. But if I want to get a massage a week or send my mom a plane ticket for her birthday, I just do it. I can't imagine living any other way."

I still thought it was weird, probably for the same reason purple hair and those gross earring holes the size of quarters still strike me as weird: I am a creature of habit and I don't really embrace change. In my mind, marriage is when you throw all of your respective shit—your cats, dogs, pots, pans, furniture, quirks, neuroses, and checkbooks—into one house, where the whole mess magically morphs into a home. Call me crazy, but I like the perks of commingled currency. You know, the familiarity and consistency, knowing someone's got my back, not having to write a dozen checks a month, oh, and having unrestricted access to half of someone else's money.

• • •

CHAPTER TEN

It's My Potty and I'll Cry If I Want To

After seven years of marriage, I am sure of two things:
First, never wallpaper together,
and second, you'll need two bathrooms.
Both for her. The rest is a mystery.

•DENNIS MILLER•

Though I have found that my husband can insult and infuriate me in just about any room in the house, the injustices that I suffer in the bathroom are uniquely revolting. I say this while fully acknowledging the fact that Joe never *ever* leaves the toilet seat up means that relative to many women, I am married to a living saint. (I had one boyfriend who never *ever* put the damned thing down. You'd think that after a year or so of plunging ass-first into the frigid bowl in the darkest hours of the night, I'd have learned to check the seat status before sitting down, but that's where you'd be giving my half-asleep self way too much credit. His recurring response was, "At least I'm not peeing on the seat." Gee, dear. Thanks for the surplus of courtesy!)

It was actually a restroom incident that almost thwarted

• • • • •

my relationship with Joe before it ever really even started. It was our very first date, and Joe came to my apartment to pick me up. We may have enjoyed a glass of wine on the patio or a quick chat on the living room couch, I can't recall. What I do remember is Joe asking if he could use the bathroom before we left for dinner. Naturally I'd spit-shined every inch of my apartment in anticipation of his visit, so I led the way to the tidy little jewel in my apartment's admittedly dinky but nevertheless spotless crown.

He was in and out in a flash, and off we went to dinner. The food was lovely and the conversation flowed easily; Joe steered me through the crowded restaurant with his hand placed gently on the small of my back. I felt like royalty. When we finished dinner we made our way back to the car and shared our very first, very memorable kiss in the corner of the parking garage. Afterward Joe drove me home, kissed me again (even more memorably, for the record), and left. I bolted to the bathroom to make sure I didn't look like Courtney Love after our little liplock, and there it was, a neon sign heralding my utter incompatibility with this otherwise staggeringly perfect man: The soiled hand towel, scrunched up and wadded down behind the towel bar like an oversized terrycloth spit bomb.

Oh bloody hell, he's a slob! was my first thought. Why would I think anything else? I hadn't seen his apartment yet (not that that information would have helped in his defense), so all I had to base my judgment on were two meetings where he'd managed to project an orderly appearance and seemingly meticulous grooming practices. But anyone could pretend to

• • • • •

be neat and conscientious *twice*. I wasn't sure if I should see him again.

"Are you out of your demented, irrational mind?" my sane friend Andrew asked kindly. Andrew had enjoyed the privilege of listening to me gush about Joe since the day I had met him, and even though Andrew wasn't gay (he had a very nice girl-friend himself), he had been almost more excited about this date than I was. Which was saying a lot. "Jenna, you've had the hots for this guy for months!" my friend went on. "Maybe Joe's *not* a pig. Maybe he was just so excited to get back out of there and be with you that he wasn't thinking clearly. Maybe he really *is* a filthy, disgusting slob. Who cares? You're neat enough for fourteen people anyway. You can't seriously be considering writing him off because of a scrunched-up towel!"

Because Andrew had effectively made me feel like a three-armed circus freak, I promised him I'd give Joe another chance. (I should probably mention here that Joe emphatically denies any recollection of or involvement in Towelgate. But why on earth would I have dreamed this up? I'm telling you, I was smitten.)

" At Least You're Not Married to Him "

Every single time my husband uses the bathroom, he stays in there for twenty to thirty minutes. No one really knows what he's doing (okay, we actually do), but we know better than to disturb "the king" on his throne.

CHERYL

• • • • •

My reservations reared their ugly multiple heads once again when Joe invited me to his place. I was impressed to find that he lived in a storybook Spanish-style house in a great part of town, even if he did share it with a roommate. Then I saw the inside.

His bedroom furnishings consisted of a single mattress on the floor wrapped in a faded plaid flannel sheet, a tiny nondescript desk, and a couple of dusty plastic milk crates doubling as a dresser. A giant beach towel was tacked to the wall above the single window, where someone with a different decorating sensibility might have hung a rod with curtains on it. The living room was home to the smoked-glass coffee table and armoire he'd built in high school. (I admit I was deeply impressed by the meticulous craftsmanship, even if the style wasn't exactly mine . . . or of the particular decade we were living in at the time.) The seating consisted of a pair of itchy brown couches draped in even itchier Mexican blankets. I think there may have been a beanbag or Papasan chair, too. And then there was his bathroom.

"I didn't even know they *made* blue grout!" I said obtusely, studying the charming Spanish tile chamber closely. "Oh my God, that's not grout, is it?" But I was young and in love and Joe was like a supercharged human magnet to me. I wanted to be near him at all costs, even if it meant rubbing elbows—literally—with a room full of filthy fungi and their kabillions of tiny airborne spore-spawn. I went through gallons of mildew remover and shredded several towels in the process, but all of the elbow grease in the world plus a chemical cocktail that could kill a horse couldn't restore that grout to its former chalkiness. It was too far gone. A four-dollar pair of shower shoes was a quick and easy temporary fix; insisting on showering at *my* apartment was the long-term solution.

" At Least You're Not Married to Him "

The most annoying thing about my husband is that he has a very slight touch of OCD, which means, among other things, that I am not allowed to get the bath mat wet. Ever. I am supposed make sure my feet are dry when I step onto the mat. Isn't the purpose of the mat to *dry your feet*?

JANET

Eventually Joe and I bought a house together, and in retrospect I wonder if I was smoking crack in my sleep at the time because the 1,100-square foot cottage we traded our combined lives' savings to mortgage had but one tiny bathroom. We talked of adding another one down the road, but we didn't have the money to do it right away. (Hell, we could barely afford to put toilet paper in the one we had.) For a while we managed just fine, mostly because we were giddy new homeowners and the house was our baby and *nobody says anything bad about the baby*, even if it's got three extra nipples and a horn growing out of its forehead. The baby is perfect, and the horn just makes it more "charming." (We used the word *charming* a lot in those days; that and *quaint*. As in, "Isn't it quaint the way only one person can stand in the kitchen at a time?" And

"Look at these charming old-fashioned rope-and-pulley windows! Too bad they don't open!") But as I said, Joe and I both loved our perfect little house-baby with all of our combined might, at least until the fateful day when our digestive systems decided to operate in perfect harmony. Since my husband is far bigger and faster than me, naturally he beat me to the bowl.

"Joe!" I shouted into the door that he had just slammed in my face. "I need to get in there!"

"Well, obviously you can't right now," he said calmly, his voice muffled but still sounding suspiciously smug.

"Joe! Come on! You know I can't hold it! What am I supposed to do?" I was hopping up and down on crossed legs.

"Sorry, honey, but there's nothing I can do. The party's already started. You could go outside?" He wisely said this last bit as a question.

"I am not going to take a crap in my own backyard!" I yelped stupidly, as if I might consider taking a crap in someone *else's* backyard.

"Then I guess you're just going to have to wait," he replied.

Sixteen years passed.

"Jesus, Joe! Are you reading *Atlas Shrugged* in there?" I bellowed, banging on the door. "My insides are about to implode! I am serious, I think I might be dying!"

I did manage to hold it together (so to speak), even though it appeared that my significant other was in no great hurry to come to my aid. After I finally got my turn, I began rifling through my office drawers, desperate to find a mechanical pencil and a pad of graph paper. There was no longer any doubt in my mind: We were going to have to add that second bathroom.

66 At Least You're Not Married to Him 99

One morning (the morning poops are always eventful in our home—why is that?) while I was making breakfast for our ten-year-old son, my husband walked into the kitchen and announced, "You're not going to believe this! I just pooped a perfect porpoise!" It's important to note the look of absolute amazement on his face. As I stood there, mouth agape, he continued, "I'm not kidding! It even had the little fin on top and was arched and everything!" Needless to say, I was even more speechless when my son asked to see it. Because only a son would ask to see "it," right? I can't imagine a daughter asking to see "it." Thankfully it had been flushed out to the ocean where it could swim happily ever after.

SYLVIA

Fortunately for my bladder and bowels, I got pregnant shortly after the urgency incident, so we started shopping for a bigger house. Joe had a laundry list of must-have criteria his dream dwelling would have. This list included but was in no way limited to a decent-sized yard, a large garage, an office for him, and space for a vegetable garden. As long as the home we bought was relatively cute and in a good neighborhood and *had at least two bathrooms*, I was on board.

We wound up buying a nearly hundred-year-old farmhouse that had a majestic two-and-a-half bathrooms. Half, shmalf! This translated into *three toilets* and I felt like I'd won the lavatory lottery. Sure, every one of these rooms dramatically needed updating, and one of the toilets was actually perched precariously atop a slab of rickety plywood, and the plumbing was sketchy at best so you had to master the art of the multiple flush, and if you were foolish enough to turn on your blow dryer while anything else in the house was plugged in, you'd better know how to change a fuse. Still, I was delighted by the knowledge that I would never have to consider dropping trou in my own yard again.

Even with three distinct and far-apart rooms in which to do our respective business, there were land mines to navigate. One of our new home's bathrooms—unfortunately the one that would have to be deemed the "master bath" because of its adjacency to the "master bedroom," although there was certainly nothing masterful about either of these rooms—had a second door that opened directly across from the main entrance to the house. You know, the front door. *The front, glass door.* Talk about a design flaw. More than once I found myself sitting there happily perusing the Pottery Barn catalog when the room would flicker with the telltale shadow play that meant someone was walking up the front path. In a panic I'd leap up, ankles bound by Lycra lace and hands crossed fig-leaf style across my lady parts, shuffle sideways toward the door, and give it a hearty slam. The UPS guy loved me. When it was Joe busting me in this indisposed position, he'd be furious. "How hard is it to remember to close a stupid door?" he'd want to know. And I admit, before I had given birth these instances were particularly traumatic. But it turns out that after you have crapped *on a table* in the presence of a dozen or so strangers, lots of formerly degrading activities don't really bother you so much. Like the book says, *everyone poops*.

Because of its aforementioned proximity to our bedroom, it was that ill-planned little cubicle of a room that Joe and I wound up fighting about the most. Mostly, the arguing was simply about who was in there first, as it really wasn't big enough for both of us. There was a single sink, which meant if Joe was brushing or flossing or shaving or pondering his enviable brows, I was out of luck. But the worst part was the horrible prefabricated fiberglass shower/tub combo that had a shower head that had been installed at the perfect height—if you happened to be a family of gnomes.

Sadly, the second shower upstairs was even worse. The shower nozzle was set at the same little-person height as the "master" shower, only the box itself was about as big as a coffin. If you dropped the soap you were screwed, because bending literally wasn't an option. You also had to remember to close the room's lone window before stepping inside the shower, as the slightest breeze would plaster the shower curtain to your body and you'd never be able to get it off again.

So mornings became a race for the better of the two showers, and the shower of choice became like the TV. If you thought you were going to want it at any point in the next several hours, you'd race to turn it on.

"Oh, shit! I was just about to get in there," the other person would say.

"I'll be quick," the first would lie.

" At Least You're Not Married to Him "

When our young son began to get mobile, my husband started baby-proofing the house. I came home from work one day and was about to die because I had to go to the bathroom really badly. To my dismay, the toilet was locked down with some big plastic contraption and I couldn't figure out how to unlock it. Since no one was home I was left with the choice of not being able to figure it out or peeing in the sink. I decided that force might be the best thing to use and started pushing and pulling every little piece and part I could. Magically it opened just in the nick of time without me having to rip the lid off its hinges. For the next few days I fumbled with these things like you can't believe, cursing every time and hearing my husband laughing at me and asking if he should get our son to come show me how to do it. *Not* funny.

DEILIA

The other thing about the not-so-masterful bath was the storage space. Essentially, there wasn't any. The single cabinet under the sink was home to an eyesore of ancient, rusty plumbing, and there was no medicine cabinet—just a mirror—so all of our crap had to fit into two wobbly drawers. Fortunately Joe didn't (and still doesn't) have a lot of personal necessities, just a brush, razor, shaving cream, deodorant, and toothbrush. That's it, his entire grooming arsenal. I, on the other hand, had more creams, bottles, lotions, potions, serums, and sprays than an embalmer. Those poor drawers were packed to the gills with perfume and peroxide, sunblock and self-tanner, all of it stuffed in alongside a tangled nest of hair accessories and appliances—because God forbid I walk out into the world with the tresses He gave me.

"You don't use half of this crap!" Joe was fond of accusing.

"I use all of it and more," I insisted. "Have you seen the overflow in my office closet?"

This continued to be a futile and frustrating argument, because I am married to a man who insists I am beautiful just as I am—which is plucked, dyed, faux-bronzed, and tattooed within an inch of my life. (I was unfortunately born with approximately eleven eyebrow hairs so I went ahead and had some nice brows permanently inked on, in addition to two small and tasteful decorative tattoos.) It's not like I'm some Lady Gaga when it comes to makeup. I like neutral shades, stick mainly to tinted lip gloss, and wear mascara a handful of times a year at the most. But Joe doesn't seem to understand that it takes time, effort, and a munitions store of beauty products to achieve the "natural" look he adores.

" At Least You're Not Married to Him "

When my husband gets out of the shower, he insists on blow-drying his butt. Apparently he likes it *very* dry. I don't mind this in theory, but it's not exactly a turn-on to watch him do it. Plus, this isn't why I forked over a fortune for an ionic dryer. The worst part is, I think our teenage son is now doing it, too. I'm afraid to ask.

LORI

For my fortieth birthday—and also because it would dramatically increase the value of the home we'd been painstakingly renovating for the previous eight years—Joe built me a glorious new master bathroom. It is spa-like and serene and ridiculously big, and we each have our very own sink and several drawers and cabinets to do with as we please. (His are practically empty so you'd think he might offer me some of this coveted real estate, but he doesn't and I don't complain. Much.) Then he transformed the old, hideous, cracked-linoleum blot on our home's landscape—the former "master bath"—into a lavish walk-in closet. *Just for me.* It's got plush chocolate-brown carpeting, a floor-to-ceiling shoe rack, wraparound shelves, and a smattering of valet hooks. There's even a lock on the door, so I can hide in there and talk on the phone, and it sometimes takes the kids ten full minutes to find me. When I die, I want to be buried in there.

"Dude, where's *your* stuff?" his friends will ask Joe when he proudly shows off the result of his carpentry (and husbandry) skills.

"Happy wife, happy life," he says with a shrug.

This is actually one of his favorite sayings, and—for obvious reasons—it's one of mine, too. (Sure, it's typically something grumbled under his breath as he's doing something he would much rather *not* be doing, such as trying to figure out how he's going to strap the chipping, rickety armoire—the one that we don't need but I insist on buying anyway at the yard sale he doesn't want to stop at in the first place—to the roof of the SUV without killing anyone. At that moment in time, does he *want* to be risking a herniated disk for a piece of superfluous, secondhand crap? Of course not! He's simply choosing possible debilitating pain over the sort of emotional torture—and let's face it, the withholding of sexual favors—that only a wife can inflict.)

Fortunately, the infamous towel incident from our first date turned out to be a fluke. In the thirteen years we've shared this sacred space since that day, Joe hasn't left a single scrunched towel in his wake. He still sometimes turns the light off when I'm in the middle of shaving my legs, but he doesn't leave floss splatters on the mirror or whisker shrapnel in the sink. When he has the audacity to use the room for one of its primary intended purposes, not only has he mastered the art of the "courtesy flush," he even installed a fan *on a timer* right next to the toilet. Occasionally he even lights a candle. He uses the shower squeegee I bought, and sometimes even complains when I leave a little speck of toothpaste on the neck of the tube. I have permanent teeth marks on my tongue from biting it when he nags me about my slovenly toothpaste ways—*as if!*—but all things considered, I think I can live with that.

" At Least You're Not Married to Him "

My number one pet peeve occurs when I am indisposed. My husband suddenly needs to know where I am. He will come into the bathroom (no knocking), stand directly in front of me, literally within an eighteen-inch circumference, and say "What are you doing?" Honestly! You're probably thinking he's stupid or something, but he isn't! He would otherwise be thought of as a wonderful, caring, intelligent, hard-working man, and I do adore him. But what on God's green earth does he *think* I am doing?! This happens *all the time*. Does he think I have a secret life in there? There's not even a window where I could escape if I wanted to. I don't think I spend an inordinate amount of time in the bathroom, although it does have the potential to be a nice little respite with some privacy and some quiet time away from the kids. Oh well.

DONNA

CHAPTER ELEVEN

Should We Just Skip the $200 Dinner and Duke It Out at Home?

My wife and I have the secret to making a marriage last.
Two times a week, we go to a nice restaurant,
a little wine, good food. . . . She goes Tuesdays, I go Fridays.

· HENNY YOUNGMAN ·

England's *Daily Mail* recently reported the results of a truly depressing survey I'll call "The Honeymoon Is So Totally Over." The researchers polled five thousand couples—each of whom had been hitched at least a decade—about their daily connubial lives. Sadly, 83 percent of the respondents had stopped celebrating their anniversary together after three lousy years, while 60 percent said they hadn't enjoyed a single romantic evening since the day they tied the knot. The number of couples who held hands even occasionally dropped from 83 percent in the first year of marriage to just 38 percent ten years later. (Luckily for me, I didn't have to wait around for the slow and painful decline. "I'm not really much of a hand-holder," Joe told me, *the day before we exchanged vows*, information I promptly shoved deep into the Would Have Been Good to Know Yesterday file.) With a sample size as large as this study's, unfortunately one can expect the results to be fairly representative of the population at large.

The often-recommended solution to marital apathy is the infamous Date Night, which ostensibly offers couples a regular chance to reconnect, unwind, and—at least the guy is hoping—have gnarly, passionate monkey sex.

Here's the thing. When you go to the great trouble of putting on mascara *and* shaving your legs and you're shelling out a king's ransom to some teenager to eat your food and keep your kids alive for a few hours and not burn the house down, you sort of hope it's going to be worth all the effort and expense. Sadly, the fact that it rarely is doesn't keep most of us married folks from getting our hopes up and going for it anyway, time and trying time again.

It's not anyone's fault, really. Think about what's involved in getting two very busy, very different people to one restaurant or movie theater or concert. First off, you have to pick a date and a time, and agree on where you'll be going and what you'll be doing. That in and of itself could take months. Most couples start with dinner, using some variation of this time-honored, romantic line of reasoning: *We'd both have to eat anyway, and at least we won't have to do any dishes afterward.* Invariably the fact that you love Thai and he prefers Italian will come up and you'll have to determine whose turn it is to call heads in the coin toss.

"Last time we went out we went to My Thai and I burned all of the skin off the roof of my mouth on that ridiculous pickled-tofu-curry thing you ordered," he'll insist.

"No, we went to Mama Mia and you got marinara sauce on the cuff of your brand-new white shirt, remember?" you'll counter. Since you're the one who famously recalls birthdays and library book due dates and where the lint brush lives, he'd be a fool to argue with your innately superior memory.

You'll try to agree on a neutral third cuisine that has an affordable restaurant in your zip code, but the odds are there is no such thing. Because your preferred-order eatery lists are in direct opposition, it will take you seven years to get to the place where they intersect, at that joint that neither of you really likes nor hates, the model of mediocrity. You'll consider wearing pants and skipping the whole shaving thing altogether.

Will reservations be needed? If so, who will be responsible for making them? For once, you concur that it should be whoever didn't do it last time. But neither of you can remember who that was because it was thirteen eons ago, so the stalemate continues.

Screw dinner, you think; it's too complicated. You'll just go to a movie instead. Because *that's* not fraught with contention, right? Action, adventure, comedy, drama, or horror? Diet or regular Coke? Aisle or center seats? Plain popcorn or a greasy bag of swimming-in-disgusting-has-more-fat-than-thirty-two-Whoppers-fake-butter nuggets?

HIM: "I'll see anything but a chick flick."

HER: "Define 'chick flick.'"

HIM: "Anything with kissing or a plotline or Meg Ryan."

HER: "I'll see anything that's not gory."

HIM: "Define 'not gory.'"

HER: "Anything with kissing or a plot line or Meg Ryan."

" At Least You're Not Married to Him "

We have this pre-date routine that is as predictable as it is infuriating.
We share a tiny, one-sink bathroom that hasn't been touched since it
was built in 19-fucking-51. Usually he shaves while I shower. We bob
around each other in our stifling little bathroom, ostensibly trying to
primp for each other. (For the record, it is impossible to see one's hair,
much less style it, in a twice-fogged-up mirror.) After his shower, he
swiftly puts on the first pair of pants and first shirt he sees, slips into
shoes, and leaves the matrimonial bedroom while I have fits about
what to wear—as if it really matters. He knows it takes me "a little
longer" to get dressed. While he uses my fashion panic time to give
dinner, bath, and bedtime instructions to the sitter and maybe have a
cocktail, I am in the back of the house throwing clothes on and off,
feverishly trying to figure out what to wear. Even though I just showered,
I'm sweaty and frustrated and I can't see through the foggy bathroom
mirror to put on my eye makeup. The movie starts in twenty minutes.
I finally get it together and rush out of the bedroom to find that my
husband is nowhere to be seen. This is because he is *waiting for me
in the driveway IN THE IDLING CAR*. Thanks to him, though, we always
make it to the movie on time.

KIM

• • • • •

Even if you could actually agree on a film, then you'd have to decide which theater to see it at, which would necessitate a debate over the merits of Red Vines versus Twizzlers, because the one of you who is from the East Coast thinks Red Vines taste like those disgusting wax lips you used to pretend to like as a kid, while the West Coaster insists that the discussion is a waste of time because strawberry-flavored straws do not qualify as *licorice*. It is right around this point that you realize that if you go to a movie instead of out to a restaurant you will both *still need to eat dinner*, a reality that probably means you'll be cooking *and* doing the goddamned dishes—which is no way to spend a date night seeing as you may have already shaved your legs. So you're back to the restaurant conundrum. Bob's Underwhelming Bistro, here you come.

Only, not so fast. First you have to line up a babysitter. This requires a week's worth of phone calls before you realize that no one born after 1989 actually talks on the phone anymore, so you resort to texting, which you hate but *I'll be damned* they get right back to you so at least that's taken care of. You're bitter that this job is yours by default—your husband can text, too, after all, and you did painstakingly create a detailed baby-sitter file with all of the necessary contact info and even made a copy for him—but you stuff the resentment way down by reminding yourself that your beloved probably begrudges mowing the lawn and hardly ever complains about it, so you're mostly even.

Finally it's the big date night! Your legs are smooth as a new-born baby's apricot-oiled bottom, and you even got a blow-out,

• • • • •

which you didn't really have the money or the time to do but the last time you went out with your girlfriends your husband got all bent out of shape because you "never make that kind of effort" for him, so you felt obligated to do it. You stuffed the girls into a push-up bra, skinnied into your Spanx, and are clanking around the house doing last-minute tasks in those goddamned heels you know make your calves look good, so it's worth the crippling pain in eight of your ten toes. The sitter is only fifteen minutes late and your husband only rolls his eyes eleven times as you go over the details of the evening routine and only one kid latches herself barnacle-style to your leg as you try to get out the door. Relatively speaking, the night is off to a winning start.

"Red or white?" the man you have shared thousands of cocktails with asks, perusing the wine list.

"White, please," you say, biting your tongue. He *knows* you don't like red, doesn't he?

"Really?" he asks. Evidently not.

"Let's just each get a glass of what we want," you say.

"It's much cheaper to buy a bottle," he insists.

"Then get a bottle of white," you chirp. Naturally this is meant to be sarcastic, because *you know that he doesn't like white.*

You scan your menus while waiting for your individual, overpriced glasses of Chardonnay and Merlot to arrive.

"What are you getting?" he asks nervously when you close your menu and push it to the side of the table.

"The filet," you respond. "You?"

. . . . .

"Well, I *was* going to get the filet . . . ," he says, trailing off and looking infinitely annoyed.

Is this meant to make you feel guilty for stealing his order? You resist the urge to point out the blazingly obvious—you could both order the damned filet!—because you know how his mind works. He figures you'll eat maybe half of your dinner, if not less. Therefore it makes more culinary sense for him to order something different, even though you'd very much like to take the uneaten portion of your meal home to have for lunch tomorrow.

He orders the lamb chops, unquestionably out of spite because although he can't seem to remember that you don't like pepper on your eggs or that you take two sugars in your coffee, he has committed to memory the fact that you won't eat any sort of animal flesh—veal, rabbit, venison, duck, and of course lamb—that once belonged to an animal that falls into the "cute and cuddly" category. Ordering the baby sheep means he won't have to forsake even a single morsel. Bring on the mutton.

"You want a bite?" he asks sweetly, nodding down at his gamy plate.

"No, thanks," you mutter, tucking into your steak (because you grew up in the country and know for a fact that grown cows aren't cute or even the tiniest bit cuddly).

"You sure?" he repeats.

"Positive," you grumble.

"It's delicious," he adds, smacking his lips.

You are left with no choice. You eat every last bite of your filet. You feel violently, miserably full afterward—far too full to fool around when you get home, which is the singular reason the lamb lover forked over for your filet in the first place. *Serves him right,* you think, rubbing your aching belly.

" At Least You're Not Married to Him "

After dinner—and the setting doesn't matter; it could be a business meal or a wedding reception—he presses his fingertip into the crumbs or drops on his plate, then licks his fingertip and does it again.

TRICIA

When I say *you* in all of these instances, for the most part I mean *me.* In fact, if we weren't already married, my very last date with my husband could well have been our very last date, period. We had cleared the day/time/babysitter hurdles, and I even whipped out a brand-new razor for the occasion. I was busy trying to hunt down a decent-looking pair of panties when Joe texted me midday.

JOE: Where should we go?
ME: I don't really care. Somewhere fun.
JOE: How about Chez Ornate?
ME: I said *fun.* That place is a blue-hair convention.
JOE: Well, where do *you* want to go?
ME: Café B?

JOE: That's your idea of fun? They have like six tables.

ME: Yeah, but it's cozy and loud and I like the funky walls.

JOE: You are picking a restaurant based on the *walls*?

ME: No, I like the food, too.

JOE: Any other suggestions?

ME: What about Stinky Fish?

JOE: I never get enough to eat when we go out for sushi.

ME: Then order more.

JOE: That's it? Two suggestions?

ME: That's twice as many as you've had.

JOE: I guess we can decide later.

Two or three more times during the day the topic came up, with Joe repeatedly asking me if I wanted to try Chez Ornate, and me making it painfully clear that *no, I did not*. By the time the babysitter arrived—on time, no less—and innocently asked where we were going, we were both in pretty crappy moods. The man I promised to honor and cherish for all of eternity had the gall to look taken aback at her question.

"We haven't actually decided," he said to her, and then turned to me. "Hey, do you want to go to Chez Ornate?"

"No, I do not want to go to Chez Ornate!" I exploded, storming out of the room, but not before catching a glimpse of the poor sitter looking at me with that knowing *What the hell is wrong with you, lady, your husband is offering to take you to the nicest place in town and that's how you reply?* look that is

normally reserved exclusively for gangrenous panhandlers and unappreciative, lunatic wives.

"You ambushed me," I spat once we were both in the car.

"What are you talking about?" Joe asked innocently as he backed out of the driveway.

"I am pretty sure I made it perfectly clear that I did *not* want to go to Chez Ornate! And then you throw it out there just so you can look like Mister Big Spender and make *me* look like a miserable bitch. You know what? I don't even want to go to dinner with you. I don't want to sit across a table from you and pretend that I like you, because right now I do not. At all. Take me home."

"No," was Joe's reply.

"No?" I screamed, my roadside stint in Hawaii all but forgotten. "No, you won't take me home? I don't believe this! Turn this car around and *take me home.*"

A millennium passed.

"So where do you want to eat?" he asked, all annoying calmness. Nothing makes me crazier when I am already on a tear than relaxed indifference. *Nothing.*

"I WANT TO GO TO HOME!" I bellowed Linda Blair–like, my head spinning around in circles on my neck for emphasis.

"Too bad," he said. "And we're not going to Café B, either."

If I had had a cup of ice in my hand, you can bet your ass an imprint of it would have been etched deeply into his temple.

We drove without exchanging another word, and eventually

Joe pulled up in front of a benign little Mexican joint. We walked inside in stony silence, a half-dozen arm lengths apart, that couple you see looking so miserable you wonder why they even considered spending an evening together, no less a lifetime. I sat across the table and made no effort to pretend that I liked him. Instead, I checked my e-mail on my iPhone out of spite, knowing that the activity infuriates him even when we're not in the throes of an epic sparring match.

"This is fun," he said with a sardonic smirk.

"I told you to take me home," I sneered back, not looking up from my phone. If they gave out awards for the adult who can best imitate her toddler, I'd have a mantel crowded with golden trophies.

Had we been at home, I could (and most likely would) have locked myself in my office or bedroom and made an elaborate show of avoiding any accidental eye or body contact. But when you're a born motormouth and you're stuck in a chair in a public venue, eventually you cave in and speak. I can't recall who actually set the verbal ball rolling, and I can guarantee you that the first few exchanges were clipped and curt if not a tad nasty. But by midmeal (another margarita, please!) we were speaking again. When the check came we were actually sort of laughing about the whole thing. In the car, we even agreed to stop for a nightcap on the way home, as in *intentionally opting to spend even more time together*. Apparently, my husband understood better than I that the fastest route to reconciliation would be forced face time. It wasn't fun *or* pretty, but it worked.

" At Least You're Not Married to Him "

My husband chews his food *really* loudly, no matter where we are. When I call him on it, he says, "Hey, I'm just enjoying my meal!" We've only been married for a year so I still think it is kind of funny and a little bit endearing, but I can see how it has the potential to become *really* annoying down the road.

ELLI

I have an amazing aunt and uncle who have been married—happily—for forty-five years. That's *sixteen thousand, four hundred twenty-five days* of having to stare at the same (aging) face, negotiate control of the remote, and pretend to be interested in stories you've heard dozens if not hundreds of times. I asked them once what they thought their secret was. Shared goals and values? One leader and one follower? Financial compatibility? A daily shag? "You have to have fun together," Uncle Jack told me simply; Aunt Linda squeezed his hand in agreement. I thought about their retired lives: They traveled the world together, but they also went grocery shopping and cooked dinner as a team. They rode matching snowmobiles at their winter house and went fishing at their summer house. (And although having gobshites of money probably hasn't hurt their marital bliss, we all know plenty of rich, miserable folks, too—so that can't be the causative factor here.) Researchers at the University of Denver recently confirmed what Aunt Linda and Uncle Jack have spent a lifetime proving to me: Couples who play together stay together.

Of course, it's not as easy as a weekly bowling game or a

shared fondness for horseshoes, because the key is that each individual couple has to agree on what is "fun." If her idea of a rip-roaring good time is a four-hour debate about health care reform—in French—and his get-your-rocks-off activity is pounding beers and racing remote control cars around a track, there's not really a middle ground. She suggests badminton; he counters with mountain biking. What's the compromise? Pinochle? Ping-Pong? Pac-Man?

Perhaps you haven't hit on your bonding hobby because it's something unknown to you both. Studies have found that engaging in a new, exciting activity together (and tuning in to the *Idol* finale doesn't count, even if neither of you has ever seen the show before) fosters closeness and ultimately strengthens the marital bond. Based on the one time Joe and I went white-water rafting together—him grinning merrily and *woo-hoo*ing at the top of his lungs, me crouched down in the raft's muddy bowels, white-knuckling the sides and praying silently for another day on earth—I'd add that the new, exciting activity should be carefully considered.

For Joe and me the answer turned out to be tennis. Sure, I didn't take up the sport until I was thirty, and I basically picked it for the cute outfits, but the activity once reserved for English nobles has been life- and marriage-changing for both of us. After a few failed attempts at having Joe give me "lessons," we were smart enough to realize that there was no way in hell he could be both my husband and my coach, so I enlisted a professional. (For some reason, comments like "Now try to get the ball *over* the net" and "Who glued your shoes to the court?" sting a lot less when they come from someone you are not having sex with.) Joe and I hit the courts weekly from the beginning, and it wasn't until eight or nine years later—when I tried to "play" with a novice friend—that it occurred to me what a gift that was.

"How could you stand going out there with me when I missed every other ball and half of the ones I did hit went clear out of the court?" I demanded of Joe.

"I wanted us to have something we could enjoy together for the rest of our lives," he said, adding sheepishly, "besides sex." I was happy to hear he thought *that* was going to continue to be a good time several decades from now.

Today we play at least once a week—which is sometimes more often than we have sex, so it's a blessing we discovered this joint interest. We hardly ever fight on the twenty-minute round-trip drive to the tennis club, and I've gotten good enough that we can sometimes carry on a casual conversation as we play. Sure, I've never, ever beaten him or frankly even come close. But I don't mind. He's a natural athlete and I am not. It's a damned good thing about the cute outfits, is all I can say.

• • • • •

• • •

CHAPTER TWELVE

It's the Thought That Counts (but Thanks for the Blender!)

When women are depressed, they eat or go shopping.
Men invade another country.
It's a whole different way of thinking.

• ELAYNE BOOSLER •

The very first birthday I spent with Joe, we happened to be in New York City for a friend's wedding. He had brought my gifts along to be opened in our hotel room, and I was giddy with anticipation. Was he practical or romantic? Showy or sweet? The sexy-lingerie sort (please God, no) or the plane-tickets-to-Paris type (pretty-please God, *yes*)? I didn't yet know. I love giving and getting gifts equally and have proudly maintained a long-standing family tradition of blowing birthdays (or rather, *birth-months* as we liked to call them growing up) ridiculously out of proportion with parties and presents and an embarrassing excess of hoopla. Knowing all of this, Joe tortured me by holding out until after an endless, decadent birthday meal to present my

• • • • •

gifts to me. I immediately noticed and appreciated how precisely he'd wrapped them; he even knew to fold the ends over before taping them to achieve the most streamlined and professional look possible. I was already head-over-heels in love with him, but this nearly put me over eternal devotion's farthest edge.

I delicately worked at the wrapping (newspaper, of course) on the first package, resisting my typical urge to tear into it like a greedy, wild-eyed kid on Christmas morning. (No sense letting my hopeful future fiancé see *all* of my ugly habits before the deal was sealed.) It was a lovely leather journal, which he hadn't inscribed, but I forgave him for this oversight because he'd mostly grown up without a mom and he wasn't a writer, either. How could I expect him to realize that the inscription is more important than the book?

The second package was roughly the same size as the first and wrapped just as meticulously. I wondered if it was a novel or memoir or some other thoughtful tome, my favorite kind of gift (besides cash, which would have been slightly creepy at that particular juncture in our relationship). I opened the box and was shocked to find what could only be a kinky, wearable sex toy. I gingerly lifted the elastic contraption from the box, turning it around to inspect it more closely. It basically looked like an industrial and not at all comfortable pair of thong underwear with a small metal box affixed to what I assumed was the crotch. *Were these those vibrating panties that were making the bachelorette party rounds?* I wondered, purposely avoiding Joe's gaze and hoping that the look on my face didn't reveal the depth of my horror and disappointment.

• • • • •

"What do you think?" Joe asked, not even the slightest bit self-consciously.

I dared to look up at him and was surprised to see he hadn't donned a leather S&M mask.

"What is it?" I finally asked, defeated.

"It's a head lamp!" he replied.

"A *what*?" I stammered.

"A head lamp," he repeated. "You know, a flashlight you wear on your head when you go kayaking into caves or spelunking."

Oh, right. *When I go kayaking into caves or spelunking.* Who was this man? And more important, who the hell did he think I was?

I considered the gifts I'd given him—the embroidered wallpaper-print shirt, the Euro-styled whip-stitched sandals, the massage gift certificate to my favorite day spa—and realized that a lot of the time, we subconsciously give our significant other gifts that will benefit us in some way. I clearly wanted Joe to be slightly edgy and the tiniest bit metrosexual; he wanted me to have an outdoorsy, adventurous spirit and an urge to get dirty. We were both screwed.

" At Least You're Not Married to Him "

My husband is an absolutely horrible gift giver, to the point that I've come to dread any holiday where the exchange of presents is involved. I've received gas station stuffed animals, perfume roses, knickknacks that play music, and myriad other treasures you probably wouldn't even attempt to regift. We've talked about it, I've begged him to take one of my friends shopping with him, and one year I went so far as to print out a list with links to websites *and* visual aids. It didn't help. This Christmas, the highlight was matching elf costumes: Supercenter sweat suits (two sizes too big) in Santa red and Christmas tree green. ("But I just wanted you to be comfortable," he said.) My friends literally wait for the report now every birthday and Christmas.

ALLISON

Over the years Joe has become somewhat famous for heading out in the afternoon on Christmas Eve to "start his shopping," and sneaking out of the house as I'm making breakfast on my birthday to procure my gift. This is not passive-aggressive behavior meant to torture me. In Joe's mind, it's not rocket science; that's just when you shop. No sense dragging the whole affair out for days or even weeks, right? Plus, by its very urgent nature, a last-minute shopping trip is guaranteed to end with a purchase. Not necessarily a mind-blowing or even marginal purchase, but a purchase nonetheless. Mission accomplished.

When you have a million friends and a couple of kids and a dozen or more nieces and nephews and gigantic blended families, gift giving can get out of control. Therefore, Joe and I long ago agreed that holidays like Valentine's Day and Mother's Day and Father's Day were really nothing more than artificial Hallmark holidays and therefore not something we would recognize with physical tokens of our affection. Because our anniversary falls in the busiest gift-giving season of our lives—we have both kids' birthdays, my birthday, Mother's Day, and the annual celebration of the one and only time we'll ever host an open bar for two hundred people all in a five-week span—more often than not, we use the occasion as an excuse to purchase something large that we were going to buy anyway but otherwise would have felt guilty about. Which means that one year I got a flat-screen TV for our anniversary (and you may recall that I don't watch TV), and another year Joe got a giant antique mirror that he wasn't particularly fond of even before he discovered how outrageously overpriced it was. *Happy anniversary of that other year we gave ourselves something* I *didn't want, dear!*

When we do exchange gifts, I have to admit that his are always both thoughtful and generous—if not necessarily things I might ever buy for myself. He's not the type to go for the Tiffany-box, ten-karat display of fondness, nor is he the homemade-card sort of sap. He tends toward practical items that would nonetheless be considered splurges because nobody in their right mind could ever claim to "need" any of them. There was the coffeepot with the built-in timer (note: we had a perfectly good model at the time, minus the clock) because he knew I hated waiting for my caffeine fix in the morning; the microwaveable Brookstone slippers and matching buttery robe that together cost a small fortune; the ATM-size high-tech towel warmer because "who doesn't like getting out of the tub and wrapping up in a nice, toasty towel?" He stuffs my Christmas stocking with not one tube of body lotion but seven, a symbol that he loves me despite my finicky nose, and also tangible proof of his relentless desire to find at least one scent that might please it. The year I mentioned I wanted a sewing machine, Joe spent countless hours researching various machines and their features, and ultimately forked over a sum that could get you a decent used car for a digital model nicer than the one the seamstress that I go to uses. It took me a week to figure out how to turn it on, and several months of lessons before I could load the thread and wind a bobbin. I made some curtains that year, and pretty they were not. It turns out that sewing in a relatively straight line is a lot harder than it looks. Sadly this was before we had children (which is probably why he was buying me pricey machinery), so I couldn't even pawn my lopsided, ill-fitting window coverings off as one of the kids' handiwork. My overly generous husband is still bitter about how much dust my electric stitcher collects, but in my defense I didn't *ask* for the bloody Lamborghini of sewing machines. If he'd gotten me the Fisher Price model I'd had in mind, its disuse wouldn't be an issue.

"I went out on a limb this time," he'll tell me, handing over another expertly wrapped box. "If you don't like it or you won't use it, you have to promise me you'll take it back."

"I promise," I vow solemnly.

Oh dear mother of the infant baby Jesus, what is *that*?

"I don't like it and I won't use it," I admit. Well, I *promised*.

"Really? You won't? You don't even want to try it? Why don't you just try it?" He looks hurt and I feel awful. But I truly don't like it and I definitely won't use it and if you didn't want the brutal honesty you asked for, you should have married someone else.

• • • • •

I know that many husbands shower their wives with precious metals and semiprecious gemstones at every gifting occasion. Mine is not one of them. Other than my wedding and engagement rings—purchases about which it's not like he had much choice—Joe has bought me jewelry exactly once: a pair of diamond earrings when I gave birth to our first child. (And I am pretty sure that if creating, carrying, incubating, and then delivering another life into the world doesn't earn you something sparkly, nothing ever will.) It took me less than two weeks to lose one of them—I was very busy not losing our new *baby*, thank you very much—and I have never heard the end of it. I would bet my last dollar I never will. Whoever came up with that catchy "Diamonds are forever" line clearly wasn't married to me.

" At Least You're Not Married to Him "

My husband is a terrible shopper. In fact, he never shops unless he knows exactly what he needs to get. He never browses, and when he does it just to be accommodating, I feel so stressed because he always asks, "Are you done? Are you ready to go?" Because of this he also is a terrible gift giver. He has gone so far as to give his mother money to buy things for me. When our daughter was small, he had her pick out my gifts so everything I got was exactly what a six-year-old girl wanted (horse-head pendant, mini-hoop gold earrings). Now, every year I get the same thing: a Yankee candle and new slippers, plus anything else that I very specifically ask for.

ROSEMARIE

• • • • •

I love buying gifts, probably because to me shopping is a fun activity, an inherently pleasant way to pass the time that sometimes even ends with a purchase. I like products and packaging, and I am a sucker for any sort of marketing claim. I'll see a tube of Blackest Black mascara and feel a rush of hopeful joy, because I have only True Black, Dark Black, and Very Black. But *Blackest Black*? How could I have lived my entire life without enjoying this extreme of blackness? Thank God I found it! Similarly, it matters not that I already own two dozen bottles of hair conditioner; when I see that Extra Super Thick and Glossy Conditioner on the shelf, I am helpless to resist it. I like drugstores and hardware stores, sock shops and supercenters. Joe will mention that he's going to pick up some paint and I will beg him to let me tag along.

"I'm just getting paint," he'll say.

"That's okay, I just want to keep you company. Plus I like looking," I tell him.

"At what?" he genuinely wants to know.

"All of the stuff!" I explain vaguely.

At the paint store, he waits mostly patiently by the counter while I bustle about the place, accumulating must-have gadgets that we didn't even know were out there waiting to make our lives easier and that we therefore must purchase immediately.

"What the hell is that?" Joe asks, inspecting a little rubber nub I've placed on the counter.

"It's a tool for cleaning the rim of the paint can!" I explain excitedly.

"Did you ever hear of a rag?" he asks, shaking his head.

· · · · ·

But to me, if they make a product *specifically for one task*, it must be one of those wonderful things you *could* live without, but you probably wouldn't want to. Like a cheese slicer. Before the cheese slicer came along, sure you could always use a knife to saw off a nice hunk of Jarlsberg. But once you've experienced the bliss of identical, uniform slices of your favorite curdled milk product, there's no going back. You know it and I know it and if your cheese slicer broke tomorrow you'd haul your ass right over to Target and buy another one.

"What's *that*?" he asks, pointing to another item in the pile.

"It's an edging tool," I inform him.

"Does tape ring a bell?" He is starting to get a little pissy with me, which isn't very nice seeing as I came along to keep him company and all.

"But this is made just for edging," I argue. "Tape can be used for anything."

"You really will buy anything, won't you?" he says sadly, handing over his credit card to the cashier. "Next time, you're staying at home."

He's right. I will buy anything. Our drawers are clogged with Chip Clips and egg separators, wine aerators and dryer balls. We have a pasta maker, a bread maker, and a yogurt maker (into which you must put *yogurt* plus whatever fruit you want in it and the machine then conveniently mixes it for you; you know, like a spoon might), plus a spatula for every dish and cooking surface ever invented, including a pan-size one for omelets and a dozen pointy ones for pie. In an effort to clear up some kitchen cabinet space, I finally sold the $100 George Foreman Grill in our garage sale. I got a whopping ten bucks, but I honestly never used the thing so I was relieved to see it go. Within months, I'd purchased a shiny new panini press, which fit perfectly in the spot left vacant by the George Foreman—because, it turns out, *they are the same fucking appliance.*

" At Least You're Not Married to Him "

My husband—a prominent architect—keeps buying these ugly printed jackets with tigers and such on them at the swap meet. He insists on wearing them in public because he thinks they are cool. I'll sneak into his closet and throw them away, but he just keeps buying more. Is this male menopause?

ILEANA

Joe doesn't like accumulating stuff, so it makes sense that he doesn't much care for trolling for it in the first place. To my husband, braving any sort of retail establishment is a task to be endured when you absolutely, critically need something, like sour cream or a raccoon trap or underpants without holes in them. If my husband determines it is time to buy, for example, new basketball shoes, he drives straight to the nearest sporting goods store, tries on three or four pairs of sport-specific sneakers, purchases the most comfortable one, and goes home. That's it! He never gets sidetracked in the pool-toy aisle or sucked into trying on a dozen or more pairs of sunglasses or considers how his ratty old socks are going to look

• • • • •

with his shiny new shoes. He doesn't stop to wonder if there might be anything else in the store worth checking out; once he's made his predetermined purchase, the goal is accomplished and he can head back home to putter in the garage. Honestly, it must be nice.

Although he's not a born shopper, Joe has made great strides in the area during our marital tenure. For instance, when we're on vacation, not only will he occasionally suggest a stroll through the local shopping district to check out the native wares, but he has even learned to feign interest in the items I show him, and he hardly ever hovers anxiously in my shadow, checking his watch every thirty seconds and sighing dramatically. Definitive proof of how far he has evolved in this area came on the morning of our ten-year anniversary, when he presented me with a thick envelope. Inside the envelope was a lovely card, and inside the card was an even lovelier surprise: Ten crisp one-hundred-dollar bills. Now, a Benjamin a year for all of the compromise and sacrifice and that forsaking-all-others business—plus doubling the size of our little family at the expense of ever being able to bare my abdomen in public again—may not seem like all that much, but my husband knows that I rarely spend money guiltlessly (although I admit I somehow still manage to squander an unseemly ton of it on God only knows what), so I was a pleasant combination of stunned and delighted.

"The deal is," he said, immediately putting the brakes on my growing giddiness, because I just *knew* he was going to say we had to do something awful with it like put it in the bank or use it to stock up on unstained Tupperware with matching lids and a new water heater, "you have to spend it before we get home tomorrow." We were going away for a whopping thirty-six hours to a romantic little town an hour away. In order to spend that kind of dough, the next day and a half would have to feature a *lot* of shopping. That, gentle readers, was the real gift.

We bought two cast iron urns for the front porch first— something I'd wanted since we bought the house, but there was always something on the endless home-improvement list that seemed more urgent. Or maybe I'd just not happened across the right pots, but *there they were* and conveniently I had a fat wad of cash in my pocket. Then we found a quaint little garden shop and chose flowers to plant in them. Up and down the main drag we traipsed, passing up only the stores that sold taxidermy or old-lady clothes. I splurged on an impractical floor-length skirt, three pairs of nearly identical earrings (without even a single eye-roll from Joe), and a gold Buddha wall plaque for the garden (again, not even a sarcastic smirk); while I wasn't looking, a pair of ceramic lovebirds flew into my shopping cart. "How much do you have left?" he'd ask excitedly after each purchase. I know what you're thinking—that he just wanted the whole thing to be over and done with so we could go back to the hotel and have sex. But it wasn't like that, I swear. He was noticeably enjoying watching me enjoy myself, and he even insisted on paying for all of our meals out of "his" money (which was technically "ours" but not, you know, *mine to do with as I pleased without asking for his input or permission*), because the grand was specifically earmarked for extravagance. He even made a game out of it, saying things like "You got that, moneybags?" when it was time to pay, and shrugging as I handed over one crisp bill after another as if to say, "My lady likes to blow the dough. What can I say?" I have never loved my husband more than I loved him that day and a half. Like I said, I know that money can't buy happiness, but it turns out it can rent it for a while.

· · ·

CHAPTER THIRTEEN

If It's Broken . . . Please God, Don't Fix It

For fixing things around the house,
nothing is handier than a man with a checkbook.

· ANONYMOUS ·

(BUT IF NOBODY CLAIMS IT SOON, I AM TOTALLY CALLING IT)

When Joe and I moved from our last house to the one we're in now, we decided to do all of the packing and boxing ourselves and then hire a moving company to take care of the transport. But when you have two Type As living and working together, here's what happens: Three days before the movers are scheduled to arrive, you have padded, packed, and labeled every single household item you own, including the pots and pans, phones, plates, trash cans, TV, towels, litter box, and bed linens. The only article in the house that's not nailed to something you're leaving behind is a single, rapidly disappearing roll of toilet paper. So you walk around in the empty-but-for-stacks-of-boxes space aimlessly until one of you grabs your cell phone and calls U-Haul and rents a truck. You know it's probably overkill, but you have to do *something*.

· · · · ·

"We'll just get a head start on things," you tell each other.

Five hours later every single picture, pillow, and piece of furniture you own, plus the leftover packing supplies and a smattering of potted plants, is neatly crammed into the truck's spacious cargo hold.

"All that's left is the garage," he'll say proudly. "Do you think the movers are going to be mad?"

"Who cares?" you'll say. "We just saved ourselves at least a thousand bucks. Plus there's plenty of stuff in the garage, isn't there?"

Um, yeah. There's plenty of stuff in the garage, all right. You've got containers, shelves, and boxes teeming with flat-head and Phillips screwdrivers, a dozen nearly identical regular hammers, and several of the ball-peen, claw, club, and sledge variety. You've got crates stuffed with clamps, crowbars, chisels, and caulk guns; vises and wrenches and pliers (oh my!). Every size and shape of screw, nut, bolt, brad, hook, anchor, latch, and tack is generously represented and sorted into neatly labeled drawers. There is one entire wall studded with enough cutlery to fillet an ocean of fish, an impressive collection that includes drywall knives, putty knives, pocketknives, taping knives, finishing knives, and whittling knives (oh yes, he can whittle; go ahead and cue the dueling banjos from *Deliverance*). The garden section rivals Home Depot's, with mowers, blowers, hoses, hoes, shovels, sprayers, rakes, edgers, pruners, trimmers, and a smattering of spades and shears. A tangle of wire cutters, wire strippers, earmuffs, and goggles hangs next to several pairs of work gloves attached by carabiners to warped,

• • • • •

worn old tool belts. Over there you've got your trowels and torches (because you never know when setting something on fire might sound like a good idea), brushes and rollers, tapes and staplers, levels and ladders—and all of that mess looks like a kid's plastic play set next to the power tool section, home to the loud, lethal gear that requires protective eyewear and prayers to operate: the drills, drivers, saws, sanders, planers, routers, crushers, and grinders that are absolutely, without question, going to claim one of your husband's limbs—or at least a digit—sooner rather than later.

" At Least You're Not Married to Him "

I adore my husband. He loves to do fix-it tasks and building projects all around the house. Unfortunately he is the most disorganized human on the planet and cannot remember where he puts his tools. He is constantly asking me if I have seen his measuring tape/hammer/head/whatever, and I do my level best not to say, "Well, if you think of the last place you used it, walk there and look down, and you'll see it!" I do refrain, because I adore him, and I greatly benefit from all of his work, once he finally finds his tools.

JULIE

As it happens, the movers had more than enough to do. It took a team of four burly men twice as long to load up the garage as it took Joe and me to pack the entire contents of our three-bedroom home. We congratulated ourselves on our obsessive collective initiative and bantered about some ideas for how we might spend the money we had saved by doing so much of the work ourselves.

"What would you do with my tools if I died?" Joe asked in earnest one day as we surveyed his thousands of dollar's worth of construction paraphernalia tidily arrayed in the new garage.

"It's my dowry," I said jokingly. I was still marveling at the fact that he didn't say his "business" or "truck" or even "cremated remains"; that his biggest posthumous concern would be his garage full of mystifying gizmos.

"That's one lucky son of a bitch," he replied, shaking his head wistfully.

"Can we not talk about this?" I asked. I was already feeling a little maudlin—moving does that to me, plus being pregnant added a whole new layer of hormonal sentimentality—and the hypothetical bereavement and remarriage discussion wasn't helping.

The thing is, Joe loves his tools. And he uses them not only often and eagerly, but with great skill. He doesn't like it when I touch or move them, and lending them out is not even an option. (It's not that he's not generous, but ever since I let a girlfriend borrow one of his *nine staple guns* to hang some stupid curtains and neglected to get it back, he's gotten a little guarded.) Even when I use my own tools—yes, I have a few *and* I know how to use them—he hovers annoyingly behind me, asking exasperating questions like "Are you sure that's level?" and "You're not hanging that on a paint chip again, are you?"

• • • • •

"You are *so lucky*," everyone who has witnessed the fruits of his handiwork is fond of telling me. And for the most part, they are right. Joe can wire an entire house, install plumbing, outfit a walk-in closet with professional-looking shelves, and build a door frame—that's square, even—from scratch. He can put up crown molding, switch out light fixtures, and cut and lay tile. He knows how to frame a room, throw up a wall, and hang, tape, sand, and patch drywall. Friends and family alike marvel at his proficiency, and I don't begrudge him the praise. He absolutely deserves every bit of it. But every once in a while, I'd like to be able to simply *call a fucking plumber*, just like everyone else.

❝ At Least You're Not Married to Him ❞

My husband is the handiest person I know. He will fix anything and does a great job at it. But when he says he needs to put something together, the kids and I run the other way. He has this habit of getting really mad at the person who is helping and no matter what you do, IT IS WRONG! You can do everything right and if one thing goes wrong—such as a screw that won't go in right—it is your fault for not holding something right or for not handing him the screwdriver right.

KRIS

On any given Saturday, I might suggest one of a million possible fun family activities: a trip to the zoo, a day at the beach, a drive up to wine country, some margaritas in the backyard.

"Sure, sounds fun," Joe will reply absentmindedly. "Only I *was* going to build you that bookcase you wanted . . ."

Oh, how I want that bookcase. I crave it with every atom in my being. I've mentally outfitted it with just the right ratio of knickknacks to books and chosen the photos I'll display on top of it. It'll be beautiful *and* functional, a workhorse and an heirloom all wrapped up in one spectacular maple package. That bookcase is the answer to my organizational prayers. Having it will change my life! So I load up the car and the kids and head off on another single-parent adventure—and I can't even complain about it, because when I get home, the tools are put away, the sawdust is a memory, and my new, expertly crafted display of woodworking is bolted securely to the wall I had chosen as its home. It's a beauty, too. The edges are meticulously mitered, the top and sides are sanded smooth, and the entire piece is perfectly plumb in every way possible. Ethan Allen, kiss my ass.

It's not just my decorative whims that demand my husband's every spare hour. The bigger culprit is the parade of home repairs of which our charming little vintage farmhouse is in perpetual need. Rarely does a week go by when a toilet doesn't plug, a pipe doesn't spring a leak, or some aging appliance or other doesn't stage a mutiny.

"Sink won't drain again!" I'll shout to anyone or no one, cursing softly under my breath at the pool of stagnant, soapy water before me.

"I'll fix it later," Joe's voice reverberates back to me from somewhere in the silently decaying bowels of our home.

I survey the piles of syrupy breakfast dishes and sticky utensils and coffee-stained mugs, and let loose another string of whispered profanities.

"Later *when?*" I bellow. The deafening silence in reply is all I need. *Later when I get around to it because it's not like I'm sitting around watching* Glee *and popping bonbons over here, in case you hadn't noticed.* It's not that I don't believe that Joe can fix the sink; I've seen him do it enough times to be utterly confident in his abilities. It's just that like a lot of husbands, he has this annoying thing called a *job*, and most days he's expected to show up at it. So off he trots to work, closing the door on his troubles for the next nine hours as he goes. I'm the one stuck looking at the mess, and it makes me want to tear all of my hair out.

I pour another bottle of Drano down the sink. Nothing. I add some baking soda because I think I read in one of those forward-forward-forward e-mails that it might help. Nothing. I add some vinegar and *Holy sulfur dioxide, did I just make a bomb because that is some toxic shit right there.* My eyes are bleeding and I can't breathe. *I could call a plumber and pay him in cash and just tell Joe the clog worked itself out.* The next time you find yourself wishing your husband were as handy as mine, pause and enjoy the fact that you will never, ever have to hide a plumbing receipt from him or use the money you've been squirreling away for Botox to get your sink fixed.

Any time I suggest we buy something for the house, Joe insists he can build it—better, cheaper, and faster to boot.

(Maybe cheaper, possibly better, but *no way* faster. I can type seventy-five words a minute, and potterybarn.com is only one.)

"Honey, you cannot build a leather couch," I try to argue.

"How do you know? I haven't ever tried. I bet you I can," he insists. "How hard can it be?"

"I know that you are extremely talented and amazing with your hands," I agree. "But you *cannot build a couch*. Or at the very least, not the couch *I* want, with antique casters for feet and a tufted back and a million hand-hammered brass studs all over it and big, rolled arms. Skilled tradesmen spend entire lifetimes learning how to craft a couch by hand, and half of the time they still turn out looking like thrift-store crap. Google 'homemade sofa' if you don't believe me."

"Wow," he'll say. "I had no idea how little faith you have in me. It would have been a kick-ass couch, just so you know."

He truly believes this, too.

" At Least You're Not Married to Him "

My husband's father offered him a "fixer-upper" boat. It didn't work then, and I knew it never would; that it would sit in our driveway for ten years just as it had at his dad's. I tried to fight it, but my husband side-stepped me by going straight to the kids. "What do you think of the new boat Daddy (he uses *Daddy* when manipulation of their emotional imma-turity is necessary) is going to bring home? Mamma doesn't think we should. What do you guys think?" Okay, are you *kidding* me? You did NOT just say that to the kids (knowing he did, but trying to stay sane).

Oh, and did I mention that shards of the boat are all around it—part of the interior, a vinyl-covered torn-up seat, the cover—on the ground? Every single day I have to look at this old, nasty, mold-ridden boat, sitting on top of a trailer that is propped up on cement blocks. *One time* he tried to get it to work . . . and of course it didn't. It's been there for a year and a half. We've officially stepped into white trash territory.

LEAH

The funny thing is—and by *funny* I mean "annoyingly ironic"—as handy as my husband is, there's one singular task he loathes, loudly complains about, and tries to put off indefinitely, every single blessed, blustery year: putting up the godforsaken Christmas lights.

"We don't need to do the outside lights again this year, do we?" he'll try.

"Yes, we do," I tell him.

"But we did them last year," he reminds me.

"And we're doing them this year, too," I insist.

"But don't you think they sort of detract from all of your beautiful *inside* decorations?" he says, trying a new and admittedly clever tack. I have to think about that one for a second.

"Nope, they're totally separate. If anything, they *enhance* my beautiful inside decorations, which by the way, thank you for noticing. Plus I love the lights, so we're doing them." I am firm. It's a tradition—the arguing about it as well as having them there on the house. I witnessed my own parents having this debate every yuletide, too, and have vivid memories of my mom high atop the roof, sweltering in her reindeer sweater (it's typically around eighty-five degrees in Florida in December), *doing it her goddamned self* while Dad drowned out her thunderous, angry footsteps by twisting the volume on the TV as high as it would go. We could all still hear her, but we pretended not to.

"We could totally distinguish ourselves by *not* doing outside lights." Joe is grasping now. "Hey, we're not even religious! Why do we even do Christmas decorations at all? Isn't putting up Christmas lights when you don't celebrate Jesus' birthday sort of hypocritical?"

"Christmas lights have nothing to do with Jesus," I say calmly, ignoring his blasphemous suggestion that we eschew decking the halls entirely as a statement-making act of agnosticism. "It's not like I'm asking you to build a life-size, working manger on the front lawn and borrow a baby and some livestock to put in it. They're *lights*. And in case I haven't been clear about this, we are going to put them on the house, this year and every year after it, for the rest of our lives. The only way it will ever be up for discussion is if your *next* wife wants to get into a debate about it with you. Are we good?"

A sad shell of the confident, cocky man I married stares back at me, shoulders slumped. Man, this guy *really* doesn't want to put up those lights. I decide to throw him a dry, admittedly unappetizing bone. "You know, I'm happy to call the Christmas Light Guys if it's really that big of a deal."

That's their real name, the Christmas Light Guys. We've never actually seen the Guys in person, but I picture a rogue band of seasonal, skill-specific handymen with ginormous beer bellies sporting dollar-store Santa hats. "Sorry ma'am, we only do lights," a portly Guy tells the bent-over little widow when she asks if he might be able to fix her creaky screen door while he's there. The Guys' little lawn signs and flyers pop up all over town right around Thanksgiving, and every year I am tempted to give them a call. Like I said, we don't know any Guys personally, but Joe does not like them, not one little bit. (Maybe it's just me, but the Guys seem to demand a Seussical sort of syntax for some reason.)

"I just don't like getting up on that twenty-foot ladder," Joe finally admits to me. *He would not, could not, on a ladder. Tell me, tell me, what is sadder?*

"Seriously?" I scoff. "You prance around on the forty-five-degree roof like a nimble old billy goat without a moment's pause, you rock climb and mountain bike for fun, and you once jumped out of an airplane—on purpose—but you're scared to climb up a silly ladder?"

He huffs and he puffs and eventually, after I've dragged two hundred feet of string lights onto the front lawn so that he can't turn on the sprinklers until they've been moved, he climbs up onto the big, scary ladder.

"If I start screaming or you see sparks coming off me, grab that wooden broom and push me off the ladder with the handle end," he says somberly. "And make sure that you don't touch my body."

"Yeah, okay, got it, get the broom, no touching the body," I indulge him, bracing the ladder against the house with both hands. "Now up you go!"

Sometimes Joe takes the lights back down as soon as I start

undressing the tree, but I can almost always count on him taking care of the removal by my birthday in May. One year we were sprucing up the place for a Fourth of July party and realized they were still up. Seeing as we were past the year's halfway mark—albeit barely—I told him they could stay up. I thought he'd leap at the chance to get out of putting them up the following holiday, but Joe has tremendous pride and he was suddenly mortified about those stupid lights, so he climbed up the dreaded ladder in the heat of summer and ripped them down and I didn't even need to save his life with a nearby broomstick. Christmas sure seemed to come early that year.

" At Least You're Not Married to Him "

When one of my boys was a baby and we were on a tight budget—some things never change—I saw a really cute highchair in the shape of a lifeguard stand. It was $350. My husband decided he could make it for me. I call him Tool-Time Tim because he thinks he is handy but he is not. The next thing you know I am rushing him to the emergency room after he ran the circular saw over his hand. By the time we paid his medical bills and for physical therapy, I could have bought that chair ten times over. It took my husband several other incidents before he finally accepted the fact that he is not a do-it-yourself guy.

MIA

I have many a friend who likes to lament the fortune her husband has assembled in fancy, dust-covered tools and plenty who complain about half-finished paint jobs and faucets that have been dripping for seven years. (Can you say Chinese-effing-water-torture?) Pals bemoan the countless hours their significantly delusional others spend in their "workshops," from which concrete evidence of any sort of "work" transpiring there does not exist. Comparatively, I won the handy-husband lottery and I know it. I just miss hanging out with him. It's not easy being a home-project widow, either.

Five years ago, my brother bought a house in foreclosure. He got a rock-bottom deal and was giddy with his new pad's upside potential, which was pretty limitless seeing as the place was totally trashed when he bought it. When the broke and bitter former owners begrudgingly moved out, in an effort to salvage as much of their investment as they could, they took every light-switch plate, towel bar, and toilet-tissue holder with them. They stripped the windows of their coverings and even took the knobs off the stove, which seemed unnecessarily vindictive to me. They didn't just leave with the bulbs that were in the light fixtures; they left gaping holes and dangling wires where the fixtures and ceiling fans once hung. Apparently, before they went belly up they had toyed with the idea of fixing up the joint, as witnessed by the way they had taped off the window trim in several rooms with thick blue painter's tape. The holes, the wires, the knobless stove, the *open electrical sockets*, the tape: It's all still there. For one thousand, eight hundred twenty-five days, my brother has been living in this house without making a single change. "I don't really even notice it anymore," he says when I ask casually how the repairs are going. He's a great guy and one of the funniest men I know and he has a heart the size of Texas and I love him fiercely and unconditionally. And at least I'm not married to him.

• • •

CHAPTER FOURTEEN

Friends and Family: Not Just a Phone Plan

Happiness is having a large, loving, caring,
close-knit family in another city.

• GEORGE BURNS •

As Exhibit Y in the virtual trial of Jenna's Big Mouth versus
Joe's Inability to Absorb Anything That Comes Out of It or
Share Anything in Return, I present to you this classic anecdote:
My husband has played basketball for eighteen years, every
single Thursday night, with the same group of guys. The only
two instances I can recall when we were actually in town and
he did not participate in this weekly ritual were the two times
I experienced the joy of induced labor. Serendipitously, on each
of these occasions the doctors arbitrarily offered Thursday as
the first viable opportunity, and both times Joe tried to gently
persuade me to hold off "just one more day" so that—and I am
not making this up—he could *play basketball as scheduled*, never
mind that by the second time we had this conversation I had
been pregnant for a cumulative 13,440 hours and was about

• • • • •

sixteen miles and thirty pounds past my breaking point. When I insisted that his coming to the hospital with me was not up for discussion, he actually had the gall to try to negotiate a midevening hall pass by reminding me that labor was a long and grueling process (as if I didn't know this?) so it wasn't as if the baby would "come right away." I must not have smacked him hard enough, because he doesn't even have a scar. But I digress.

"Kent's getting married in Mexico and we're invited," Joe announced out of the blue one day. "Do you want to go?"

I had a brief moment of utter blankness, and then a tiny, low-voltage lightbulb went off. "The Kent you play basketball with that I've never met?" I asked, not really caring about this small detail as I was too busy mentally picturing myself on a tropical Baja beach sipping a frosty margarita and wearing a sexy white slip dress (that I didn't technically own and that I'd have to starve for a week to wear in public, but it was a *great* dress so it was totally going to be worth it.) It briefly crossed my mind that I didn't know that Kent was even single, but then I also realized that I knew absolutely nothing about *any* of Joe's Thursday night buddies, one of whom felt close enough to my husband to ask him to fork over several thousand dollars to watch him utter a barefooted "I do" on foreign sand.

I suppose I should have assumed that the entire basketball team and their families—and not just my husband and ours— would be invited to this shindig, but to be honest I really didn't give the wedding itself a whole lot of thought. The other guests were nameless, faceless people and they had nothing whatsoever to do with my upcoming tropical holiday, which was going to be all about me save for a quick little exchange of vows by a pair of strangers somewhere in the middle.

We arrived at the resort to find that the thoughtful bride-to-be had assembled dozens of sand buckets into darling little welcome kits and left them at the check-in desk. There was sunblock and bottled water, a generous selection of snacks, and even a pair of massage gift certificates. Oh, and a three-page, jam-packed-with-back-to-back-events-and-excursions itinerary spanning the better part of the upcoming week.

As we shuffled behind the valet into the sweeping glass elevator, I was livid. "Why didn't you *tell* me it was this kind of wedding?" I wailed, already knowing what Joe's answer would be.

"I had no idea what kind of wedding it was going to be!" he spat back. Well, of *course* he didn't. Because it never would have occurred to him to ask.

"Have you even met Robin?" I asked suddenly, referring of course to the thoughtful mystery bride.

"Sure," he said. "She comes to watch Kent play ball some-times. She's great."

"You never told me that any of the *wives* come to watch you guys," I said angrily.

"Oh, they don't," he replied. "Only the girlfriends."

For some reason this infuriated me. All of a sudden I felt like Joe had this whole secret life that I knew absolutely noth-ing about, a life that only *girlfriends* were invited to partici-pate in.

"I think you'll really like Matty and Tony's wives, too," he added sheepishly, struggling to mollify me. *Who?* And just like that it dawned on me: This wasn't going to be the romantic little getaway I'd envisioned; it was going to be a flipping five-day bachelor party and I was going to be stuck with a posse of equally bitter and bitchy wives with whom I would surely have nothing in common or else why hadn't I ever been introduced to them before? I snatched both massage certificates out of the bucket and told Joe I'd be back in a few hours.

The first big pre-wedding fiesta of many in the exhausting schedule of events was that night. I met the impending new-lyweds, and they were shockingly lovely. Then Joe introduced me to the rest of the guys and *their* wives, and again I couldn't believe how cool everyone was. How on earth had my husband kept all of these people from me, and more important—why? We were always looking for other couples to double-date with and invite over for barbecues and swap free child care with; I just didn't understand why Joe had never arranged a meeting.

"We play basketball," was Joe's nonsensical response.

"I can see how you might not be running up and down the court talking about your deepest feelings or sharing your best marital advice or bragging about how amazing your wives are in the sack," I conceded. "But you guys go out after you play every single week! What do you talk about all night?"

"Talk about?" he asked, genuinely perplexed. "We don't really talk. We just, you know, drink beer and watch whatever game is on in the bar."

My husband has a theory about friendship that I don't quite

share, and after careful consideration I have decided that it must be a guy thing. Distilled down to its essence, Joe's philosophy goes like this: "You don't really know someone until you play sports together." I get what he's saying in theory—that a person can claim or even pretend to be honest and fair and considerate and all of that crap, but if he's a ball hog on the court or the type to cry foul when the play was obviously good or isn't a gracious loser, his core is rotten so you might as well save yourself the trouble of getting to know him any better. But I have hundreds of friends (not even counting Facebook and Twitter and MySpace and LinkedIn) and I've known many of them for decades and would swear that I "know" them as well as you can ever know another human being, even though we have never once tossed a Frisbee back and forth or swatted a tennis ball at each other or even gone for a nice Rollerblade together. I have forged lifetime alliances with these women (and a handful of men, despite what Harry told Sally) through long, meaningful conversations, shared play dates with our kids, hairdresser recommendations and breakups, endless recipe and book exchanges, miserable lice outbreaks, summer camp carpools, and in many cases an ocean of wine. We call each other on our birthdays, celebrate each other's achievements, bake each other lasagna when we have babies or surgery or just a little extra time, justify each other's purchases, borrow each other's champagne flutes and cowboy boots and suitcases, hold each other's hair when the other has to puke even if we're putting ourselves at risk because the puking is from the stomach flu and not a wild night out on the town, and mourn each other's losses—whether it's a breast or a parent or a job or a worthless cheating spouse that's gone—as if they were our own.

My husband? Not so much. He can probably tell you the year, make, and model of the vehicles most of his friends drive, and whether they are left- or right-handed. (It's a sports thing.) He might know where they went to college, if that establishment had or has a decent hockey/football/basketball team, and if they've ever spent any time in jail. Beyond that, his buddies could be a bunch of banjo-playing cross-dressers and Joe would be oblivious to it.

"Did Kurt find a job yet?" I'll inquire.

"I dunno," Joe replies.

"You had lunch with him yesterday," I remind him.

"Yeah, I forgot to ask," he admits.

"What did you talk about?" I ask.

"Stuff, the Celtics, I don't know," Joe mumbles. "I think he said he got a dog, or he was thinking about getting a dog or maybe his dog died."

Because of our fundamentally different approaches to forging and maintaining friendships, you can imagine how fun it is when we are courting a new couple.

ME: "Want to have Jack and Meg over for dinner on Saturday?

JOE: "I don't know Jack at all. Does he mountain bike?"

ME: "Our kids have been in school together for three years and we've seen them six hundred times and sat with them at every freaking Spring Sing and potluck picnic.

I can vouch for Meg, and we've both always said that Jack seems nice. I have no idea what he likes to do for fun; why don't we invite them over and you can ask him?"

JOE: "Can I see if he wants to go hiking or hit some golf balls first?"

ME: "Really? It's two days from now. How are you going to make that happen? I'm not asking you to marry the guy, just sit through a two-hour meal. He doesn't have to be your soul mate, for crying out loud."

My husband hems and he haws and he rumbles and he grumbles and I just know that having them over won't be any fun at all because I'll have to carry the entire conversation ("You're the social one," Joe always insists), which is exhausting, so I say good-bye to my group-vacation fantasies starring Jack and Meg. They have a boat, too, damn it. It truly is a shame.

" At Least You're Not Married to Him "

Like most people, we have Caller ID at home. If my husband doesn't recognize the caller's name or if he doesn't *like* the person calling, either he won't answer the phone or he'll pick up the receiver and then immediately hang it up. This has to be the hardest thing for me because I think it's terribly rude. He says, "It's my phone and I'm not talking to anyone I don't want to talk to." It's very annoying.

THRESEA

A landmark study out of UCLA a few years ago confirmed what scores of women could have told the researchers before they sacrificed years of their lives to gathering data: Women rely on their friends to reduce stress. Before this particular study—when the majority of stress-related research had been performed exclusively on men and then the results had been incorrectly been extrapolated to pertain to women, too—the theory was that stress in *both* sexes resulted in the infamous "fight or flight" response. In other words, whether you had a penis or a vagina, when the going got tough you either stood up and faced the music or bolted to safety. But the UCLA study found that the complex female brain actually has a larger behavioral repertoire than the male brain. A woman under stress produces the hormone oxytocin, which makes her want to cuddle her children and gather with other women. (Men produce the bonding hormone, too—but the extra testosterone they crank out when anxious or upset all but cancels out the attachment urge.) The more a woman engages with her kids and her cronies, the more oxytocin she releases, which further mellows her out while fueling her need for even more closeness. It's a lovely and positive little cycle that plainly illustrates how good begets good and proves that women, therefore, rock. This is why we gals, after mulling a marital spat over with our girlfriends for a nonstop day or two, are usually ready to move on, while our partners are over there teeming with testosterone, pounding their fists and sprouting new body hairs and humping the arm of the couch.

My friend Leah and I were discussing the differences

between male and female friendships, and we decided that it all boils down to our *Homo habilis* roots: Men hunt, women gather. Hunting, by nature, is a pretty noiseless pursuit. Talking shop while you're stalking prey just isn't a pastime that's going to pay off out in the field or in the forest. But for the ladies, what's the sense in biting our tongues while we gather? There isn't any! We are free to gossip and grouse because it's not like we're going to scare the cherries away. We discuss what we're gathering, why we're gathering, and how we're gathering. We talk about the most energy-saving, time-efficient, and economical ways to gather. We discuss who's not gathering enough and who's gathering too much and who could really use a bigger loincloth, if you know what I mean. We ask our friends, "Does this basket make me look fat while I'm gathering?"

Because Joe is biologically built to hunt and hump and not congregate with other men to forge deep and spiritually fulfilling friendships, he has a hard time understanding many of mine. He marvels at the fact that I know so many of these women's phone numbers by heart and can recall the names of their hundreds of spouses and billions of collective children.

"Jerry?" he'll whisper quietly, even though we are alone in the car.

"Jason," I sigh. We're on the way to dinner at the home of our friends Jason and Cheryl, where we've been a half-dozen times before. Sure, Cheryl was my friend first, but Joe and I met Jason at exactly the same time—more than ten years ago.

"And what's the son's name again?" Joe asks.

"Twin girls, Abby and Ashley," I say, shaking my head.

"Right, Abby and Ashley," he repeats. "They play water polo or something, right?"

"Track," I deadpan. "They run track."

"And Jerry's in sales of some kind?" he asks.

"Jason *is my doctor! You saw him last year when you had strep throat and you couldn't get in to see your regular doctor. You talked to* Jason *about buying his office building last time they were over for dinner.* Jason *played college football with some guy you knew growing up.* Jason's *mom went to the same high school as your dad but five years later, so they never met. Is any of this ringing a bell?*"

"Jesus, Jenna, no wonder you can never find your car keys," Joe says. "You've got all of *that* crap in your brain."

" At Least You're Not Married to Him* "

My adorable, wonderful husband refuses to engage when it comes to acknowledging special occasions for *his* family. Every birthday, Christmas, or anniversary, it's up to me to send a card or gift. And if it doesn't get done, I get this weird sense that it reflects poorly not on him, but on me! He's always like, "Well, I'll call them." For real? We are going to throw them a last-minute phone call? Why is my awesome man such a goober in this one area?

DIANE

*But you probably are, because don't all husbands do this?

At least we can choose our friends; family is another matter. And when you marry someone, it's not a one-shot deal. You get the whole famdamily, for richer or for poorer, for better or for worse. It's one of the greatest benefits to hooking up, in fact. If your families are equally fabulous, you get to share in the wealth; if one or both of them suck, at least now you've got someone to commiserate with and who can help diffuse the misery.

Beyond the basic male/female differences, saying that Joe and I were raised with dissimilar parenting styles in divergent environments is like saying mice and snakes sometimes have trouble snuggling. The youngest of four kids raised mostly by a very stoic, old-school dad, my husband is uncomfortable with conflict and tends toward all things conservative. Before I met Joe Sr. for the first time, my future husband described him thusly: "My dad doesn't talk a lot, but what he says matters." My own parents, on the other hand, fought and swore openly and robustly, and the definitive "winner" in any family argument was the one who yelled the loudest or slammed the door the hardest. Dad was a hilarious and extremely quirky son of a bitch, the sort who used the words *Democrat* and *Communist* interchangeably and found it sidesplitting to greet my new boyfriends with a friendly "So, are you banging my daughter yet?" At the dinner table we talked about having periods and smoking pot, and if you had an opinion you shared it without daring to care that someone else might disagree. On Christmas morning, whoever woke up first hollered until the rest of the family was good and awake, and then we raced to the tree and tore into our gifts simultaneously like a school of ravenous piranhas attacking a pile of bloody limbs. In Joe's highly civilized household, everyone took turns slowly opening and appreciating one present at a time, often after showers had been taken and the breakfast dishes had been cleared. I don't envy his past, nor does he pity mine; they simply were what they were, and we are what we are because of them. Which has made years of family get-togethers interesting, to say the least.

"Everyone is so . . . quiet," I whispered to Joe upon first meeting his brood. I was starting to feel itchy.

"Do they ever stop talking?" Joe whispered to me upon first meeting mine. He was beginning to sweat.

For a while there, it took a paper-scissors-rock showdown to decide which group we'd spend our precious holiday and vacation days with, as each of us fervently preferred the comfortable companionship of our own (some of them admittedly crazy) kin. But a decade and a half later, both Joe and I have learned to embrace the benefits of our relative differences. I've come to appreciate how easy Joe's family is to be around, and—especially now that we have kids of our own—I find their near-silent civility delightful and refreshing. Learning to mind my mouth and my manners has made me a better mother (although I still swear like a sailor in private—and in print—so I hope none of them are reading this, because that would certainly blow my carefully constructed cover). For his part, Joe has loosened up considerably, stockpiling his dirtiest jokes and most inappropriate stories to share with my people when they gather to drink too much. Because that's what you do when you love someone.

. . . . .

CHAPTER FIFTEEN

If You Build It, There Will Be Many, Many Arguments

If you want to sacrifice the admiration
of many men for the criticism of one,
go ahead, get married.

• KATHARINE HEPBURN •

Even if you're not as ballsy (or naïve or stupid) as Joe and me and you don't decide to buy a second house you can't quite afford and completely gut and renovate it with money, time, and skills you don't really have *on national television* (more about this later) so that all of the world can bask in your ballsy, naïve stupidity, chances are at some point in your marriage, you and your husband will attempt to assemble something together. It might be a Barbie Dream House for your daughter's eighth birthday or a Ping-Pong table you splurged on in anticipation of your First Annual July Fourth Tequila, Taco, and Table Tennis Blowout, or maybe it will be a simple IKEA bookshelf comprising four particle-board pieces that "snap together in seconds, no tools required!" All I can say is, don't say I didn't warn you.

You'll go into your construction project pumped and prepared, having had the forethought to assemble several thousand tools plus a few rags, a handy tarp, the video camera for posterity, and of course a couple of cocktails. (The cocktails are crucial.) You will probably forget to check to see if the product packaging contained everything it promised that it did, but since screw A looks identical to screw B to you and you have no idea what a washer is in this context, you'll figure it doesn't matter so much anyway. You lay everything out neatly, in what feels to you like some sort of order, and the process begins.

"Can you hand me an Allen wrench?" he asks.

"What's an Allen wrench?" you reply, surveying your temporary tool corral and looking for something that might resemble Alan Alda or Alan Greenspan or even Woody Allen.

"The hex key," he says.

"The what?" you ask.

"Allen wrench, hex key, it looks like a little L," he replies impatiently.

"Why didn't you just *say so*?" you demand, handing him the stupid L, which looks nothing at all like an aging actor-activist or a bald economist or a screwball Jewish screenwriter/director, for the record.

"Okay, now I need the main body piece labeled number six," he instructs.

You scan the boards you've laid out smartly, but there is no number six.

"There is no number six," you inform him.

"There has to be a number six," he insists.

"Well there isn't," you maintain with all of the confidence in the world, swallowing half of your vodka and cranberry. You have a college degree and once even worked as a math tutor and you're pretty sure you can recognize the number six when you see it. Which you are positive you don't.

"It's right there," he barks, pointing at a piece of particleboard.

"That's not a six, that's a ni—" You stop midword and mentally kick yourself. Why didn't it occur to you earlier, when you were arranging these things meticulously in numerical order, that it was sort of strange that the parts were labeled one, two, three, four, five . . . and nine? Of course that's a fucking six, it's just upside down so it looks like a nine. It's a mistake anyone could make, really. At least that's what you tell yourself. But at the moment you hate this project and you hate your husband and you grab the slab and hand it to him and then you knock back the rest of your drink. Four hours later you are extremely buzzed and barely speaking to each other, but the thing is mostly assembled and fairly sturdy and you decide not to worry about the extra hardware because obviously they just put a few spare pieces in the box. How very thoughtful of them.

" At Least You're Not Married to Him "

I learned long ago to not even be in the room when my husband works on a project. Last Christmas we attempted to put together a play kitchen for our then two-year-old. My job was simply to put on the stickers; I let him do everything else. After one too many "suggestions" from the husband about my sticker application technique, I left and hid in the bathroom trying not to cry. Perfection is overrated!

TJ

If you want to really test the strength of your marriage and your sanity, flip a house together. No really, it's fun! (If you like having daily squabbles in front of dozens of strangers at various building-supply stores and watching your hair fall out in clumps.) It's rewarding! (Wow! Look at this killer place you've lovingly created for *someone else* to live in.) You can make a lot of money! (You can also lose your life savings *and* your mind, but if it was easy everyone would do it, so don't be such a wuss.)

Using the only money we had—our handy equity line of credit—Joe and I bought a full-on fixer-upper, a bargain at not much over seven figures. Yes, *those* seven figures, a reflection of entry-level prices in our hometown hamlet of Santa Barbara at the time, which was probably the pinnacle of the decade-long real estate boom. The house itself was a Brady Bunch special, only smaller and much more run-down, complete with a choppy, dysfunctional floor plan; ancient, rusty appliances; stained, threadbare carpets; a shoebox-size "master" bathroom;

and lattice-covered windows that, judging by several similarly "original" homes still standing in the neighborhood, must have been very chic in the 1950s. It had a hideous, dated roofline that would have to be somehow altered without compromising the integrity of the structure it covered, and the yard was a jungle of weeds surrounded by a feeble chain-link fence. We gave ourselves six weeks and what we thought was a decent chunk of borrowed change to do the necessary work, which basically entailed rebuilding the thing from the ground up.

Quit laughing; it's rude. We really thought we could renovate a dilapidated house and not blow our meager timeline or our ridiculously tight budget, okay?

It wasn't like we were rookies—we practically had our own parking spot at Home Depot—and it wasn't as if we came up with the time and money figures arbitrarily, either. We created elaborate spreadsheets based on actual figures and past experience, and we even padded the expenses *and* the timeline to include the things we might have overlooked. But construction is unpredictable. Vendors are unreliable. Inspectors are impossible. Opening up a single wall is like ripping the lids off a thousand cans of worms and setting the slimy bastards loose at your feet. Parts sell out, people flake out, and paint colors look *nothing at all* on a wall the way they do in a can or on a two-inch card. And when you're experiencing a hundred just such frustrations every single day alongside the person with whom you share a sink *and* a bed over at your other house—the one that is in sad need of attention because who the hell wants to work on *two* houses at the same time?—that person becomes your own personal punching bag. (Emotionally at least. I'm proud to admit that other than the ice-to-the-temple incident, neither Joe nor I have ever laid an angry finger on the other.) What's more, each of you begins to feel that whatever part you are contributing is the one that really matters the most.

"I need the sink hardware today," Joe announced to me as he was walking out the door to "work" one morning. Never mind the fact that we both had full-time jobs and two small children; time is major money when you're carrying two mortgages, and that flip was one nasty, demanding boss. (We're both self-employed, so at least our other bosses were being semireasonable.)

"I bought it online and it hasn't come yet," I informed him.

"Well, then please go down to the plumbing store and get another one because we need it today," he said, visibly struggling to speak without snarling.

"The girls have dentist appointments this morning and I was going to bring them with me to the tile store afterward to pick out the backsplash," I tried to explain. I left out the part about the actual, paying work that I should be doing but that was once again getting bumped for a flip-related task.

"You want *me* to pick it out, then?" he asked, knowing what my answer would be.

Well, of *course* I didn't want him to do that. We each had a clearly defined role in this project, and those roles were based on our individual, indisputable skill sets: I was form, he was function. He made it work, I made it look pretty. If we were going to get tippy-top dollar for this pad—which we damned well had to or we'd be living in our cars on an all-rice-and-beans diet at the end of it all—it could not have the clearance rack passé-brass faucet set Joe might be inclined to buy.

"I'll reschedule the goddamned dentist and do the tile store tomorrow," I sighed.

To be fair, the whole flip thing was a fluke. We knew someone who knew someone who worked for the show, and when this friend-of-a-friend heard we'd bought a house to renovate and sell, she suggested we apply. We wouldn't be compensated financially for our willingness to look like nationally televised idiots, but we *would* get professional input and hopefully the cameras would add an unnecessary element of urgency. We discussed it only briefly, too consumed with the actual work before us to imagine the possible consequences of completing it in front of an audience. "It'll be fun to watch someday!" we agreed, not quite realizing it might take many, many decades before we would be able to view it without cringing.

Imagine wallpapering a room or installing a new ceiling fan with your significant other. Now multiply that little project times infinity plus thirteen and throw in a camera crew following you around 24/7, and you'll have a tiny, vague idea of what those fourteen weeks—yes, it took 2.3 times longer than we had estimated—looked like. And the cameras weren't relegated to the property; oh no. They tagged along on every paint store and dump run, rolled tape during every meeting, filmed us frantically trying to stay on top of our respective nonconstruction jobs, thoughtfully documented both of our daughters' birthday parties, and even followed our family as

we hiked up a mountain one beautiful Saturday morning in
an effort to escape the toxic cauldron that was the job site.
Thankfully the final cut of the show featured only a handful
of the hundreds of marital arguments, both minor and massive,
that transpired during that highly stressful time. Sometimes
just knowing that those endless hours of unused raw footage
may still be out there keeps me awake all night.

" At Least You're Not Married to Him "

I love my husband and we have been happily married for ten years.
That being said, I don't know why his projects are always more important than mine. Example: I am sitting at the table with about a thousand
pictures in a thousand piles trying to organize the last five years of our
lives, and he is going to hang a picture (that has been sitting on the
floor in the hall for about ten months . . . another story completely!
Christ.). He gets the picture and gets the ladder and is holding the
picture up to the spot on the wall where he thinks it might look good
and then bellows to me from the hall. "Shell, can you get me the
picture-hanging thingy? And can you grab a hammer? And do you see
the level in your toolbox?" Which is yet another story that I have to
have my own toolbox . . . which I hide for my own protection, because
he never puts anything away and can't ever find his own fucking tools.

SHELLY

Having survived that emotional and mental tsunami (which
earned us enough money to take a whole week off to celebrate
and survive reentry into the real, sawdust-free world), you'd

think we'd have learned how to co-construct harmoniously. I wish I could say that you were right. We still argue over fixtures and finishes and wants versus needs and *how much is it going to cost* and whether we should attempt to salvage the old materials and hardware when we fix up a room or splurge on nice, shiny new ones.

"These windows are fine," Joe insists, running a hand over the chipping paint and splitting wood framing the nearest one. "We have an old house, Jenna. It's not supposed to be perfect."

"I'm not asking for perfection," I maintain. "It's just that now that the walls are so smooth and the paint is so clean and everything, the windows look even worse. Plus wouldn't it be nice if we didn't have to put buckets under them when it rains and stuff towels around the sills when it's windy?"

"Next time don't pick a hundred-year-old house," he huffs.

"Next time don't build a fancy, supersized bar with a beer tap out back, and we'll have plenty of money for new windows," I fire back.

The biggest problem is our priorities. Maybe it's because I'm a Taurus, or perhaps it's because I've lived in New York and Paris and L.A., or maybe it's because my dad was a builder so I grew up around model, showcase homes, but I like my house to look nice. I can't help it. Joe, on the other hand, thinks that aesthetics should always and forever take a backseat to practical matters. Which means when he discovered that half of the house still featured antiquated, unsafe knob-and-tube wiring (that's K&T to us builder's brats), he took the money I'd been hoping to spend on a new couch—a fancy one without claw marks and everything—and spent it on stupid electrical supplies. Crap you couldn't even *see*.

"You'll thank me when the house doesn't burn down," he insisted.

"If it burned down, could I get a new couch?" I asked.

He ignored me.

"So if it *doesn't* burn down, you're saying I am going to be living with this faded, stained, cat-clawed couch for the rest of my life?" I asked.

"They're *your* cats," he reminded me unnecessarily.

"This couch is twenty years old!" I repeated for the kazillionth time. "I just think we deserve a new one."

"And I think our daughters deserve to live in a safe home," he countered solemnly. Damn him! Whipping out the old children's-best-interest card. That was just low.

"Well, I hope they don't get poked with an old rusty spring from the fucking couch and get tetanus and have to have a limb amputated," I said, stalking from the room.

❝ At Least You're Not Married to Him ❞

When we were renovating our house, my husband was a complete obsessive-compulsive. Every decision took weeks. Decisions about tile, molding, trim, carpet, fixtures, windows, doorknobs, etc., were each painful episodes in our relationship. Ultimately, I would fold. If I had an opinion that varied from his, he would beat me down with questions about my reasoning. And it didn't end there; even after I

• • • • •

explained my rationale for my choices, he would suggest alternatives.
I couldn't deal with most of it and would just give in. It's easier to just
maintain the peace, right? We had agreed that I was going to be the
one to choose all the paint colors, but I wound up in the hospital with
severe abdominal pain in the middle of the project. As I writhed in pain
in the hospital, my husband and the contractor spread paint color
samples all over the bed and I made my selections. Seven days later
I was home, after two surgeries and missing a gallbladder—and my
husband had changed almost every single thing I'd chosen.

VICKY

Not even including the flip house, Joe and I have undertaken
hundreds of construction projects together. I'm not talking
about putting together a swing set or building a doghouse or
outfitting a pantry with new shelves (although we've done those
things, too). I'm talking about full-scale, live-in-it, multi-
month, add-a-room, move-a-wall, rent-a-jackhammer, wash-
dishes-in-the-bathtub-for-weeks endeavors. Our single
refrigerator lived in the garage for so long during one kitchen
remodel that I'd automatically shuffle sleepily outside every
morning to get the cream for my coffee even months after the
project was finally finished. Despite having more than a decade
of experience under our well-worn tool belts, our very last joint
venture—the building of the aforementioned and long-awaited
Zen retreat of a master bathroom in the house my husband
insists we are going to live in until we die—wasn't without its
challenges.

Every night after the kids went to bed, we'd meet in the
dirty, dusty space of our future sanctuary and debate the

infinite design possibilities. Before long, we dubbed our nightly meeting the "FUF," short for *Fuck-You Fest*—because invariably, no matter how hard we each tried to be flexible and understanding, that's pretty much what it was.

"You ready for the FUF?" he'd ask, handing me a very full wineglass. It's absolutely not a FUF without adult beverages.

"Bring it," I'd reply with mock antagonism, accepting the goblet and clinking it against his beer glass.

"Where do you want your main light switch?" Joe asked one night at the onset of the evening's FUF. Christ, he already sounded impatient, and we were just starting. I took a hearty swig of my wine.

"Right here," I said, carpenter's pencil poised to make a big fat X at the center point. I'd sneaked into the construction zone earlier and mentally arranged all of the hardware and outlets and accessories to determine the perfect placement. I knew that when Joe was working, he liked immediate answers, and I was ready. Plus when you grow up as a builder's daughter, you know how these things work.

"You can't have it there," Joe said plainly. "There's a pipe running behind that wall."

"Oh, okay," I stammered, unprepared for this kink in my carefully thought-out design.

I thought for a moment, surveying the space.

"I guess it could work here," I said, moving my pencil toward the only other even remotely acceptable spot on the wall. *Damn it all to hell, that's going to look like ass and it isn't a functional place for a light switch at all*, I thought to myself.

· · · · ·

But I was trying to be flexible—something that's not in my nature.

"Can't have it there, either," Joe replied, shaking his head. "Once I put the trim piece on, there won't be room."

I started to seethe.

"Well, why don't you just tell me where I *can* have it," I snapped.

"Pretty much right here," he said, indicating a seemingly arbitrary, centered-on-nothing point on the geometric plane that was the wall, in precisely the spot where I had planned to hang the robe hooks.

"Perfect," I said sarcastically.

"Where do you want your outlets?" he asked in all sincerity.

"Is that a trick question?" I demanded. "Because ideally I would like them centered over the backsplash."

"Yeah well, that's not to code," he replied.

"Then put them wherever the hell you want and thanks for asking," I muttered, throwing my pencil into a pile of sawdust and flouncing from the room. (I flounce from rooms a lot; it drives Joe crazy.)

"So we're done here?" he bellowed after me. I ignored him.

Pretty soon the weeks of individual, nightly FUFs started to blend into one giant festival of angry obscenities. The finished, fuzzy result was an eleven-month "discussion" about where I wanted the faucet handles and how I wanted the tile laid out and how high I wanted the top of the pony wall next to the toilet to be, all of these "discussions" were moot because there weren't actually any options. Nevertheless, Joe would ask and I would answer and he would proceed to tell me why what I wanted wasn't going to be possible at all and I'd fly off in a murderous rage, because that's what I do.

After a lengthy debate about which sort of light I *couldn't* have over the bathtub, I found and bought a darling petite crystal chandelier. It was absolutely perfect, practically made for the space.

"You can't have that over the tub," Joe said when I showed it to him.

"Why not?" I demanded, crushed.

"Because if you grab it when you're in the tub, you'll get electrocuted and die," he replied wryly.

"How could I grab it when I'm in the tub?" I asked. "I'll be sitting down!"

"Not when you're getting in and out," he insisted.

"You never said I couldn't have a chandelier there," I reminded him with a pout.

"Well, I'm saying it now," he answered.

Cue the exit music.

Eventually, every single detail had been hammered out and we could cross *master bathroom* off our endless remodel list. Remarkably enough, the finished product turned out quite beautifully, and I've gotten used to reaching behind a wall of damp towels and fluffy bathrobes to flip the light switches on and off. Most important, we're still married. I guess that's all that really matters. That and I got my lovely little crystal chandelier centered over the bathtub, and I'm still alive to tell about it.

• • • • •

CHAPTER SIXTEEN

Are You In or Are You Out?

Outside of a dog, a book is a man's best friend.
Inside of a dog it's too dark to read.

• GROUCHO MARX •

Joe and I are similar in that we both like carefully constructed systems and elaborately detailed plans. Go-with-the-flow, we are not. When I got pregnant the first time, I wondered how we would ever be able to agree on a name for our unborn future child. We had endless lists of possible monikers but nothing close to a consensus. He refused to consider Sebastian or Olive, and I put the kibosh on Jordan and Joe Jr. He scoffed when I added Hunter to the girl-name list, even after I agreed to consider Mokelumne for a boy (I'd just call him Mack). Finally I offered a suggestion, the best I could come up with besides drawing straws or paper-scissors-rock: If it was a girl, I got final say from a field of mutually acceptable choices, and if it was a boy, he'd get to make the ultimate call. It seemed fair enough and Joe agreed to it, but still I prayed for a girl. (I like to think that my two daughters are proof that God likes me and He listens.)

When we bought our first house together, I got a tiny taste of what the rest of my life was going to look like. Joe and I requested duplicate copies of every single piece of paper associated with the purchase and spent ridiculous amounts of money at Staples in order to painstakingly organize our individual forests of forms. It was an exhausting waste of time and resources, but we hadn't figured out a single record-keeping method we could co-manage without killing each other yet.

"Do you have a copy of the physical inspection report?" our real estate agent would ask us, and Joe and I would frantically tear through our respective color-coded binders, desperate to be the one who could locate the document first. We laughed together at our shared compulsiveness, but it was obvious that once we were *in* the house, there would have to be a mutually agreed-upon division of authority.

"How about I get inside and you get outside?" I suggested.

"What do you mean?" Joe asked, sounding appropriately suspicious.

"Well, we are going to have to make a million decisions about paint colors and furniture placement and fixture choices and landscaping and stuff," I explained. "I think we might avoid a lot of fights if each of us has a domain." I was waiting for him to point out that there would be a lot more decisions to be made *inside*, where we'd also be spending the majority of our time, but surprisingly he agreed. It was official: I would never have to even pretend to consider hanging a framed basketball-legend poster on my living room wall, or argue over a stupid wagon-wheel Roy Rogers garage-sale coffee table. I could hardly believe my good fortune.

"Please don't take down that tree in the back that I love," I added sweetly, referring to an adorable gumdrop-shape bit of greenery that was one of the first things I'd noticed when we looked at the house.

"That's not a tree, it's an overgrown shrub," he countered. "And it's going."

"Fine," I spat. "I hope you like your new pink bedroom."

Despite the rocky start to the inside/outside agenda, it has served us well over the years—with a few noteworthy exceptions.

One day after we'd been in our first home for a few months, I was strolling through an antiques store when I saw it: an architecturally stunning recycled garden station crafted entirely from vintage pieces. The top was a repurposed door into which a large hole had been lovingly cut to hold a weathered porcelain bowl. The back had decorative wrought iron corbels holding up a former drawer front enjoying a new life as a shelf. Best of all, the front of the reincarnated shelf was dotted with antique glass knobs—aged to the perfect shade of purple—where I could hang all of the garden tools I didn't have because technically I can't stand gardening, but I could always buy some tools, and besides, having this beautiful piece of furniture on the property might even inspire me to cultivate a green thumb after all. My lack of agricultural interest or inclination didn't diminish the appeal of this wonderfully lovely bit of recycled history in any way. The thing oozed more charm than any season's *Bachelor* ever has, and I wanted it desperately.

I have a husband now, I reminded myself. I was still in that giddy newlywed phase where I nearly wrecked my car a hundred times a day because I was busy staring at the way the sunlight glinted off of the princess-cut diamond on my left hand instead of looking at the road. *I should call Joe and ask him if I can buy it.* It was more of a formality than an actual request for permission; it was a sign of marital solidarity, my blossoming maturity, and a commitment to our new little team of two. Plus I'd need him to come down with his truck to pick it up and haul it home.

"No way," Joe said when I rang him from my cell phone and told him in painstaking detail about our new and utterly incomparable garden table.

"What?" I stammered. Maybe he hadn't heard me right, or perhaps he was answering another question I had asked earlier that day. I made my own money and I could buy whatever I wanted! Surely he understood this.

"I said, no, you are not buying that garden table," he repeated.

"But you haven't even *seen* it yet!" I argued, my head filled with a running tickertape of *You are not the boss of me.* "It's really amazing and it will look great on the back wall by the garage. I promise, you'll love it. Here, I'll take a picture with my phone and send it to you. Hang on."

"I don't need to see it," he interrupted, "because I don't want it and you're not buying it."

"You cannot tell me what I can and can't buy!" I shouted. *Not the boss, not the boss, so totally not the boss!* Other shoppers were staring at me like I was a petulant seven-year-old, but I didn't care. I couldn't believe I was having this conversation at all.

"Oh yes, I can," he said calmly. "It's *outside*."

I was furious. How dare he lord his domain over me like that! It was obvious that he was just saying no to be spiteful. He was a power-hungry SOB and I had *married* him. The finality of that decision hit me like a wrecking ball to the gut. For the first of what would be many, many fleeting moments over the next several years, I wholeheartedly hated him. The next time I wanted something I certainly wasn't going to ask, even if it meant I would have to carry the thing home on my back. I began crafting a detailed mental list of all the crap I was going to buy without requesting my husband's precious authorization first.

I stomped around the house for a few days and eventually the spat blew over. We didn't talk about the infamous garden table again for months, and then one day it just came up. I was still bitter—about losing out on it *and* that boss-of-me business—and I let him know it.

"Jenna, don't you understand?" Joe began. "You have great taste and our house always looks amazing. Whenever people come over they assume you are responsible for the way everything looks, and they're right. The outside is all I've got, and if you start putting your cutesy shit out there, too, I won't get any credit for that, either."

You really could have knocked me over with a sneeze. Blocking the garden station had had nothing whatsoever to do with power or money or just being an asshole for the sake of it; it was about pride, and I hadn't even considered that for a second. Sure, Joe could have told me his reasoning months ago and saved me an ulcerative amount of resentment—but we were both new to the soul-baring, sharing-everything aspect of marriage, and at least he was trying. I was both touched and repentant, and although I can't recall any specific details, I'm sure we had a nice go at it to celebrate our camaraderie.

" At Least You're Not Married to Him "

Every single day, my husband leaves his sock drawer open about half an inch. And every single day I close it all the way. I mean, how much extra effort does it take to close it the rest of the way if you're already closing it most of the way? I'm not exactly obsessive-compulsive; for example, I can tolerate quite a bit of dust, so it's not "my problem" that's to blame. It's just that it looks so messy left open and looks so neat closed. I don't want to even bring it up because it's not worth starting an argument over, so I shut my mouth, shake my head, and push that dad-gum drawer closed every single day.

JEANNE

As Chief Executive Officer of Exterior Operations, Joe gets to decide things like which plants will go where and whether we'll have a wild and eclectic English garden (my preference) or a neat, manicured yard (Joe's inclination) and when he will water the aforementioned jungles. On the latter front, I am convinced he has subconsciously created a watering reminder that coincides perfectly with my grocery shopping schedule. Because the joy of selecting, bagging, and lugging around hundreds of dollars of foodstuffs is compounded only by having to dart through a water park to get them safely to the front door.

I call his cell phone from mine.

"Can you please turn off the sprinklers?" I ask.

"Why?" he wants to know. "Where are you?"

"I am sitting in my car in front of the house and I have a trunk full of groceries," I explain.

"If you parked in the driveway like I always tell you that you should, you wouldn't have to run through the water," he says.

"Can we *not* have this particular discussion right now?" I demand. "Your truck is in the fucking driveway and I have ice cream melting out here." Nine hours later he saunters slothlike out front and gingerly flips off the sprinklers.

"I hope you didn't hurt yourself rushing out there like that," I mutter under my breath, struggling up the soggy path under a load of hateful grocery bags.

" At Least You're Not Married to Him "

My husband will grab items that he doesn't think are being used enough to justify having real estate *inside* the house and throw them into a box and label it KITCHEN STUFF despite that fact it has four of my books, a flower vase, a few of the kids' clothing items, a rubber spatula (the only kitchen item), and an old VHS tape. He then takes said box out to the garage and there it goes into a Garage Location Items/Witness Protection Program—never to be found again. Why, I ask?!

HEATHER

Sometimes Joe will try to goad me intentionally (or so it feels) by describing some elaborate yet hypothetical al fresco plan or another that he's considering. It took me an embarrassingly long time to learn to bite my tongue when he does this, but I've gotten quite good at not engaging—because I know that whatever it is that he's threatening to do is likely never going to happen.

Joe: "I was thinking about moving the hot tub up onto the back deck."

Former unenlightened me: "What? That's insane! It's utterly ridiculous! We paid a fortune to lay that foundation under where the tub is now, and the deck isn't even big enough so we'd have to add onto it, and do you remember how expensive that PVC decking was? And even if we did move it, do you really want to walk out the back door of our bedroom and step directly into—or have to step around—a behemoth hot tub? Oh, and once you built the new deck and moved the stupid tub then we'd have a lovely gaping cement hole out here by the patio, and what were you thinking of putting there? A nice tetherball pole, maybe?"

The discussion would continue to escalate exponentially,

with Joe systematically deflecting my arguments with some version of "God, you are so negative," and me getting angrier and more frustrated because I knew in my heart the discussion was pointless to begin with. *It's never going to happen,* I tried to remind myself. It's not that I ever had some great epiphany or anything that caused a shift; but after a decade or so of having one variation or another of the same futile argument, I just couldn't muster the enthusiasm for it anymore. The result is that those exchanges now look a whole lot more like this:

Joe: "I was thinking about moving the hot tub up onto the back deck."

New and improved me: "Great! Good luck with that."

During yet another endless remodel (honestly, we never stop; it's a sickness), we decided to close off a doorway that went from our kitchen to a tiny dining room and move it over a few feet. The existing doorway just wasn't functional at all, and closing it off would add a few feet of usable wall space to the room, even though we hadn't exactly earmarked a use for all of the newfound real estate. As Joe began to frame out the former doorway, I had a vision.

"Wait!" I practically bellowed into his ear.

"I'm right here, Jenna," he replied exasperatedly. Joe seems to think I have a volume problem when I speak, and he is therefore constantly reminding me of his proximity. It drives me nuts because can I help it if I'm half Italian?

"Sorry," I said, trying to be nice because I was about to ask him to do something for me. "I was just thinking that we should leave the old frame intact and you could drywall the back and then build some little, shallow shelves."

"Shelves for what?" he demanded.

"To put stuff on," I told him. Wasn't this obvious?

"What kind of stuff?" he asked slowly, suspiciously.

"I don't really know yet, but I'm sure I'll think of something," I assured him.

"I'm not going to build you an entire wall of shelves just so that you can put a bunch of shit on them," he informed me.

"Well, why else would you build shelves, then?" I asked, trying to tone down the sarcasm that I know he can't stand.

"I just mean if they're going to be *functional* in any way, I'll be happy to build you some shelves," he insisted.

"Honey, they're *shelves*," I said patiently. "Shelves are designed for the singular purpose of *putting shit on*."

"Do you mean decorative shit or functional shit?" he asked. He wasn't even kidding.

"Does it matter?" I demanded.

"Absolutely," he replied.

"So if I promise I'll only store a bunch of unsightly, *functional* crap on there—maybe the blender parts and an assortment of sippy cup lids and that ugly-ass serving platter one of your friends gave us for our wedding—then you'll build me the shelves?" I asked.

"Yup," he said.

"Deal," I lied. Once I had those shelves in place, I knew there really would be no further discussion. You know, because they were *inside*, in my domain.

• • • • •

" At Least You're Not Married to Him "

My husband has piles of stuff everywhere, and they all have to be at right angles to each other. There are books, CDs, and papers on every available surface in our house, and nothing is in any kind of order, but everything is very neatly piled and exactly perpendicular. If I need to find something, it's hopeless to please him because there's no way I can pile things up as neatly as he wants them. Also, he rotates the following items in the cabinets or drawers, as the case may be, so they "wear evenly": socks, underwear, silverware, and plates. It's almost funny if you don't let it get to you.

JANE

Joe is better than me at many, many things: snowboarding, working the TiVo, grilling meat, mowing the lawn, carrying cases of soda and tubs of cat litter, playing tennis, parallel parking, and fixing computer glitches instantly leap to mind. But the thing I kick his ass in when it comes to our respective domestic spheres is finesse. See, when Joe decides it's time to alter something outside, he tends to announce it in a very direct, definitive way. "The ivy's coming out this weekend," he'll say, hands on his hips, the singular raised brow and puffed-up posture together screaming *I double-dog-dare you to try to talk me out of it.* This of course makes me immediately defensive and argumentative, which is rarely a good starting point. In other areas of his life, Joe has learned the art of subtle diplomacy. Just last night, in fact, he asked, "What would I have to do for you in return if you let me go to the Lakers-Celtics playoff game with Brian this weekend?" Not,

"Guess what? I'm going on an expensive boys' getaway in two days and leaving you alone to deal with the kids," or even, "Can I go on an expensive boys' getaway in two days and leave you alone to deal with the kids?" This is because the man I married is smart enough at least in this situation to know that careful wording that includes a promise of future payoff is going to earn him a much more favorable response. But when it comes to his beloved exterior, the same guy can be a bit of a dictator.

Now consider my approach. I've gotten away with some pretty extravagant interior splurges over the years by mastering the delicate, dying art of combining patience with subtlety. I start by planting a few seeds, which usually entails extolling a thing's *functional* value, over and over, until Joe wholeheartedly believes that we need it as badly as I want it. The wine bar in our kitchen is a perfect example. If you asked him whose idea it was to buy the gigantic, overpriced, six-piece wall-length Pottery Barn unit, he'd probably say "Ours." And that's just what I want him to think.

As soon as I saw it on the cover of the catalog, I knew that wine bar would wind up in our kitchen. We'd just moved yet another wall and, serendipitously, the bar was exactly the right size to fill it; so much so in fact that it would practically look like a custom built-in. I was foaming at the mouth for it but I didn't go out and buy it or even ask Joe what he thought. I simply ripped the page from the catalog and taped it to the wall.

"What's this?" Joe asked immediately upon noticing the temporary artwork.

"Oh, it's something I saw that I thought might work on

• • • • •

that wall, but it's pretty expensive and I'm not sure it would even work anyway," I replied.

"Why not?" he asked.

"It's not the cabinet space, because it's got plenty and that would certainly be nice added storage, like you're always saying we need," I said carefully. "And it holds a ton of wine, so we could move the boxes out of the garage that are constantly getting in your way. But I just don't know if it will fit . . ."

"Well, did you measure the space?" he asked, leaping into handyman mode.

Who did he think he was dealing with, some kind of rookie? Of course I measured the space and it couldn't be a more perfect fit. It wasn't really *going to be this easy, was it?*

"I was going to," I told him. "I just wanted to get an idea of how it might look there." I know, lying to your husband is terrible, but that wasn't technically a lie because I *was* going to measure it—and then I did. Besides, if I looked too eager, I knew I'd never get the thing. That was where the patience came in.

Within seconds Joe had the measuring tape out and was appraising the space.

"Wow, Jenna, this would fit *perfectly* here," he announced.

"Really?" I replied with mock shock. "Because if you think so, it *is* on sale but only for a couple of days. Were you thinking of ordering it right away?" Did you see how I did that? How I turned it on a dime and now the whole thing was Joe's idea in the first place so he couldn't even argue it? I know, I'm brilliant.

Despite a few similarly manipulative little stunts, for the most part I think I am both respectful and gracious in the way I handle the "inside operations." I might replace a few faded throw pillows or buy a new vase at Target without running the transaction by my husband in advance, but more often than not I seek Joe's input before making a major change or purchase. I consider his towering height when hanging mirrors so that I don't accidentally position them so low that he can't see his own forehead in them. I narrow curtain and paint and bedding options down to a handful I can live with and then ask whether he has a favorite. (Sometimes he even does.) I try to remember to fawn appreciatively when he plants this or prunes that or otherwise busts his ass trying to spruce up the outside. For the privilege of having the house look exactly how I want it *and* never having to mow my own lawn, I figure it's the least I can do.

CHAPTER SEVENTEEN

Vacation:
All I Ever Wanted

Most travel is best of all in the anticipation
or the remembering; the reality has more
to do with losing your luggage.

• REGINA NADELSON •

In a former life—well, it was technically this one, but it feels like a different one altogether because I was young and wrinkle-free and rarely carried snack-size bags dusted with pretzel crumbs plus a dozen or more crayons in my purse—I did a lot of travel writing. One of the great perks of travel writing is that you get to see the world and also you get a ton of free shit. When you are gainfully employed in this capacity, generous companies eagerly furnish you with first-class plane tickets, sprawling presidential suites, petrifying paragliding lessons, and as many gourmet meals as you can shovel into your cake hole in the hopes that you might recommend their resort/ airline/cruise ship/death-defying activity to three or four mil- lion of your closest friends. For the very reasonable price of a smile and an assignment on official magazine letterhead, I have

• • • • •

scaled walls of rock in Utah and mountains of ice in Colorado, plumbed the depths of the Kauai coast with a scuba tank on my back, and practiced yoga poses on a blindingly white beach somewhere in the West Indies. Getting paid to pretend you're a rich tourist is a sweet gig all around, save for occasionally having to sacrifice an hour or two of your critical "research" time to dine with an annoying PR person.

Call me spoiled (I admit! I was!), but after you've experienced the VIP vacation treatment, it's hard to go back to the budget-traveler lifestyle. Especially when your new husband thinks that *camping* actually falls into the vacation category.

"Do we have an air mattress?" I asked, surveying the towering piles of camping gear, every last bit of which seemed to be the same shade of camo-puke green. I'd been camping exactly once in my life, as a child, and the only thing I remembered about the experience was the neat orange shag carpet that lined the roof of the Winnebago. I had dabbled in Brownies but didn't quite make it to Girl Scouts, and I had never slept in a tent in my life. You could leave me alone in a room with nothing but two sticks for all of eternity and it would never occur to me to rub them together and see what happened. I'd said yes to camping easily, because I hadn't really given the idea any thorough thought. Once I had, I have to admit that the knowledge that the only thing between me and the God-knows-what that was lurking in the forest was a flimsy sheet of nylon unnerved me more than a little bit. Plus, what if it was cold? What if it was hot? What if it rained? And how *did* a bear shit in the woods? But I was trying to be game, so I purposely employed the "royal we" construction there, because we were married now—and apparently *we* were campers.

"We have inflatable sleeping mats," Joe replied.

"Can I see them?" I asked, trying really hard not to sound too skeptical.

Joe handed me a tiny bag.

"What's this?" I asked.

"Our sleeping mats," he said.

I looked at the sack in my hand. It was smaller than the lingerie bag I take on a long weekend away.

"I'm going to get an air mattress," I informed him.

When we were all packed up, the truck looked like it belonged to a family of nine about to embark on a cross-country expedition. We had lanterns and propane tanks, firewood and bear spray (Dear God, we had *bear spray*?), bug repellent and biodegradable soap, hiking boots and hydrocortisone, a cooler full of booze and a massive three-room tent we had affectionately dubbed the Taj Mahal. Oh, and a king-size pillow-top air mattress that I planned to lovingly envelop in our butteriest sheets and top with a fluffy down comforter.

"You're not serious," Joe demanded when I'd set up the Taj's master suite. The luxurious bed was flanked on either side by a pair of upturned crates serving as nightstands; on top of the crates stood matching lanterns. Our pillows from home perched happily at the bed's head; there was a small rug at the foot of it all for our dog, Sam, to curl up on.

• • • • •

"What's wrong?" I asked, hurt. I thought the whole thing was impossibly cozy.

"We're *camping*, Jenna," Joe reminded me unnecessarily.

"Oh, I didn't realize that meant we had to be miserably uncomfortable and sleep on a bed of rocks and freeze our asses off," I pouted.

"It doesn't mean *that*," he replied, sounding more than a little defensive. "It's just that it doesn't really feel like camping if you bring the whole goddamned house with you."

"So it *does* mean that!" I accused. "You think it's a more *authentic camping experience* if we are cold and uncomfortable and drink disgusting instant coffee and eat beans out of a can instead of steak on a real plate. Admit it."

"That's not true," he said, utterly without conviction. And then the last part of my statement seemed to register. "Did you bring plates? And *steaks*?"

"Of course I brought plates and steaks!" I howled. "And Starbucks coffee and half-and-half and homemade lemon scones. Do you have a problem with that?"

"You're unbelievable," Joe said, shaking his head.

I was unbelievable? Unbelievable!

After roughing it up and down the California coast, I have to say that one of my favorite rustic retreats is a central California hotspot called El Capitan Canyon, conveniently located about twenty minutes from my front door. Technically a campground, the canyon claims on its website to cater to "luxury campers," which if I have to classify myself as any sort of camper, that's the one I'd choose. You're welcome to pitch a tent at El

Cap, as it's known, but why would you when you can bunk in a charming two-room cedar cabin that features a fireplace, full-size refrigerator, wraparound deck, enormous soaking tub, and a handy gas grill? Before you say "What's the point?" let me draw your attention to the fact that the deluxe cabins have skylights *and* outdoor showers *and* huge glass French doors, so there are ample opportunities to enjoy all of nature's wondrous bounties that surround your pastoral pad. Plus the cabins don't have honor bars or room service, which means you have to remember to bring your own Pringles and smoked almonds, and if you forget your corkscrew, there's no bellhop on the property to rescue you, so it's not like you're staying at the Bellagio or anything.

"Do me a favor," my sister said after I sent her the link to El Cap's website and told her we'd be spending two nights there during an upcoming visit. "Call it 'staying in the cabins,' not *camping*."

"Okay, but why?" I asked.

"Because if my husband and kids think you can camp like this, I'll never be able to get them to sleep in a tent again," she explained.

It took the better part of a decade to help Joe revise his camping definition to look a little more like mine, and on more than one group outing we have sat hungrily watching our friends inhale their hot dogs and beans while waiting for our prosciutto-stuffed chicken breasts and marinated portobello mushrooms to cook. But in the morning, it is always *them* asking *us* if we can spare a cup of French roast or a splash of cream; never the other way around.

" At Least You're Not Married to Him "

My husband and I travel quite a bit, and he can endure discomfort much better than I can. Because of this I have had quite a few meltdowns, including one very famous one at Kensington Palace when I had had enough walking and wanted to take a cab; you know, a car you pay money for? My husband had a big problem with cabs . . . until my meltdown in front of Princess Diana's palace. It was loud and quite legendary. Now he knows that wherever we are, if I say the C-word he starts whistling.

RANDEE

Regardless of whether you are pitching a tent or shacking up in deluxe accommodations, vacations are fun! You get to see the world, take a break from your hectic life at home (although you will have your laptop and your BlackBerry and your iPad along so that you can still feel "connected" to the home you couldn't wait to get away from), enjoy unfamiliar cuisine, and fight in an entirely unfamiliar setting over new and different things. If you go somewhere exotic—and by exotic I mean anywhere the road signs aren't also written in English or they drive on a different side of the road than you're used to—the opportunities to claw at one another's eyeballs are virtually endless.

Over the years Joe and I have defaulted to pretty static travel roles: He is the pilot and I am the navigator. And I have to say we are both extremely competent in our positions. Nevertheless, because he won't let me buy a new car that has that sultry gal who tosses out handy navigational tips living inside the dashboard, there is unfailingly a midjourney moment (or seventeen) that looks like this:

JOE: "You're going to tell me when I'm supposed to exit, right?"

ME: "Yup, it's coming up here pretty quickly."

JOE: "Just tell me when to exit."

ME: "Soon, so get ready."

JOE: "Which side is the exit on?"

ME: "What am I, telepathic? Am I supposed to have a 3-D GPS tracking chip in my brain? Hang on a second; let me try to visualize the exit . . . Ooh, there it is!"

JOE: "You're funny."

ME: "You just passed the exit! I told you, *there it is*! What are you doing? Why didn't you get off?"

JOE: "I thought you were *fucking visualizing* it. If I get off at the next exit, can I flip around and get back on the highway?"

ME: "Are you serious?"

JOE: "Give me the map."

ME: "The small roads aren't *on* the map."

JOE: "Well, why did you buy that stupid map then? There were thirty maps to choose from and you picked the one that doesn't have any actual roads on it. Perfect."

ME: "So it's my fault you missed your exit?"

JOE: "If you say so."

ME: "Oh my God, I hate you."

JOE: "Right back atcha, babe."

" At Least You're Not Married to Him "

Let me just start by saying my husband and I have very different definitions of the word *vacation*. For starters, he is a resort guy. His happy vacation is Hawaii or Palm Desert, whereas mine is New York City or San Miguel de Allende. I go away to see new cool cultural and art things; he goes away to relax and play golf. As I write this, we are in Palm Springs. He is on the balcony, which overlooks the eleventh hole (that's a golf term), and he's watching live, in-person, amateur golf. How fucking boring is that? Not to use a cliché or anything, but watching paint dry has *got* to be more interesting than watching golf. I've been referring to our balcony as the Golf Channel. I think he could sit there all day. He talks to me about golf (players, tournaments, shots), and he'll even say "I'm boring you, aren't I?" Of course he's boring me. Bugging me? No. Boring me? Totally.

KIM

Although we almost always spar when we're en route somewhere, usually we are speaking again by the time we reach our destination. This is handy because it absolutely takes two people to corral the kids and collect the bags and dole out the dollar bills to the fourteen people who are patiently waiting for a tip before you've even put the car in park.

"So what do you want to do?" I always ask as soon as Joe has finished unpacking his bags. Yeah, he's that guy who fully moves into a hotel room immediately upon entering it, even if he's going to be there for only one night. He always insists on taking the side of the bed nearest the door, too, an extremely chivalrous move born of the watertight "the axe murderers will have to get by me to get to you" argument.

"We're doing it," he replies, stretching out on the bed and clicking on the TV. "Grab me a beer out of the honor bar, will you?"

One of the things I love most about my husband is how generous he is on vacation. Not that he's ever stingy at home, because he absolutely isn't, but he goes from being the poster boy for practical, conservative spenders everywhere to Drinks-Are-on-Me Dude, and it's one of the best reasons to go through the hassle of going somewhere besides vacation sex.

"You want it?" he'll ask when he sees me fondling some trinket or another in the hotel gift shop. "Get it!"

"No, I don't want to split an appetizer," he'll say as we scan our dinner menus. "Get your own. And save room for dessert!"

"Wow, they actually charge fourteen dollars for a can of macadamia nuts," he'll remark, tipping back the diminutive container and downing at least eleven dollars' worth of nuts in a single swallow.

Even though we fight and probably because he lets me buy a lot of stuff, Joe and I have taken some amazing trips over the years and have had pretty great travel luck. We rarely lose our luggage, we've never regretted not forking over for the rental car company's added collision insurance, and I only *once* had to go to the ER in a foreign country for a shot in the ass after waking up with what I was convinced was a brain aneurysm but turned out to be vertigo. Our family did spend a miserable week stuck in a cabin in Tahoe when a nasty stomach bug tore its way through our collective intestines, but we were staying with friends so at least we had someone to bring us Gatorade and fresh sheets and towels.

> ## " At Least You're Not Married to Him "
>
> My husband is lazy, plain and simple. He is a travel writer and gets a ton of free things from his trips. He brings them home and leaves them lying around. These free things are not items that he wishes to keep; he is just too lazy to throw or give them away. I have offered to discard some of them, but he is particular and says that he would like to do it himself. But he has never hit me or cheated on me, and in spite of his annoying habit of being lazy, he sometimes carries my heavy bags up the stairs of our apartment after long trips.
>
> LAURA

At the risk of stating the blaringly obvious, taking a trip requires a colossal amount of work, and I'm not even including the years you have to toil away at a soul-numbing job to make enough money to afford one. I'm talking about everything that leads up to that moment when your bags are packed and waiting by the front door, the mail has been put on hold, the gas has been properly shut off, and you are *out of there*! Just as soon as you find your fucking keys.

I have a pre-vacation to-do checklist that spans several days and includes admittedly ridiculous things like "pack clothes."

It's not as if I've ever found myself checking into a hotel room and had the porter ask if he could help me with my bags only to discover that I had forgotten to pack any. Having this task on my list, however, provides another handy item I can cross off when it's finished, resulting in a false sense of accomplishment that I rather enjoy.

If you're anything like me, here's how the pre-trip preparations look. Let's start by assuming that the destination is a given, for example the annual trip to see the in-laws in Florida. (Because if you're going away purely for sport, you can factor in an additional 357 glitches, issues, and arguments such as a debate over the merits of really experiencing the rain forest versus not having wireless Internet access from your room.) Picking a date is fun, if you enjoy spending days on end trying to juggle work and school and soccer and gymnastics schedules. Just when you think you've got the ideal itinerary, you remember your husband's weekly, nonnegotiable basketball game, which means you can never be anywhere but home on a Thursday night. Ever. You settle for the backup itinerary, the one that has you traveling at unholy hours with a total of four five-hour layovers and two plane changes—which you loathe because you hate flying, especially the taking off and landing parts—but what can you do? You add *Get Xanax prescription refilled* to your list.

The actual packing takes you several days, because (a) you are packing not just for yourself but for everyone in the entire house (although at some point you will either boycott packing for your husband for obvious reasons, or quit inviting him on your trips), and (b) everyone in the entire house is a high-maintenance pain in the ass. This one can't crap without her daily dose of Miralax and that one has allergies that require different daytime and nighttime medications. They both need hair ties and Band-Aids and water shoes and sunblock and a noise machine to sleep to and do you think they can actually agree on a single toothpaste flavor? You should be so lucky.

And you haven't even cracked your *own* suitcase yet. Oh sweet Jesus, it's overwhelming, isn't it? First you have to try on every single outfit you own, because even if you wore something just yesterday, there's no guaranteeing that it will fit you today, and besides you need to be *wearing* it in order to assemble the proper accessories and undergarments. You will pack all of your staple, uniform, go-to pieces, and then you will continue to stuff random items of clothing into the suitcase, including several that have been hanging in your closet for decades and still have the tags on them because *hey, you never know, they might be perfect in Florida!* When your suitcase is bursting at the seams, you will realize that you forgot to pack your panties. Or did you? Shit, you can't remember so it all has to come out again anyhow. It turns out that you *did* pack the unmentionables after all, but now that the whole lot is spread out across your bed, it all seems out of style and seasonally inappropriate and wrong, wrong, wrong. You used to have cute, trendy clothes, didn't you? You would almost swear on your life that you did. But you don't have the time or money to shop for a new wardrobe before you leave, so you angrily shove it all back in. This time you do forget the panties.

● ● ● ● ●

The clothing part taken care of (sort of), you will start amassing the rest of the stuff that you can't live without for two or twelve days. You always start with tampons, especially if you are going anywhere near a beach or a pool, as you will absolutely get your period just as soon as you are officially en route to your destination, even if you are nowhere near due and have an ovulatory cycle you can otherwise set your watch by. However many tampons you think you need, double it and you'll probably only have to make one emergency drugstore run on your trip. The must-haves are staggering. You pack three books (that you'll never crack), five magazines (that you'll have finished skimming before you board your plane), and an eighteen-pack of condoms (if you're lucky you'll use one). You can't sleep without earplugs, you can't figure out how to go anywhere with fewer than four pairs of shoes—sneakers, flip-flops, heels, and casual walking shoes are the rock-bottom bare minimum—and your humidity-control plan for your hair (two different types of gel, one ionic blow dryer, paddle brush, round brush, the as-seen-on-TV ceramic tourmaline straightening iron that has changed your life and you wouldn't think twice about trying to rip from an armed robber's grip, a bottle of silicone serum, and an assortment of holding sprays ought to do the trick) takes up an entire carry-on bag all on its own.

You scan your list. You've lined up a house sitter and arranged for the mail and newspaper to be put on hold. You have left checks for the dog walker and the gardener and double-checked the timers on the lights and sprinklers. You have created a snappy yet vague "out of the office" e-mail auto-reply, unplugged all of your small appliances, watered your plants inside and out, and hauled your trash and recycling cans to the curb. You checked the car's fluid levels and tire pressure and have your printed boarding passes in hand. You make one final sweep of the place to make sure you haven't overlooked anything. You haven't. Of course you haven't.

"Ready to go, honey?" you shout, because now that you think of it you have no idea where your husband is.

He materializes out of nowhere. "Yeah, just give me a sec while I throw some stuff in a bag," he says.

Bon voyage!

. . .

CHAPTER EIGHTEEN

He Can't Help It, He's a Guy

See, the problem is that God gives men a brain and a penis,
and only enough blood to run one at a time.

• ROBIN WILLIAMS •

My husband, Joe, was raised to be a consummate gentleman,
to open doors for women and stand when one enters a room.
He has impeccable table manners, shines his shoes when they
get a little scuffed, and hardly ever forgets to apply deodorant.
With all of this going for him, you can understand why it still
shocks me when he delivers this ridiculous-to-me request:
"Show me your boobs."

Really? Show you my boobs? While I'm scrambling eggs or
struggling into a pair of jeans or tearing through the house
trying to find the cordless phone that's ringing somewhere,
suddenly you would very much like to see my breasts? And
you think that I will think this is a fine idea, too, and just whip
them out for you? Once he even offered me fifty bucks for a
peek, which I probably shouldn't have taken, but come on, it

. . . . .

was *fifty bucks*. The whole thing is so absurd it's almost comical, especially when I occasionally give in (trust me, when you live with it every bloody day, eventually it wears you down, even when there's not cash involved) and he actually looks as giddy as Charlie when he won that ticket to the wonderful, whimsical Wonka factory. *My* boobs do that to him. Like I said, comical.

"Aren't you glad that I'm still so attracted to you?" he'll ask when I express my disdain for the frequent peep-show demands.

"Well, sure, yeah, of course," I tell him. "It's just that I honestly don't get why you need to look at my sad, deflated, postbreastfeeding breasts all of the time."

"I can't help it," he replies. "I'm a guy."

Indeed, a recent study (because we needed a *study* for this) out of New Zealand's University of Wellington found that when men are shown photos of a woman, nearly a solid half of them will check out her breasts first. One third of the fellows will home in immediately on her waist and hips, while less than one in five gentlemen is even remotely concerned whether she has a face that looks like Rocky's after Apollo Creed beat up on that shit. Some speculate that boob gazing is evolution at work, a manifestation of a man's innate attraction to these twin symbols of fertility and youth, which clearly is a bunch of bullshit because like I said, Joe really likes looking at *my* breasts. (Or maybe it's just that they're the only ones he has any likelihood of seeing without an embarrassing pay-per-view charge showing up on the cable bill.) So because most of the time I rather like being married to him even though he can be a juvenile pain in my ass, I try to let him have this small thrill every once in a while.

The problem is that *looking* at them is rarely enough. No sooner have I dropped top than the next request rolls in.

"Can I touch them?" he pleads.

I have tried innumerable times to explain to him that the sudden copping of a feel does nothing for me. In fact, it does worse than nothing; it makes me want to recoil and run screaming in the opposite direction. It's essentially anti-foreplay. He knows this, but he insists that he can't help himself.

"So you can still thoroughly enjoy feeling me up, knowing that I can't stand it in this context?" I ask.

"Totally," he insists.

Day in and day out, Joe finds any and every opportunity to brush his hands across my baby feeders. He sneaks up behind me as I'm brushing my teeth or surveying the refrigerator contents for an acceptable snack option and cups them from beneath. Even a nice morning hug by the coffeepot habitually ends with a double hand-slide up the sides of my torso, fingers lingering just a little too long around the bosom region. The funny part is he actually thinks he's being sly when he does this. I always see it coming and have mastered some pretty clever—and effective—deflective moves of my own. To watch us you'd think we were a pair of dancing octopuses with all of the skim-block-slide-stop business. When subtlety doesn't work, I usually resort to a calm, rational request.

· · · · ·

"Would you get your fucking hands off of my boobs?" I command.

"I can't help it," the refrain goes. "I'm a guy."

" At Least You're Not Married to Him "

The worst, most ridiculous, annoying, frustrating, brazen, pompous, chauvinistic, childish, and idiotic thing that my husband does to me— so often that it has become habit—is flick my boobs. Actually it is usually just one boob. The "flick" is a little upward stroke of his index finger delivered right under my somewhat sagging postbaby breast. Of course he thinks this is hysterical and endearing at the same time. Needless to say, I enjoy it about as much as he would enjoy a flick of his testicles. Telling him to stop at this point only fuels the fire. Plus I refuse to give him the satisfaction of even acknowledging the flick; it's the Pavlovian response that seems to keep him going. We've been married eleven years and have two daughters. I expect to endure about 7,382 more flicks from this otherwise very loving and handsome man.

CARRIE

Would that it were only my breasts that had such magnetic qualities, but apparently my ass is also utterly irresistible. (I know, I should be flattered. If you've seen my flat, shapeless, pancake-like ass, you know this to be true. And on an intellectual level I guess I *am* flattered. But unfortunately that doesn't make the pawing any more pleasant.) He'll swat at it, cup it, slap it, snap his towel at it, play air drums on it, jiggle it, and pat-pat it (oh my precious, heavenly God, the *worst*) whenever the opportunity presents itself, which is often, seeing as we live together and everything. And then there's the morning poke.

An inveterate early bird, most days I leap from our cozy marital bed at some unholy hour and launch into what Joe has dubbed my whirling-dervish routine. I plump pillows, pack lunches, check e-mail, peruse Facebook, shuffle papers, dispose of the many cheese wrappers that are undoubtedly still scattered about the house from Joe's midnight snack attack the night before, and of course Tweet about the whole exciting affair. Eventually I whirl back into our bedroom, coffee cup in hand, ready to scoop up laundry and eager to make the damned bed already.

"Come cuddle with me," Joe says sleepily, every single time.

"Can't," I tell him. "I'm on a roll."

"You're always on a roll," he replies. "Come on, come cuddle with me."

Occasionally I oblige, setting my coffee cup on my nightstand and reluctantly tucking back into bed. I try not to squirm too much.

Fifteen seconds later: "You feel great," Joe tells me, his pair of hot paws heading on autopilot up my top.

"Thanks," I reply, getting wiggly.

"Wanna get naked?" he asks.

"Can I take a rain check on that?" I ask him, eyeing the laundry basket in the corner.

"Come on, it'll be quick," he pleads.

"Hard to turn down such a compelling offer, but I have

stuff to do," I say, trying to roll away from him, an impossible task seeing as he has my entire lower body in a scissors grip.

"Why are you always so agro in the morning?" he asks, hurt, clamping down even harder.

"I am *agro* because I was in the middle of doing something productive, and also after thirteen years of having you stick your boner in my ass-crack under the guise of 'cuddling' it's starting to get a little old," I say into my pillow.

"I can't help it," he says, hungry octopus hands all over my body, desperate for one final brush against my boobs. "I'm a guy."

" At Least You're Not Married to Him "

If my husband is walking behind me or I am bending over gardening, in the fridge, whatever, he has to brush up against my butt. I guess I am glad he still likes it, but it is irritating.

L.H.

You know what's funny to me? That the ass-grabbing, gas-passing, breast-fondling man I married gets absolutely bent out of shape when I talk on the phone. Of all the potentially annoying wifely sins I could commit, personally I think this one is pretty benign. To hear Joe bitch about it though, you'd think I walked around banging a gong and singing "I'm Henry the Eighth, I Am" in a bad British accent all of my waking hours.

"Who are you talking to?" he'll ask in an excruciatingly

loud voice that my friend Kim, with whom I am trying to have a nice chat, could probably hear from Colorado *without* the phone.

"Kim," I reply, covering the mouth part of the receiver with my hand and foolishly trying to hide the fact that I'm having two conversations at once.

"What's new with Kim?" he'll ask, ignoring one small detail, which is that I am *still on the phone with Kim*.

"I'm trying to find that out," I inform him, marching out of the room. Of course he follows me. If I throw myself down on the bed, suddenly he gets the urge to organize his sock drawer. If I go out to the back patio, he abruptly remembers that he has some straightening up to do outside. The only place that is safe and sacred is my walk-in closet, which is dark and windowless but otherwise delightful and nearly soundproof. You'd think that the fact that when I'm on the phone at least I am blabbering *to someone else* would be a great relief to my husband, but still it bugs him, and trying to figure out why has proven pointless.

ME: "Why do you hate it so much when I talk on the phone?"

JOE: "*When* you talk on the phone? You're always talking on the phone. And you are right, I totally hate it."

ME: "I'm not talking on the phone right now, am I?"

JOE: "Well, practically always."

ME: "I don't talk on the phone at dinner, and I don't talk on the phone in bed, and I don't talk on the phone in

the shower or bath, and I don't talk on the phone at
work—except for work stuff—and I don't talk on the
phone while we're having sex—"

JOE: "Hey, can we have sex right now?"

ME: "Sorry, I have to make a phone call."

It's really not as if the phone is glued to my ear 24/7. I talk
on the phone when I'm doing other, mindless things, like
unloading the dishwasher or folding laundry or putting away
yet another load of groceries or doing my tedious portion of
the meal preparations. Invariably as I am doing one of these
things, Joe enters the room and sees me cradling the cordless
receiver with my shoulder.

JOE: *[dramatic, disappointed sigh]*

ME *[into phone]*: "Hang on a sec—"

ME AGAIN *[covering the mouthpiece with my hand and giving
Joe the horse-look I have perfected where I pull my ears back
until they are practically touching behind my head; it's a
talent]*: "What? Do you urgently need something from
me or can you wait until I am finished with my call?"

JOE: "You're never finished with your call. You just call
someone else."

ME: "Then I guess I'll never talk to you again. It was nice
knowing you."

It pisses me off that he gets prickly when I'm on the phone
because to me the implication is that I should be sitting around

waiting for the moment he is available to generously grace me with his presence. He can't multitask, so therefore I shouldn't. (Actually when *he's* on the phone he paces back and forth the entire time—typically in whatever room I happen to be occupying at the moment—which is super relaxing to watch and doesn't make me want to trip him or anything.) Perhaps the most ironic bit is that when I eventually wrap up my conversation and hang up the phone—and I know you saw this coming—he has absolutely nothing to say to me.

ME: "What did you need?"

JOE: "Nothing specific, I just wanted to talk to you."

ME: "So shoot."

JOE: "Never mind."

ME: "Are you serious? I hung up because I thought you needed to talk to me."

JOE: "Well, now I don't."

ME: "You are absolutely impossible, do you know that?"

JOE: "I can't help it. I'm a guy."

" At Least You're Not Married to Him "

My husband has a gas problem. I don't know where it all comes from and if this is normal, but he will pull one butt cheek for these releases of trapped air—maybe to increase the chances of it being silent? It's not like you can't see what he is doing.

LYNN

• • • • •

Even though my husband is a blameless, testosterone-driven being, I really do love him a lot. And also sometimes—in particular when I'm trying to send him a sly, subliminal message—I wish he would get a fucking clue.

Once again, evidently it's not his fault. Studies have shown that women experience significantly more "communication events" per day than men do, referring to those subtle body language gestures we use to convey volumes to one another without saying a single word. A gal can lift her eyebrow a millimeter and wordlessly convey to her friend, *Holy shit, I cannot believe that skank had the nerve to show up here with* him *wearing* that *when everyone knows what she did* without even a smirk. Being a man, my husband is utterly unable to give *or* receive anything resembling a covert message. It would be bad enough if he chose to simply ignore me when I'm trying to telepathically communicate something urgent like, *Oh my God, check out the huge fake boobs on that chick over there* or *You may or may not have a large visible booger in your left nostril.* Instead, he has this thing he does whenever I try to whisper something to him or give him a knowing look or heaven forbid attempt to employ some other sly way of catching his attention in public.

"Did you just kick me under the table?" he'll ask full volume, a mere second after I have done precisely that, even when I've gone to the great trouble of looking elsewhere and appearing utterly spellbound by a lint speck on the tablecloth.

"What?" I reply, trying to sound shocked and feeling a band of sweat beads popping out above my upper lip that I'm certain are visible from the next zip code. "Of *course* I didn't kick you under the table. Why would I kick you under the table? I mean, if I *did* kick you, it was purely accidental, so if you felt a kick I'm sorry if I accidentally did it." At this point, I have a great urge to kick him, although his shin wouldn't be my first target.

When we are finally alone, it's the same exchange every time.

"I can't believe you called me out!" I shout at my husband. Needless to say, I have never had to have this conversation with a single girlfriend.

"You know I hate it when you kick me under the table," he says, not even the tiniest bit contrite.

"What is the *big stinking deal*? I was just trying to get your attention," I try to explain. "It's not like I'm round-housing you with a pair of golf spikes or anything."

"Well, I don't like it," he pouts. "It makes me uncomfortable. Whispering makes me uncomfortable. Your horse ears make me uncomfortable."

"I thought we were supposed to be a team," I remind him. "What is so wrong with me wanting to share a little secret look or an inside joke with you sometimes?"

"Jenna, can't you think about something—anything—and then just enjoy that thought and keep it to yourself?" he asks.

"Well, of course not!" I reply. "The whole point of having a thought is to share it."

"Oh my God," he says, and I can practically see the lightbulb going on above his head. "You really think that, don't you?"

"Well, of course I do," I huff.

He looks at me with genuine bewilderment, a mystified Martian stumbling across unfamiliar, rocky Venusian terrain.

"I can't help it," I add. "I'm a girl."

"I noticed," he replies with a lecherous leer, all thoughts of shin kicks forgotten. "Can I see your boobs?"

CHAPTER NINETEEN

· · ·

You're Merely the Sperm Donor, Dear

It sometimes happens, even in the best of families,
that a baby is born. This is not necessarily cause for alarm.
The important thing is to keep your wits about you
and borrow some money.

· ELINOR GOULDING SMITH ·

Few would argue that raising children is a challenging endeavor. As a parent, you have to keep your spawn relatively clean and regularly fed, and make sure they are breathing and that they stay out of jail and don't get (or get anyone else) pregnant. You have to teach them to read and to swim and to ride a bike and to wipe their own asses and that very bad things can happen when you stick metal bobby pins into electrical outlets. (Thanks a *lot*, Mom and Dad.) You have to outfit them with car seats and soccer cleats and braces and bras or cups and occasionally, regrettably, casts and crutches. You've got to clip their tiny fingernails and remember to get all of their shots and help them write 1,497 papers and make 892 dioramas and craft at least one working papier-mâché volcano

· · · · ·

out of chicken wire without poking anyone's eye out. (Good luck with that!)

And will the brood you beget be born oozing sportsmanship, able to be graceful in both winning and losing? Hell, no. Courtesy coaching is but one of your countless parenting jobs. You will be responsible for modeling kindness and empathy and generosity and compassion, and because your kids will be far too busy imitating every move you make to listen to a word you say, you might want to start watching that potty mouth. You'll remove splinters, resolve arguments, and pay good money for clothes and shoes that will never get worn and eventually get donated to Goodwill with the tags still on them. You will become proficient at administering Tylenol and time-outs and declarations of "We don't like tattling" in your sleep. You'll chauffer your progeny to Texas and back every week, dry a river of tears every month, and prepare them for that bittersweet day when they move out of your home and into their own, which will look a lot like yours because they'll take half of your furnishings with them. Trying to juggle all of these highly complex tasks is hard enough in and of itself, but when there's *another person constantly getting in your way*, the whole thing is almost enough to drive a gal to drink. Or at least, drink more than she normally would.

For me and Joe, the custodial debates started long before we even considered tossing caution—and birth control—to the wind. You see, Joe couldn't wait to have kids, whereas I was decidedly on the fence about the whole issue. It's not that I dislike children (only some of the more annoying ones); I just

· · · · ·

could see myself being happy with or without them, and I sort of felt that if you were going to create a new person inside of your very body and then squeeze it out of your vajayjay and into the world where you then were going to be responsible for its every need, you should really, *really* want it. Plus kids were expensive. And defiant. And very, very messy. Judging from my own childhood, parenting was a tiresome, thankless gig that had very little payoff. Why anyone did it was a bit of a mystery to me, frankly.

"It's just that I know that the bulk of the child care responsibilities will fall on my shoulders, and I guess I resent the idea of being the primary caregiver," I explained to the stranger we were paying $150 an hour to mediate this impossible debate and in effect, decide our future.

"Well, you *will* be the primary caregiver, so you'd better get over the resentment," the rat-faced counselor replied dryly. I kid you not, that's what she said. I couldn't decide which one of them I hated more: Her or the asshole sitting across from her whom I had obviously made the great mistake of marrying.

"*He's* the one who wants to have kids!" I shouted, pointing at my smug bastard of a husband.

"It doesn't matter," the sexist, overpaid analyst informed me with just a little too much blasé for my taste. "You're the mom. Details like dentist appointments and sleep schedules and how long to breastfeed and what sort of child care you'll have typically default to the child's mother. That's just the way it works."

"Well, if that's the way it works, then it *isn't going to work at all,*" I replied, storming out of her picturesque office and thinking she could have made at least a grand off us if she'd waited a few more sessions to drop that invariable little bomb. It would be several years before I acknowledged the fact that not only was she unequivocally right, but even given a dozen or so alternative options, I wouldn't have it any other way.

" At Least You're Not Married to Him "

Why don't dads move when the kids say they need something? When our children say "I want some water" at the dinner table or "I need to go potty" in the backyard, my husband just stares off and continues eating his dinner or whatever . . . Hello? Why assume *I'm* going to answer the call of the wild every single time?

ANNA

By the time we brought our first newborn daughter home from the hospital, Joe and I had discussed and debated and deliberated every hypothetical parenting situation we could imagine. We knew where she was going to sleep and how we were going to co-manage her midnight feedings and had decided not only where we would stage the first family photo but what we were all going to be wearing in it. I actually thought we had it pretty dialed in. Of course, trying to envision what your life with children will be like before you have them is sort of like attempting to picture yourself at ninety. It's just not possible to factor a zillion unknown and frequently unpleasant variables into a mental image. Just as you'd never visualize your ninety-year-old self being completely infirm or dead (two distinct possibilities), no woman fantasizes about the far-off day when her lap-held child has an exploding poop—the kind that results in crap up the kid's back and down her blouse—on an airplane or her preschooler's pristine skin gets stuck in the zipper of his snowsuit, even though both of these things are bound to happen. In my carefree, childless days it would never have occurred to me that I might one day find myself routinely referring to my husband as *Daddy* or issuing ridiculous ultimatums a thousand times a day ("If you do this, I'm gonna do *that*!"). I pictured tea parties and pedicures and Nobel Prizes, not a jam-packed family production starring Mom in the roles of chauffeur, Sherpa, referee, and ATM. And let's get one thing straight: Even my darkest, most frightening pre-parent nightmares never featured a single lice comb or bottle of Rid.

At first most of the child-related disagreements Joe and I had were based on subjective data. He wasn't holding her right. I overdressed her. He wasn't doing enough around the house. We never had sex. I didn't think watching TV together should "count" as bonding time. He thought I should "shut the fuck up." But once we lowered our respective expectations and got more comfortable and confident in our own parenting roles, we began having tiffs that looked like this:

JOE: "Want to go out to dinner tonight?"

ME: "Sasha didn't take a nap today so she should go down by six o'clock."

JOE: "Says who?"

ME: "Say the sleep books."

JOE: "Do you believe everything you read in that library of parenting books you've accumulated?"

ME: "Well, if you ever read *anything*, maybe you could—"

JOE: "I could what? Quote some idiot's totally unproven theory about something I don't really give a shit about?"

ME: "How can you actually sit there and call people who are far more educated than you *idiots*?"

JOE: "It's easy. I don't need a Ph.D. to know when I should put my kid to bed. I have instincts and a brain, and I am pretty sure that when she's tired, she'll fall sleep."

When the kids were little and hadn't yet mastered any discernible language, at this point in the discussion I would simply smile sweetly and unleash a string of impolite profanities, delivered in the most syrupy voice I could muster and punctuated with the appropriate, corresponding hand and finger gestures.

Now that our daughters are older and mobile and speak English so they can tell us when they want a snack or need a ride to Nola's house, they are fodder for an entirely new breed of marital discord, namely over those things we don't just disagree on but over which we sit at diametrical, polar opposites of the spectrum. For instance, he thinks I'm overprotective, and I think he's reckless. He accuses me of spoiling them; I'm constantly berating him for being too hard on them. I think they should make their beds; he feels that if they're going to do chores, they should be chores that *matter*. I don't make them listen. He refuses to apologize to them, even when he's patently wrong. I let them walk all over me. *If he spent one eighth of the time with them that I do, he'd be singing a totally different tune so I don't really want to hear it, thank you very much.* And then there is the massive distinction between what I now refer to as Daddy rules and Mommy rules.

More often than not, the difference between my policies and Joe's boils down to hygiene, decorum, or some combination of the two. Allow me to illustrate Daddy rules in action with a handy example: We have a hot tub outside, and most nights after dinner Joe takes the girls for a soak while I clean up the kitchen. If it sounds like he's getting off easy here or forcing me to play some dreaded retro-hausfrau role, let me assure you that I relish this quiet time by myself to scrub and scour and load the dishwasher using my preferred and undeniably superior method without anyone getting in my way or asking me for a single blessed thing. I can talk on the phone and check my e-mail without any dirty looks or an ounce of guilt. Plus I don't have to put on a swimsuit or get my hair wet. I live for this hour.

Anyhow, one day Joe was out of town and the girls begged me to take them in the hot tub. *Why not?* I thought. They usually seem to be having a lot of fun out there. I could be the cool pool mom for an hour or so.

No sooner were we submerged than they began an exciting game that involved gulping large quantities of murky, chlorinated water and spitting it at each other.

"Girls, stop that!" I demanded. "That's disgusting! Our filthy feet not to mention our *bottoms* are in this water, and it's filled with dirt and bugs and all sorts of toxic chemicals."

They looked at me in confusion, murky ass-water dripping down their chins.

"But," they stammered in unison. "*Dad* lets us do it."

I shook my head sadly. Of course he did.

"I have to pee!" one of them announced next.

"Okay grab your towel and walk carefully—don't run—to the back—" I didn't get to finish my sentence because she was already standing spread-eagle on the deck, her bikini bottom pulled expertly to one side while she *emptied her bladder right there on the deck*.

"What are you *doing*?" I shouted, aghast.

"Peeing!" the fruit of my womb replied with a what-do-you-*think*-I'm-doing look.

"On the deck?" I moaned, wondering what on earth else went on out here when I was inside scraping macaroni and ketchup shrapnel off the table.

"What?" she asked back. "*Dad* lets us do it." Her sister nodded in confirmation. I had found out just the week before that Dad also sometimes lets them ride in the back of his truck—only on our street, but still—which about gave me a heart attack (even though I grew up riding in the back of *my* dad's truck, frequently perched back there on a folding lawn chair, because it was a different, safer world back then, and you and I both know it).

It must be nice to be the good cop. What fun that would

• • • • •

be! You could teach your kids to make obnoxious armpit-barking sounds and let them stay up until midnight watching *Weeds*. You could agree with them that if they promise to brush their teeth "really, really, super good in the morning" then it probably won't kill them to skip brushing them tonight. They'd like Sprite and brownies for breakfast? Well, hell—who wouldn't? Fizzy chocolate bombs for everyone, coming right up!

Alas, I feel strongly that kids should only be allowed to have one laid-back legal guardian who lets them drink chlorinated water, shun sunscreen, and sleep in their wet bathing suits when that bizarre urge strikes, and Joe clearly rocks that job. As the self-appointed guardian of my children's little lives and limbs, I spend most days detailing the many things they *can't* do and cataloging the gruesome consequences that will most surely befall them if they ignore my sage advice and do it anyway. It's exhausting and they often call me *the meanest mom ever* because of it, but seeing as they are both still alive and boasting the same number of digits they were born with, I will continue to wear my bad-cop badge with pride.

Let me make something perfectly clear: It's not that Joe isn't concerned about our children's well-being, because he most certainly is. He would wrestle a hungry grizzly bear to protect them. It's just that he isn't nearly as afraid of blood, vomit, or infectious diseases as I am.

Just the other day, one of our neighbors had stacked half a dozen large metal crates by the street. Before their current stint as a roadside eyesore, these crates had been home to a large family of bearded dragons, which are giant alligator-lizards that feed on live crickets, roaches, mealworms, and occasionally their own tails. What had happened to the crates' scaly former tenants was anyone's guess, but precisely why their erstwhile habitats were bound for the landfill was not something I wished to explore.

"I'm going to go ask them if they're giving those crates away," Joe announced one afternoon, motioning toward the house next door.

"Why?" I asked, curious as to what he could possibly have in mind for our neighbor's contaminated trash.

"I thought they might be fun for the girls," he said.

"For *our* girls?" I asked incredulously. "To do what with exactly?"

"To play in," he said.

"To play in?" I repeated stupidly, nearly gagging on the words. "Uh, *no*."

"Uh, *yes*," Joe replied, working the single brow arch like a madman and folding his arms across his chest.

"They're filthy and disgusting," I pointed out. "I am not letting our children *near* those cages."

"You need to lighten up," he answered me. "They're going to love it. I'm asking."

"You can't just make a unilateral decision and then decide that it's final," I told him, getting angry.

"Why not?" he demanded. "You just did."

"I said *you* can't," I reminded him with a satisfied smirk. At least he had the good sense to laugh.

• • • • •

"But seriously," I added. "We're not bringing those germ-infested crates over here."

"You are one stubborn, opinionated bitch," Joe said to me, shaking his head.

"You should have realized that before you married me," I replied.

" At Least You're Not Married to Him "

He forgets our kids! We have three children, ages ten, nine, and six, and he sometimes forgets to get them from the bus when I cannot get there in time. One time I told him he had to be there in fifteen minutes, and he said, "Okay, no problem," and thirty minutes later my phone was ringing to notify me that no one showed up at the bus to get them! He got caught up mowing the lawn or something to that effect.

MAGGIE

The very same man who feels as if he needs no wisdom or input from parenting professionals has a mantra that causes more arguments between us than an army of in-laws: "Experience is the greatest teacher," he'll say. I understand the "free-range parenting" concept in theory, and I'll admit that more often than not I am guilty of leaning (hard) toward the overprotective end of the spectrum. But I'm not going to let my kids lay their tiny hands on a scalding appliance so that the impact of "the stove is very hot" will be magnified.

Joe thinks kids are hearty and resilient; I worry constantly about the countless hidden dangers that lurk like hungry sharks waiting to maim my babies. One menace in particular is a certain upstairs window in our home that opens—if I were to allow it to be opened, which I rarely do—directly onto the flat roof of our master bathroom below. In my fantasies, one day we will enclose the roof with a sturdy railing and swap the window for a nice French door and have ourselves a cozy little rooftop terrace from which, if the goddamned neighbors would ever bother to trim their trees, on a crystal-clear day we might enjoy a sliver of an ocean view. In the meantime, with its unprotected edges and a sheer twenty-foot drop on three sides, it's an absolute off-limits death trap. I have spent years convincing our daughters that if they so much as leaned even an inch out of that window they would burst into spontaneous flames and perish on the spot. Because of this, they have never even considered asking for a roof pass, as it obviously wouldn't be an option. Relieved, I confidently scratched *kids climbing out onto the roof* off my long worry list.

So you can imagine the shock and horror I felt the day I walked up the stairs and caught sight of the two of them out there dancing and laughing and twirling while their dad stood several frightening feet away, clapping and laughing and egging them on.

"What in God's holy name are you *doing*?" I shrieked, hauling myself through the window and grabbing one of each of their tiny arms in a death grip.

"Oh, I was replacing a shingle and the girls wanted to come out and see what it was like," Joe replied casually.

· · · · ·

"It's fun!" shouted one.

"We like it out here!" chimed in the other.

"Great idea," I said sarcastically, shuffling the protesting pair back through the window to safety.

Later that night I tried to explain, rationally, how upset I was about the whole incident. "Honey, I think I did a really good job scaring the shit out of them about going *near* that window, and now you've completely ruined it," I scolded.

"I was out there with them, Jenna," he replied. "And I think it's wrong to make them think their heads will fly off if they step out onto the roof. Besides, I told them that they are never to do it without me."

"So you think they aren't going to do it because you told them not to?" I demanded. "Children believe they are immortal and invincible and every last one of them defies their parents' rules. It's their job! Before it wasn't a rule they were tempted to break to see what might happen, it was something they were utterly terrified of, and I liked it that way. A little healthy fear is good for them."

"You have to let kids live," Joe insisted, whipping out yet another of his hateful parenting clichés.

"*Live* is what I'm trying to make sure they do," I spat.

"Sounds like a lot of fun," he replied sarcastically.

"And just so we are clear, when they climb out there when you're not around and fall off, it is *all your fault*," I added, mentally etching *kids climbing out on the roof* back onto the damned worry list.

" At Least You're Not Married to Him "

My husband of twenty-five years loves to debate and approaches many conversations as if there will be a winner and a loser. This is typical at his job. At home, he constantly asks questions that I can't answer. For example, we are discussing one of our grown kids:

ME: Darling Daughter is going to do XXX.

DARLING HUBBY: Why would she do that? Has she thought of A? Has she considered B? Is she first going to do C?

ME: I don't know.

DH: [*just asks the same questions again*]

ME: You're asking the wrong person.

DH: But why does she even want to do XXX?

ME: CALL YOUR DAUGHTER AND ASK HER!! I HAVE NO IDEA! And lose the demanding 'tude when you talk to her.

DH: I'm just worried about her, and I really want to know why she is going to do XXX.

ME: [*putting my hand to my forehead and doing a Carnac the Magnificent impression*] Obviously just to piss you off.

BETH

Before you got married, you might have made sure that your views on religion and finances and sex and politics were compatible with your future husband's. But if you're like me, you forgot to bring up a thousand or more seemingly benign possible dissimilarities like your take on whether or not it matters if SpongeBob SquarePants is gay and a child's absolute right to an annual celebration of his or her nativity.

"What should we do for the girls' birthdays this year?" I

• • • • •

remember asking Joe one day. I am sure it was far too early in the year to be planning two hypothetical celebrations that wouldn't happen for months, but I had meant it as more of a generic, input-gathering question than a strategic planning session.

"What are you talking about?" Joe replied blankly.

"Their birthdays," I said, drawing out the word *birthdays* with annoying slowness for emphasis. "Like, should we do big family-style barbecues or maybe something at a park? I guess we should ask them before we plan anything because they might want a slumber party or to take a bunch of friends bowling or something like that."

"We had parties for both of them last year," Joe stammered, confused.

"We sure did," I said. "What's your point?"

"Are you suggesting that we should throw a birthday party for each of them every single year?" he wanted to know.

"You're not being serious, are you?" I asked. "Of course that's what I'm suggesting! Kids have birthday parties every year that they have a birthday, which last time I checked was *every year*."

"Who says?" he wanted to know. Joe defaults to "Who says?" a lot, and even if I could cough up a relevant biblical passage ("And then the Lord said to Little Sally, 'Fear not, my child, for ye shall haveth a bouncy house and a strange balloon animal guy and a mountain of gifts to behold on each anniversary of thy creation . . .'"), I know that it still wouldn't satisfy him. Because "Who says?" isn't actually a question, not even a rhetorical one. Translated literally into Joe-speak, it means *I don't give a flying flip what anyone else does because I think it is stupid and I'm not doing it, the end.*

The thing is, our daughters aren't even into the double digits yet, which means we still have the bras, braces, dating, driving, drinking, boyfriends, birth control, cell phones, and college debates ahead of us. These years will not be easy on any of us, I fear, but I am confident that my marriage can survive them because Joe and I agree that our children are the most important thing in the world to us. When we are at a frustrating future impasse, we have vowed to remind each other that our daughters' happiness, safety, and general well-being will always come first. We can agree on this because everyone knows that blood is thicker than water. It's also much harder to get out of the carpet.

• • •

CHAPTER TWENTY

See? It Really Could Be Worse

All husbands are alike,
but they have different faces so you can tell them apart.
• OGDEN NASH •

My husband, I am proud to say, has a sixth sense. He does. He knows unequivocally, without the faintest shadow of a doubt, that *my fucking shoes are going to be the death of me.* Interestingly I do not own just one pair of poisonous footwear. Pretty much all of them but my tennis shoes and hiking boots fall into the lethal-shoe category, and really he's only express- ing his immeasurable concern for my well-being, not accusing me of *putting my very life at risk with my vain desire to be slightly more fashionable than the gal we buy our avocados from at the farmer's market.* Nevertheless, I have to hear over and over how violently he disapproves of my sandals/slingbacks/slip-ons/ stilettos. Because he is clairvoyant, okay?

Apparently the mentally elite are drawn to their own kind, because Joe also insists that I have a unique superpower of my

• • • • •

own. You see, I can jinx things. Stop! I'm serious. By merely taking the time to verbally acknowledge some blessing—"Wow, what a beautiful day! I'm glad that wind finally died down," or "Can you believe the girls have been playing quietly for two solid hours?"—I automatically flip an invisible switch that powers up some mysterious and malicious force of nature that will put a swift and ugly end to the stroke of luck in question.

"It's supposed to be gorgeous this weekend," I'll remark casually.

"Aw great, you jinxed it," Joe will accuse, shaking his head sadly and looking up at the sky to scan for the thunderclouds that he expects to appear at any minute.

"I didn't *jinx* anything," I laugh. (Well, I used to laugh, when I still found it amusing that someone could actually believe that another person—let alone the person they chose to marry—could beget misery without even so much as a nose twitch. Now being called the devil incarnate on a daily basis is just fucking annoying.) "I'm appreciating our good fortune. How can that be bad?"

"Nope, you jinxed it," he'll insist. "Thanks a lot."

At least you're not married to him, right? Or any of the dozens of guys ~~brutally~~ affectionately immortalized on the next many, many pages. When you're done, go ahead and count your blessings. Despite what Joe would have you believe, it won't jinx anything. Probably.

· · · · ·

" At Least You're Not Married to Them "

I can't stand the way he sneezes. They are really loud, really dramatic, and so out-of-the-blue, they frighten me. I've lived through earthquakes that haven't scared me as much as one of his sudden, deafening nasal-passage clearings. I've learned to live with them, even though I'm completely irritated and unnerved by his each and every involuntary expectoration. But here's the big *oy*: Now that my son is fifteen years old and manly, his sneezes have started to rival his father's, decibel-wise. I pray that my future daughter-in-law has more mettle and patience than I do.

—Nancy

What's with the early morning farts as they are peeing? Sometimes I ask myself how I could love a person who pees and farts at the same time.

—Robin

He is a very messy eater! Even if he's dressed up in a suit and tie. In fact, at the last function we attended a couple of months ago, after a few drinks he ate his prime rib with reckless abandon. Fortunately, the lights in the room were dim and everyone was drinking. The next morning when I was packing, I was shocked to see his clothes looking like a two-year-old had eaten in them. He had food all over his tie—I think he dipped it in his plate. His pants were covered from front to back. I had to soak his white shirt in Biz. I made him take them to the dry cleaners because I was too embarrassed, and we still haven't picked them up. I wonder what they thought.

—Karin

He will wear a nice pair of slacks with the most worn, loose, disgusting socks you can imagine. Or he will pair super-old white athletic socks—you know, the ones that have turned dingy whitish gray and no longer have any elastic in them and may even have visible holes—with a decent pair of shorts and Pumas.

—Eileen

He has a tic—he clears his throat all the time, even while he is eating—that drives me crazy! He does it until it hurts or he is hoarse and cannot stop. It is maddening.

—Laurie

My husband completely lacks the ability to plan ahead. I'm not talking about planning a vacation or even a nice dinner out. I'm talking about anything that should happen beyond this particular moment in time. He can read the news, watch baseball, *totally oblivious* to the fact that the kids aren't dressed, the dogs haven't been fed, you know, all the usual daily occurrences that he seemingly cannot predict. He'll say he'll be home promptly at 6:00, and then after I have employed my super investigative powers of questioning, he'll admit he has a conference call at 5:45. Like he can magically transport himself home in seconds. I think I've figured this one out, though. He'll do anything I ask so as long as I just treat him like an entry-level employee, and all is well.

—Donna

It trips my liberal do-gooder guilt switch and drives me nuts that my wonderful husband won't use things up and instead will open/get out a new [roll of toilet paper, loaf of bread, jar of peanut butter, etc.] while the other one still has lots left. When it leads to things spoiling and going to waste, it really bugs me, but I know he's not going to change.

—Rose

It never fails . . . I am scrambling in the morning to put myself together in a reasonable fashion and get to work on time and it's like he has radar for what I'm going to do next or where I'm going and he gets in my way. If I see he's left the bathroom, I try to slip in and get my makeup on and my teeth brushed in privacy, but no sooner do I have paste on the brush than he walks in and starts brushing his teeth! Or I'll be reaching into the glass cupboard to get a coffee cup down and he'll stand right beside me and reach into the cupboard for something else instead of asking me to pass him something. No matter how hard I try to reverse my morning routines from his, it's almost like he's my mirror image.

—Grace

When he eats soup or stew, he siphons off all of the liquid first with his spoon first, then eats what's left.

—Lisa

When I walk into the kitchen after he has unloaded the dishwasher, my mind instantly starts playing that *Sesame Street* song, "One of these things is not like the other . . . one of these things just doesn't belong." I have found potato peelers in with the forks, measuring cups with drinking glasses, and cooking utensils shoved in miscellaneous drawers. He's not mentally challenged, either.

—Kandis

My husband dresses like he's still in college. He wears the same T-shirts he wore when we were dating (almost ten years ago). I can't get him to dress like an adult and it drives me nuts.

—Deilia

It drives me crazy when my husband takes credit for something I said or did. If I say something funny or do something amusing, he will tell the story to friends with him in the starring role. He doesn't do this all of the time, but he's done it enough so that it is annoying. I don't even think it's on purpose, so maybe I should be happy that he thinks of us as one!

—Kristin

The thing that consistently irks me that I consistently forgive is the abyss between the kitchen counter and the dishwasher. Apparently, the activity involved in getting dishes from the sink/counter/table actually *into* the dishwasher is my man's Kryptonite.

—Jenny

He is obsessive about washing his hands. He has to do it literally hundreds of times a day. I guess it's good that he's so clean, but really?

—Laurabeth

He never changes the clock in his car when it's Daylight Saving Time. I can't just look at the clock and know what time it is, I have to think about it and do math. Currently, for example, when I look at the clock and it says 6:30 P.M., I have to stop and think, wait—that means it's really 7:30 P.M. It's a small thing, but it bugs me.

—Scarlett

My husband not only passes gas whenever he feels like it, but he tenses up to "push" it out and then sighs loudly with satisfaction. Being in the same room is bad enough, but he also does it when we're cuddling on the couch. My rule about it is that it has to be away from my general direction. It hardly ever works.

—Danielle

So, we're curled up on the couch watching a really good movie when I hear this sort of crunchy, snappy sound. I look over and see my husband totally engrossed not just in the movie, but also in picking at his nails or some dry skin on his foot! I know he does it subconsciously, but man is it annoying. I try to ignore it for as long as I can . . . about forty-five seconds . . . and then I smack him and ask him lovingly to please knock it the hell off.

—Carmen

He wears shoes until the soles literally have holes in them. Once, the sole of his shoe actually flapped away from his foot as he walked, and when I got him new ones, he said, "Why? What's wrong with the ones I have?"

—Tricia

My husband is a brilliant man but sometimes his ADD gets the best of him, like the time he couldn't find the phone. He looked everywhere . . . and finally found it in the freezer. Or the time we couldn't find the garage door opener for two weeks. One day I was transferring his wash into the dryer and heard a funny clunking sound. I thought maybe it was a belt buckle or loose change. No, it was the missing garage door opener that was a stowaway in his pants pocket. I love my husband, but one of these days I'm going to strangle him.

—Rachel

He eats ice cream every single night, which sucks for me because I'm trying to keep in shape, but that's not the issue. The issue is that he leaves the damned spoon in the sink *every single night*. I mean what the hell, it's a spoon, one tiny spoon, and he can't bring himself to wash it no matter how many times I ask. So every morning I get to be reminded that *he* gets to eat ice cream every night and I don't. I swear I'm going to start leaving them on top of the remote, or under his pillow, or up his you-know-what!

—Julia

He blows his nose into the air without a tissue. He says nothing comes out, but sometimes it does.

—Lynn

He lets our yard, especially in the back, get way out of control and then he invites all these people over for a barbecue and is hustling an hour before and has it looking great for our guests. Unfortunately it's only about five times a year that we have a nice-looking yard and it's not even for *us*, it's for our guests!

—Amanda

• • • • •

He can't bend. When he looks in the refrigerator, if he can't see an item from where he is standing, it must not exist. I think he thinks he gets bonus points if he doesn't have to move anything around. I have actually labeled the refrigerator shelves so I can provide more direction: yogurt, back of B1; cantaloupe, left side of A2; carrots, right vegetable bin, under the onions. He also won't eat the last of anything. If there are seventeen chicken wings, he'll only eat sixteen and leave the last miserable one sitting in there until I throw it out.

—Cheryl

When he clips his toenails he does it on the front porch . . . like our neighbors really want to see that disgusting sight. Ick!

—JC

My husband does not know where the dirty clothes go (same place they have always gone), does not know where the dishes go (even after he got them out), has more shoes than a woman and gladly leaves them out for everyone to admire, continues to pile garbage upon garbage in the can instead of changing the garbage bag, could not put a toilet seat down or close a shower door even if his life depended on it, and leaves his spit bottles sitting wherever he last used them (he dips Copenhagen).

—Crystal

He bites his nails. I don't mean he just bites the edges off; he chews them down to the quick. He then proceeds to crunch on the pieces for hours while on the computer. It drives me crazy! Recently, he had to go to the urgent care clinic and spend $100 because his finger was so raw from his biting it that it got infected.

—Lynn

He eats sunflower seeds in bed. Then he will leave the gross bag full of spit shells on the floor so I have to clean them up. To top it off, when I'm sitting next to him, the sound is awful (crack, crunch, spit), and they kind of smell bad. Oh, he eats them on road trips, too.

—Karin

He smacks his food. Just the other day, I asked him not to. His response was, "What is 'smacking' anyway? And how do I stop?" Umm, it's chewing so loud I can hear you smack your food around. Should I demonstrate with my hand?

—Tara

I love my husband but I really want to cancel his World of Warcraft account and kick his freeloading sister out of our apartment.

—Kelly

My husband has given away many of my possessions over the course of our seventeen-plus-year marriage without asking me, including two bicycles, golf clubs, and a sewing machine. Now, his line of reasoning was that I did not use these items, but what irks me is that they did not belong to him, so he had no right to give them away! This past school year, my son needed a costume for his social studies class. I had to staple the fabric together because I did not have a sewing machine.

—Liz

He always has to move the dishes around in the dishwasher before running it. Granted, he can usually fit more in it than I manage, but this is EVERY single time!

—Stephanie

For the past twenty-seven years—as long as we have been married—my husband has brought the exact same thing to work for lunch every day (unless he goes out to lunch or has a lunch meeting): PB&J (has to be crunchy peanut butter), fruit, and a soda, although he did switch to Diet Vanilla Coke and swapped strawberry preserves for raspberry about ten years ago. I love varied lunches and it annoys me that he is so boring in his food preferences, but since I don't have to eat it, I let it go.

—Rosemarie

My husband and I work together rehabilitating birds, and we often bring our two-and-a-half-year-old daughter along for the fun. Since she's got a toddler's short attention span, one of us completes a volunteer task while the other entertains her, and then we switch off. My entertainment ideas run to making bird feeders out of pine cones and helping to cut up tofu for the resident raven. But my husband thinks it's perfectly acceptable to let our daughter walk around the center holding and petting dead rats intended for the owls' dinner.

—Melissa

The man does not blow his nose. Instead he tears off a long strip of toilet paper and shoves one end up his nostril. He will walk around the house like this, and it doesn't seem to bother him that he has a strip of toilet paper flapping in the wind in front of his face. It has to be toilet paper; even if we have tissues, he still uses toilet paper. He used to come to bed like that when he was sniffly until one morning I woke up with THE SNOTTY STRIP OF TOILET PAPER STUCK TO MY FACE! He is no longer allowed in the bed with toilet paper shoved up his nose.

—Sara

He scratches the couch with his finger the whole time we watch TV. If I smack his hand away, he'll just move it back or scratch with the other hand.

—Teri

My husband, bless his heart, does not brush his teeth at night. It drives me crazy. I mean, besides the obvious hygiene issues, I've got to admit his breath is a little rank by the end of the day, especially if there were onions or garlic in our dinner.

—Brynna

He leaves his big, bulky shoes all over the house, and it drives me bonkers. He always places them in the most inopportune places, like in our two-year-old daughter's room or in front of the couch, where I am sure to stub my toes on them.

—Lisa

My husband wears a CPAP machine at night to stop his horrible snoring. It is a sight to be seen when it is on, which is not that often because he falls asleep every night before putting it on. And when he does wear it, he will take it off in the middle of the night and hold it in his hand for dear life. Then he flips out when I try, with loving care of course, to put it back on.

—Robin

His idea of "cleaning" a table or counter is to either sweep the crumbs onto the floor (like I don't have to clean that, too!) or pick them up off of a glass top by using a wet finger.

—BJ

Whenever we are out together, my husband runs me over when he walks. It's like I have some gravitational pull, and before you know it, he's stepped right into me. It doesn't matter where we are. The last time we were in the airport and he did this to me, I told him to follow the row of square tiles—those were his, that was his space, and this row was mine. Stay in your own lane.

—Teri

My husband is a good man, but I am going to smack him with a frying pan one of these days because:

1. He smacks his gum when he chews it.

2. He likes to walk around in his underwear in the summer. We have the same "put on your darn pants" fight every year. It's worse this year, because now he does Wii Fit in his undies.

3. He keeps the bar codes from the boxes of things we buy "in case we need it," but never identifies what the bar code is for. We have tons of mystery box ends.

4. Oh, and his farts could be an Olympic event.

—Lisa

· · · · ·

Famous Last Words

(by Joe)

Jenna is a wonderful wife and an amazing mother and obviously an extremely talented writer and I am lucky to be married to her. However, in addition to swearing a lot (sorry about that, Dad), she also has a tendency to occasionally embellish details for the sake of a good story. In fact, since marrying her, I call *any* extreme example of exaggeration a "Jennaism." So I thought you should know that this book—which I have read from cover to cover and heartily endorse, by the way—*may* contain one or two slight Jennaisms. All of the parts where I come off looking generous, capable, or just really nice, *those* are all 100 percent true. With regards to the remainder of the intimate details about our life that you have just read, I urge you to use your good judgment in discerning where ~~the light leaver-onner~~ my lovely wife may have liberally employed what she calls *poetic license.*

—JOE